Gender, Feminism, and Queer Th
of Teacher Education Practices

Professional Learning
Volume 17

Series editor:
J. John Loughran, *Monash University, Clayton, Australia*

Editorial board:
Renee Clift, *University of Arizona, USA*
Ruth Kane, *Ottawa University, Canada*
Mieke Lunenberg, *VU University, The Netherlands*
Anthony Clarke, *University of British Columbia, Canada*
Donald Freeman, *University of Michigan, USA*
MOK, Mo Ching Magdalena, *Hong Kong Institute of Education, Hong Kong*
Max van Manen, *University of Alberta, Canada*

Rationale:
This series purposely sets out to illustrate a range of approaches to Professional Learning and to highlight the importance of teachers and teacher educators taking the lead in reframing and responding to their practice, not just to illuminate the field but to foster genuine educational change.

Audience:
The series will be of interest to teachers, teacher educators and others in fields of professional practice as the context and practice of the pedagogue is the prime focus of such work. Professional Learning is closely aligned to much of the ideas associated with reflective practice, action research, practitioner inquiry and teacher as researcher.

Gender, Feminism, and Queer Theory in the Self-Study of Teacher Education Practices

Edited by

Monica Taylor
Montclair State University, USA

and

Lesley Coia
Agnes Scott College, USA

SENSE PUBLISHERS
ROTTERDAM/BOSTON/TAIPEI

A C.I.P. record for this book is available from the Library of Congress.

ISBN: 978-94-6209-684-4 (paperback)
ISBN: 978-94-6209-685-1 (hardback)
ISBN: 978-94-6209-686-8 (e-book)

Published by: Sense Publishers,
P.O. Box 21858,
3001 AW Rotterdam,
The Netherlands
https://www.sensepublishers.com/

Printed on acid-free paper

To Rose and Amy

TABLE OF CONTENTS

ACKNOWLEDGEMENTS

Writing, editing, and getting a collection of papers ready for publication requires the support of many more than the authors and editors. We would like to briefly acknowledge Samantha Stiner whose work on formatting the chapters was rapid, accurate, careful, and reliable. We cannot thank her enough. We are also very appreciative of Michel Lokhorst from Sense Publishers, and John Loughran, editor of the Professional Learning Series, who welcomed the idea of the book from the outset and helped us throughout the process.

Editing a collection such as this always takes more time than one thinks. There is always work to be done, and not only during times that are convenient for others in our lives. We would like to express our deepest gratitude to our partners, Patrick and Mark, and Monica's sons Michael and Griffin. Their love and understanding have made the editing of this volume possible.

SERIES EDITOR'S FOREWORD

It is a pleasure to have the opportunity to write the foreword for this book by Taylor and Coia. As their introduction makes clear, the nature of the self-study community has been important in shaping their professional lives as it has helped to create a home for their academic endeavors. In a similar way, they have now extended that form of development to others by leading the way in the project that has led to publishing this book.

Self-study has proven to be quite alluring to many teacher educators because of its central concern to better align teaching intent and action. As a consequence, an underlying purpose of self-study - researching the development of pedagogy in ways that might better reflect the complexity of the teaching-learning relationship – is again highlighted as crucial if teacher education is to go beyond a technical-rationalist approach to practice. The manner in which Taylor and Coia have done that through this book is strong and clear. They have brought together an impressive group of authors to offer insights into gender, feminism, and queer theory through self-study in a productive way that illustrates a nice array of thinking and methodology to challenge the reader. As they have done all of this, they have also reinforced the place of community that is so important to self-study through the ways in which they have collaborated, shared, and developed new learning opportunities for their team as a whole; the fruits of that labor now being available to others through this publication. They have demonstrated what it means to lead.

The focus on gender, feminism, and queer theory addresses a concern to pursue issues of educational change for social justice and demonstrates how the editors' understanding of the sense of community within self-study matters in supporting scholars to push the boundaries of their work to genuinely seek to make a difference. It would be fair to say that, through this book, the editors and authors have created a text that may well prove to be the touchstone for others and further encourage the community to strategically pursue self-study in thoughtful and well-reasoned ways; a clear sign of scholarship.

Taylor and Coia have put a lot of thought into the way the book is organized. As an edited volume they have brought together authors with something to say; and they say it well. The work is well situated within the literature but it is not confined to the literature. Although the editors have put the chapters together in a particular way to create connections, as they say themselves, there are also other connections open for exploration. In so doing, the ideas, issues, and approaches offered in the book combine in interesting and engaging ways to create opportunities for the reader to reflect upon the research and writing and think again. That approach then encourages reframing (Schön, 1983) and creates a heightened sense of the value of noticing (Mason, 2002, 2009); two key components of quality in pedagogical reasoning and practice.

In seeing this book come together from an initial idea into the quality product offered as a consequence of the fine mix of authors and the clear leadership, direction, and support from the editors, it highlights the place of collaboration, the generosity of spirit, and the value of sharing learning in open and meaningful ways. Although the editors have worked hard to create a text of value, it is the shared sense of purpose, the collaborative effort, and the overall strength of ideas that makes the sum greater than parts for this book. That is not always easy to do in an edited collection, but when achieved, as is obviously the case here, it makes clear why it is that developing new knowledge must be at the heart of scholarship in teacher education.

Reading this book reminded me that "self-study cannot simply be about our lives, our practices, our histories. It must also understand these in relation to and through the lived realities, experiences, and perspectives of those with whom we are involved" (Kuzmic, 2002, p. 233). This book helped reinforce that message for me. I trust it is the same for you.

John Loughran
Monash University
Melbourne, Australia

REFERENCES

Kuzmic, J. J. (2002). Research as a way of knowing and seeing: Advocacy for the other. In J. Loughran & T. Russell (Eds.), *Improving teacher education practices through self-study* (pp. 222–235). London: RoutledgeFalmer.

Mason, J. (2002). *Researching your own practice: The discipline of noticing.* London: RoutledgeFalmer.

Mason, J. (2009). Teaching as disciplined enquiry. *Teachers and Teaching: Theory and Practice*, 15(2), 205–223.

Schön, D. A. (1983). *The reflective practitioner: How professionals think in action.* New York: Basic Books.

INTRODUCTION

"Just know you're not alone, cause I'm gonna make this place your home"
(Pearson & Holden, 2011).

Sometimes it is difficult to find home. This is especially true for one's academic home. It is vital for one's intellectual health and vitality to find a place where one feels comfortable and is able to express one's self in a supportive environment; a place where one can try out ideas, come to know new colleagues, find informal mentors, be introduced to new concepts, and feel the support of that community when back at one's own institution. Yet, that sense of intellectual nurture and support is not always readily available in these harsh and competitive times. In 2001, we met Jeff Kaplan at a Kappa Delta Pi conference in Orlando, Florida. We were in the early stages of our collaboration and beginning to explore a shared research agenda that combined our interests in feminism, autobiography, and teacher education. We had found each other but were still searching for a larger community to call home. Jeff was a member of Self-Study of Teacher Education Practices (S-STEP), a special interest group (SIG) of the American Educational Research Association (AERA). He saw in our feminist work on autobiography a connection with the work of S-STEP. He described the S-STEP community as one that was open, innovative, and experimental; and enthusiastically encouraged us to submit a proposal to the fourth international conference on self-study of teacher education practices held at Herstmonceaux Castle in West Sussex, England. So began our relationship with the SIG.

At our first Castle conference we felt we had found our academic home for a number of reasons. We were energized to be among others who care so deeply about their teaching and strive to examine the gap between one's teaching beliefs and one's actual practice, what Whitehead (1989) calls "a living contradiction." There was a rigor to the conversations along with a palpable commitment to teachers, teacher educators, and the profession. We were excited by the view that studying "the nature of teaching and teaching about teaching" has the potential to "improve the quality of teacher education" (Loughran, 2004, p. 30), but most of all we appreciated the warmth and inviting nature of the entire community. S-STEP provided then, and continues to provide a safe, encouraging, and caring place where issues can be explored without judgment or silencing. These are the very traits noted by Barnes (1998), an observer at the first Castle conference, when he remarked that S-STEP can be characterized by its openness, its collaboration, and its reframing of issues. Like Barnes, we were impressed by the inclusive spirit of the group, and its willingness to re-examine teaching from the perspective of the teacher educator. We began to understand how

M. Taylor and L. Coia (Eds.), Gender, Feminism, and Queer Theory in the Self-Study of
Teacher Education Practices, 1–10.

self-study leads to thinking about pedagogy differently: changing the way one looks at what is going on in the classroom, and transforming one's practice.

S-STEP is a progressive organization founded on the idea that the teacher educator is a source of knowledge about her own practice. As such, many would agree with Zeichner (1999) when he labeled self-study the "single most significant development ever in the field of teacher education research" (p. 8). It is a research community that has stood up to criticism and stood by its principles. This has been a hard row to hoe in an era when objectivism and positivism have been dominant and the role of the teacher educator has been under almost continual attack and criticism.

An inherent characteristic of the SIG is its receptiveness to new methods of analysis and ways to share research. As Loughran (2004) points out, there is no "one true way" (p. 17) to do self-study. While there may be a single purpose, namely the improvement of our practice, the community encompasses many individual aims in pursuing self-study research. Discernible among these is a strong commitment to social justice, and specifically a welcoming of a wide range of perspectives on social justice issues. As we were invited into the community, we saw a place where our views could grow to include not just our concern with distributive justice, but also how our identities as teacher educators impact our conception of, and our work towards social justice.

As we were encouraged to take paths of inquiry into our own practice and explore the many ways this can be done, we were always thinking about our commitment to an education that realizes the potential of all: teachers and students. With the support of the SIG, we turned to our own learning and teaching selves to explore how our social justice perspectives, particularly our concern with feminism and gender in general, interacted with and informed our teaching. It was during our session on feminist pedagogy at the 9th Castle Conference in 2012 that we realized the extent to which other SIG members were interested in issues of gender, feminism, and queer theory. In typical Castle style, we spent the rest of the conference talking over the ideas with our SIG colleagues, on walks in the grounds, over meals, and at the pub. Galvanized by the conversations we proposed this volume in the Professional Learning Series and invited contributors we thought would ably represent the self-study community and its interest in gender. Thus you will find here contributors who have a long history of involvement with S-STEP and others who are new to the SIG. You will also find contributors who have researched and written about gender, feminism, or queer theory before, and those for whom this is their first self-study on the issues.

FOCUSING ON GENDER, FEMINISM, AND QUEER THEORY
TO MAKE A DIFFERENCE

Change, and in particular change related to equity, access, and social justice, has been a perennial area of concern (Tidwell & Fitzgerald, 2006) to the self-study community. This is because we are educational researchers focused on studying our own practice with the aim of improving it (LaBoskey, 2004). Most of the change occurs in the pursuit of understanding and transforming the individual practice of teacher education. This is evident, for example, in the edited collection of self-studies on diversity organized by Tidwell and Fitzgerald (2006). There have also been calls for systematic and institutional change (Cole & Knowles, 2004; Craig, 2008), supporting Samaras and Freese's (2006) claim that "[s]elf-study teachers continuously examine the perplexities and dilemmas of their teaching practice, while also working to transform the institutional contexts of their work" (p. 13). There is great potential within our S-STEP community to conduct research that is directed towards change for social justice (LaBoskey, 2009). Indeed, as Hamilton and Pinnegar (1998) remind us, "[s]elf-study undertaken with rigor produces living educational theory that will lead to both reconstruction and the reconceptualization of teacher education" (pp. 243-244).

While there is evidence of interest in social justice change in the SIG, this work has mostly been focused on issues of race, ethnicity, gender, disability, and power, as well as broad conceptions of social justice that include multiculturalism and ways of knowing (Tidwell & Fitzgerald, 2006). This wide view includes the influence of gender and feminism but this is the first focused look at this issue. We believe it is an important time for us to examine these issues both because our SIG community is growing and also because of the reconceptualization of issues of gender, feminism, and queer theory in teacher education. This edited volume provides a space for members of the SIG, from founders to welcomed new members, along with the general community of teacher educators to problematize these issues through a variety of theoretical lenses.

NAVIGATING THE CHAPTERS

As with any collection, some thought has gone into its arrangement, and while we encourage our readers to follow their own interests, to enable the most effective use of the collection we provide below a detailed explanation of the ways in which the chapters are organized and short summaries of their content.

We begin the volume with a review of the self-study research that has been conducted over the life of the SIG on issues of gender, feminism, and queer theory. This creates an historical and cultural context for the subsequent chapters written by the contributors to the volume. We show that, in common with the work of self-study researchers in general, self-studies that address these issues are wide ranging in their focus and intent. In the review, we discuss how the major concepts of gender, feminism, and queer theory have been explained and examined in self-study. The review shows that there has been interest in gender from the outset, but that most often it is used as an identifier in conjunction with other self-identifiers or as part of the larger intention of teaching for or about social justice. There are, however, some self-studies that problematize gender and examine its complexities. For example, there are studies that focus on gender stereotyping in various contexts including classrooms, teacher education courses, and by student teachers. Researchers also examine the connections between gender, power, and agency. Feminism, and specifically poststructural feminism, has also been an important theoretical lens in S-STEP and has been used to look at teaching practice and pedagogy in a variety of studies. Several self-study researchers draw a link between their feminist stance and their focus on the self. As we see in these studies, poststructural feminism helps to reflect on issues of power and authority in our teaching and in particular the political aspects of our practice. Additionally, several self-studies use innovative feminist research methods that incorporate elements of narrative writing, the arts, and psychology. Finally, the lens of sexuality and more recently queer theory has been adopted to critically examine the field of teacher education. Initially in the SIG, researchers did not self-identify as queer, rather they used the term sexuality to identify sexual orientation. This was the case in terms of self-studies that focused on teaching issues of sexuality to preservice teachers in teacher education courses as well as thinking about the influence of sexuality on a teacher educator's identity. Over the last decade, self-study researchers have increasingly analyzed their teaching through a queer theory perspective.

In the second chapter, Kathryn Strom, Rabab Abi-Hanna, Linda Abrams, Charity Dacey, and Jacqueline Dauplaise, five doctoral students from Montclair State University, explore their process of "becoming" within the context of a shared sense of disequilibrium in their roles as students, teachers, and professionals. Specifically, they reexamine their previous co/autoethnographic work that explored becoming change agents and in this study focus narrowly on their transformation. Developing a self-study methodology that uses rhizomatics from a poststructural feminist perspective, they adopt Deleuzian concepts of "assemblages" and "lines of flight" to identify vehicles that enabled them to break away from their individual fixed identities and become part of a collective that allowed new perspectives to emerge. This permits a non-hierarchical and relational worldview that facilitates an examination of "becomings" rather than static identities. They deliberately use the term "becomings" rather than "findings" to imply an ongoing continual process of transformation. Interweaving their personal narratives to show rather than tell what has emerged, they describe five main "becomings" that interact with one another. Their self-study reminds us of the promise of "thinking with theory" (Mazzei & Youngblood Jackson, 2012), and in particular poststructural feminism and rhizomatics, to disrupt the binaries that constrain us in academia and provide opportunities for us to try on new perspectives and ignite new potentials.

Mary Lynn Hamilton and Stefinee Pinnegar give us another example of thinking with theory in their chapter on interpretation and its use in self-study. Developing the idea that self-study always exists in a zone of inconclusivity, they explore interpretative turns they have previously taken, using feminist, positioning, and queer theories to reveal how we can continue to learn from previous self-studies. The paper examines a self-study published in 1994 where the interpretative orientation is explicitly feminist. They then look at a reinterpretation of this work published in 2007 and show how the original interpretation shifted as the authors positioned themselves differently in relation to the original texts and their communities. Although the use of positioning theory provides new understanding, Hamilton and Pinnegar continue to re-read the study with additional interpretative frameworks, this time using queer theory to open up other gendered dimensions of the original study. In this way they can look at aspects of the self-study such as potentially binary views of gender that were less visible in the previous two interpretations. This intensive revisiting of a self-study shows how interpretation is never static and self-studies are always open to new understandings. In so doing they enrich our perspective of the role of self-study in influencing our practice over time.

The next two chapters look at an issue with which all teachers are familiar, but that has received scant attention in the literature: the role of emotions in teaching and learning. Rachel Forgasz and Allie Clemans provide an in-depth analysis of their teaching practice showing how emotion and feeling operate as important epistemological as well as pedagogical stances. Analyzing teaching incidents through feminist frameworks that focus on the epistemological dimension of emotions, they utilize their students' voices to show that despite the fact that emotions are difficult and little understood in the classroom, they are vital. Indeed, as they cogently argue, emotions offer legitimate ways of knowing. In making this argument they highlight the complex interplay between emotion and cognition, as well as other putative binaries. Forgasz and Clemans provide a model of collaborative self-study with each researcher collecting data from her teaching. In line with other self-study researchers they are explicit in their intention to positively impact their practice through their study and position the student as knower. This is very valuable to those who wish to follow Forgasz and Clemans' lead in providing a space in their classrooms for emotional knowing.

Having a similar focus on emotions but using a masculine researcher lens, Jeff Kuzmic explores the epistemological significance of emotions as a part of his researcher subjectivity and self-study methodology. This study is a retelling of a teaching incident that occurred with Madison, one of his female students. The episode has been examined and discussed twice before in previous self-studies, but never from the perspective of their identities as gendered subjects. In this chapter, highlighting how emotions are often outlawed in the literature on qualitative research, Kuzmic focuses on the oft-felt epistemological tension between analytical distance and emotional participation. In particular, he reflects on his response to Madison's anger, guilt, and anxiety, emotions that emerge in her research project as she struggles to redefine her identity as both teacher and researcher. In this self-study of a self-study, he unpacks through a masculine gendered lens why he reacted the way he did. He problematizes whether his patriarchal stance privileges researcher rationality and blinds him to her emotions, a central part of her inquiry. As he re-examines both her narratives as well as his own written responses to her, her emotions are reinterpreted and repositioned as valuable for action and validating for her as a teacher and student advocate. Throughout his study, Kuzmic attempts to "disturb his masculinity," to awaken the limitations of a gendered subject but also to disrupt the hegemonic constraints of patriarchy.

Deborah Tidwell takes a long view in her self-study, examining with the help of two critical friends, her sisters Pamela Schwartz and Janet Dunn, how her upbringing in a matriarchal family has influenced her attitudes to gender in her teaching practice. Moving between family stories, her early experiences of discussions of gender in her life as a teacher, and her current work as a teacher educator, they use personal history and narratives to create scenarios through story-telling that are examined through the lens of their family matriarchy. This leads them to identify four overarching values: being female, individuality, following one's own interests, and being independent. This original way of proceeding provokes genuine insight into Tidwell's past and present practice, as she recognizes these values in her own teaching of fifth and sixth grade students, and her current work as a teacher educator. Her intensive and systematic work on her past and how her family structure influenced her attitude to gender causes her to examine her bias towards the success of her female students and her assumption that boys will need more instructional support. This troubles Tidwell as she contemplates the potential tension between these tacit values and her explicit and heartfelt commitment to diversity and to eliminating bias. Her chapter shows the value of working honestly and collaboratively with family members to uncover beliefs through the analysis of scenarios from one's personal history and relating this to the complex world of gender and teaching.

Tidwell's exploration of matriarchy is followed by Nathan Brubaker's thoughtful analysis of contrasting cultural viewpoints in a course on diversity. Although the analysis is of a critical moment in a class discussion that addressed Christian privilege, he focuses on gender issues and how his assumptions about gendered discourse were confronted. He selects this particular teaching incident because it occurs in a context where the students are all female and primarily identify as religiously conservative. He also chooses this event because it is emotionally intense, and demonstrates his attempts to live his commitment to cultivating a community of inquiry. The challenge Brubaker faced in this situation was how to maintain his commitment to diversity. Through a careful study of the conversation that took place in the class, he identifies and examines his pedagogical assumptions and in the process grows as a teacher educator. Specifically he finds that his commitments to teaching about diversity and to democratic practice are reaffirmed through an increased sensitivity to the ways in which his own and his students' multiple identities interact in pedagogical encounters.

In the chapter that follows, Julian Kitchen explores the potential of employing a queer theory lens to examine teacher educator identity, experience, and practice. Echoing both Strom et al.'s as well as Hamilton and Pinnegar's chapters in terms of the value of reflecting with theory, he demonstrates the usefulness of adopting queer theory as a way of looking at identity anew. Providing a thorough and accessible description of queer theory and its commitment to disrupting heteronormativity, he uses the theory with two different narratives from his past to reveal contrast, create tension, and show the importance of play. First he examines a self-study that dealt with his co-facilitation of a preservice teacher workshop on LGBT issues and discovers a commonality between queer theory and self-study in their shared embrace of ambiguity and tensions. He honestly reflects on the tension between creating a safe space for his students where they can comfortably problematize their conceptions of sexual identity and pushing them to identify and critique oppressive heteronormative institutional standards. He later revisits a personal narrative reflection written 19 years ago, about his own cultural identity. Examining his past using queer theory empowers him to articulate the oppressive nature of both masculinity and heteronormativity and strengthen his commitment to social justice for his students.

In the next chapter, applying the queer theory Kitchen has so carefully described, Adrian Martin deconstructs mythological stories alongside his own personal teaching narratives to reveal gender norm conformity. Using a unique method of literary nomadic inquiry borrowed from Deleuze and Guattari (1987), he strives to travel between personal stories from his classroom and school experiences, poststructural and queer theories, and biblical stories to investigate how gender issues were addressed in his elementary school teaching. He begins with his own description of a classroom incident where he made gendered assumptions about a student. He follows with the biblical story of Genesis, drawing connections with his own imposition of gendered norms on his student and the ones prescribed for Adam and Eve. He offers the Deleuzian concept of "Body without Organs" as a theoretical tool to confront the oppressive privileging of heteronormativity. Finally, he ends with a retelling of another gendered conversation in the teachers' lounge of his school and his own powerful reflection of his silenced response and complicity. Martin thoughtfully demonstrates how ingrained gender norms are in our schools and society and how challenging and complex it is to combat these norms.

In the final chapter, we also borrow the Deleuzian concept of the nomad to explore our feminist pedagogy. Using co/autoethnography to examine the teaching of a course on gender and education, we employ a writing approach we call "nomadic jamming" that combines a focus on the inbetween with the improvised jamming of a band like the Grateful Dead. Their jamming at live concerts involved breaks in the songs to improvise and play music together in an unplanned and unscripted way. These were planned unpredictable moments in their shows. Similarly, in the teaching episodes we share in this chapter, our nomadic jamming allows us to highlight the planned unpredictable moments in our teaching. This allows us to reflect on how our poststructural feminist beliefs encourage us to embrace the unpredictable and the ways in which this helps us to try on new identities, diverse perspectives, and more complex understandings of feminisms. By doing so we are able to enact daily and in subtle ways our commitments to social justice. For us, being a feminist teacher is not about strategies or techniques, it is about continually questioning our beliefs and taking a stand.

7

Whilst the chapters have been carefully ordered to reveal certain connections there are many others to be explored, and in closing we would like to draw attention to a few of these. A fascinating aspect of self-study is how they reward being revisited from different perspectives, whether these are theoretical or practical. Self-studies are, in an important sense, never complete. Self-studies in this volume that revisit prior work include Kuzmic, Hamilton and Pinnegar, Kitchen, and Strom et al. Other studies in this volume contain, at least in part, reflections on early teaching experiences. Tidwell's chapter reflects back on her experience as a new teacher educator as do Hamilton and Pinnegar. Martin and Kitchen include reflections on their experience as K-12 teachers. In each case their work as teachers is examined through the frameworks of gender and sexuality showing how such reflection can yield insight for current practice. Current practice is the explicit of focus two chapters; those by Forgasz and Clemans, and Brubaker. Each provides a traditional self-study examining teaching practices using data generated by their students, transcripts of class discussions, along with their own reflections to create knowledge about their practice.

Not surprisingly, although used somewhat differently in each instance, feminism is an important and pervasive theoretical framework for multiple chapters within this volume. These include the chapters by Coia and Taylor, Kuzmic, Forgasz and Clemans, Hamilton and Pinnegar, and Strom et al. Masculinity is explored by Kuzmic and Brubaker who look carefully and critically at how their gender impacts responses to female students' reflections and how this affects discourse in their classes.

It is important to note that another way to read the chapters would be to focus on the vaunted collaborative relationship associated with much S-STEP work (LaBoskey, 2004; Samaras & Freese, 2006). While many of the chapters are co-authored, and all are collaborative in some sense, those by Strom et al., Tidwell and her sisters, Hamilton and Pinnegar, and Coia and Taylor provide explicit reflection on how collaboration is used to enhance self-study.

Beyond collaboration S-STEP is known, as we said at the beginning of this introduction, for its openness to a variety of approaches. Echoing this, one of the values of this book is its openness to many different readings, and we hope, rereadings.

REFERENCES

Barnes, D. (1998). Forward: Looking forward: The concluding remarks at the Castle Conference. In M. L. Hamilton (Ed.), *Reconceptualizing teaching practice: Self-study in teacher education* (pp. 9–14). London, UK: Falmer Press.

Cole, A. L., & Knowles, J. G. (2004). Research, practice, and academia in North America. In J. J. Loughran, M. L. Hamilton, V. K. LaBoskey, & T. Russell (Eds.), *International handbook of self study of teaching and teacher education practices* (pp. 451–482). Dordrecht, The Netherlands: Kluwer.

Craig, C. (2008). Change, changing, and being changed: A study of self in the throes of multiple accountability demands. In M. L. Heston, D. L. Tidwell, K. K. East, & L. M. Fitzgerald (Eds.), *Pathways to change in teacher education: Dialogue, diversity and self-study. Proceedings for the 7th International Conference on Self-Study of Teacher Education Practices* (pp. 87–90). Cedar Falls, IA: University of Northern Iowa.

Deleuze, G., & Guattari, F. (1987). *A thousand plateaus: Capitalism and schizophrenia.* Minneapolis, MN: University of Minnesota Press.

Hamilton, M. L., & Pinnegar, S. (1998). Conclusion: The value and promise of self-study. In M. L. Hamilton (Ed.), *Reconceptualizing teaching practice: Self-study in teacher education* (pp. 235–246). London, UK: FalmerPress.

LaBoskey, V. K. (2004). The methodology of self-study and its theoretical underpinnings. In J. J. Loughran, M. L. Hamilton, V. K. LaBoskey, & T. Russell (Eds.), *International handbook of self study of teacher education practices* (pp. 817–869). Dordrecht, The Netherlands: Kluwer Academic Publishers.

LaBoskey, V. K. (2009). Name it and claim it: The methodology of self-study as social justice teacher education. In D. L. Tidwell, M. L. Heston, & L. M. Fitzgerald (Eds.), *Research methods for the self-study of practice* (pp. 73–82). Rotterdam: The Netherlands: Springer.

Loughran, J. J. (2004). Learning through self-study: The influence of purpose, participants and contexts. In J. J. Loughran, M. L. Hamilton, V. K. LaBoskey, & T. Russell (Eds.), *International handbook of self-study of teacher education practices* (pp. 151–192). Dordrecht, The Netherlands: Kluwer Academic Publishers.

Mazzei, L., & Jackson, Y. A. (2012). *Thinking with theory in qualitative research.* New York, NY: Routledge.

Pearson, D., & Holden, G. (2011). Home (Phillip Phillips). On *The world from the side of the moon* (LP). Interscope.

Samaras, A. P., & Feese, A. R. (2006). *Self-study of teaching practices.* New York, NY: Peter Lang.

Tidwell, D., & Fitzgerald, L. (2006). Introduction. In D. Tidwell & L. Fitzgerald (Eds.), *Self-study and diversity* (pp. 13–17). Rotterdam, The Netherlands: SensePublisher.

Tidwell, D., & Fitzgerald, L. (Eds.). (2006). *Self-study and diversity.* Rotterdam, The Netherlands: SensePublisher.

Whitehead, J. (1989). Creating a living educational theory from questions of the kind, 'How do I improve my practice?' *Cambridge Journal of Education, 19*(1), 41–52.

Zeichner, K. (1999). The new scholarship in teacher education. *Educational Researcher, 28*(9), 4–15.

MONICA TAYLOR & LESLEY COIA

ADDRESSING GENDER, FEMINISM, AND QUEER THEORY THROUGH SELF-STUDY OF TEACHER EDUCATION PRACTICES: A LITERATURE REVIEW

In self-study of teacher education practices (S-STEP), our research begins with the self (Loughran, 2004). It is self-focused and self-directed in order to reconceptualize practice. As practitioners researching ourselves, the notion of the self is necessarily complicated, and while it would be unwise to attempt a definition of self that all self-study researchers would accept, it is clear that the self of self-study is not conceptualized as static or isolated. When we investigate the self, we are "examining one's self in relation to others" (Feldman, Paugh, & Mills, 2004, p. 971). This review of self-study research that addresses issues of gender, feminism, and queer theory starts from this perspective. To situate our review we therefore begin by providing a brief overview of the ways in which the social is significant in self-study.

In self-study, it is generally understood that the self is not a fixed entity rather it is socially constructed in the context of social, historical, and cultural relationships. As Brown (2004) clearly explains, these contexts provide conventions and practices that influence the ways in which we make meaning. We are "not simply 'influenced' by the external world," we make sense of the world through a negotiation between "the private and public, personal and political, individual and historical" (Elliott quoted in Brown, 2004, p. 528). As researchers, we bring our negotiated versions of these contexts to our self-study. Our interpretations draw from our past experiences, theoretical explorations, readings, and scholarly engagements (Hamilton, 1998). The conceptualization of the self is always social in this sense. But it is also social in a number of other ways.

We study ourselves in the context of our practice in order to understand that practice. Kuzmic (2002) reminds us that when we study the self through self-study we go beyond the self to consider our students and their perspectives. Although our self-study may result in personal changes or new ways of thinking, ultimately the intention is that what we learn will impact not only ourselves but also those with whom we work: primarily our students, but also our colleagues. As Hamilton and Pinnegar (1998) write, "[t]he evidence of our understanding about teaching should appear not just in our own practice but, also in the practice of our students, and therefore, in the lives and actions of their students" (p. 242). The focus on our selves is therefore also deeply social in that it is directed towards others.

M. Taylor and L. Coia (Eds.), Gender, Feminism, and Queer Theory in the Self-Study of Teacher Education Practices, 11–29.

Finally, self-study is deeply collaborative and open to others. Understanding the value of alternative perspectives on situations, self-study researchers have what Samaras and Freese (2006) call "a commitment to outside interpretations and a willingness to review one's existing frames" (p. 49). Self-study researchers appreciate the ways in which collaborators or critical friends help to see beyond the individual or personal worldview and reframe teaching practice. This supportive collaborative environment extends beyond traditional research partners writing and working together. The collaborative spirit extends to the S-STEP community itself. Our work has implications beyond the personal or the collaborative relationship, to the larger professional community of teacher educators. Self-study, therefore is, as Ham and Kane (2004) describe, "a study of that which binds the particular to the collective, a study of that which assumes a 'we,' a collegial society or culture of others who spend much of their waking hours being what I am, and doing what I do" (p. 116).

If one recognizes the importance of the social, then it is worthwhile to see what self-studies addressing gender, feminism, and queer theory have to say. In this review of the work of the self-study community, our aim is to show how issues of gender have been used and represented within this overarching perspective of the complex social nature of the self of self-study. We hope the themes that emerge will prove useful for those both inside and outside the community, and spur further work in this area.

METHODS OF ANALYSIS

In order to provide a good general picture of the ways in which gender, feminism, and queer theory have been addressed in S-STEP, we reviewed major publications of the organization including all issues of *Studying Teacher Education*, S-STEP Conference proceedings from 1996-present, the *International Handbook of Self-Study of Teaching and Teacher Education Practices* (2004), and S-STEP texts. In an effort to narrow our literature review and keep it manageable, we limited our research to resources that have been fostered within the S-STEP community. We acknowledge that we may have missed some self-studies on gender, feminism, and queer theory but we hope that our literature review provides an extensive thematic overview of this work.

Using the constant comparative method (Glaser & Strauss, 1967), we categorized research studies on an Excel spreadsheet according to their dominant theme of gender, feminism, or queer theory. We noted title, citation, and any pertaining quotes or references. We then examined each category individually and did a secondary analysis, looking for emerging patterns or themes. We named the themes and supported them with examples from the relevant studies. We conducted this process individually and then compared results to ensure trustworthiness.

In the following sections, we discuss the three areas of gender, feminism, and queer theory in S-STEP and identify the themes from our analysis. We look at how these major concepts are defined in the literature, and then give examples of the ways that they are conceptualized and operationalized in each study. We conclude by giving an overall assessment of how gender, feminism, and queer theory intersect with S-STEP, closing with recommendations for further work.

GENDER

In the context of the S-STEP literature, the definition of gender is frequently implicit. In line with accepted usage, it refers to a socially constructed gendered identity, i.e. male or female. This is evident in the many cases where the S-STEP researcher self-identifies, for example, as a "White, middle class female." In these cases gender is often not problematized, and is presented as a binary, functioning to position the researcher along with other social identities. However, in other self-studies where gender is either a theoretical lens or the research focus, there is some resistance to the idea of gender as a fixed or static identity. Some self-studies also explore notions of positionality in regards to identity politics (Harré & van Langenhove, 1998), however, the majority of the references to gender in the S-STEP literature come in the context of self-identification with the authors' race and class. Moreover, for most researchers the focus is on race and class, not gender. Schulte (2006, 2009), for example, in exploring her multicultural teacher education practices, states that she is "White, middle class, and female" but problematizes her race and class more intentionally than her gender. Similarly, Brown (2000, 2004) examines issues of race and class in two self-studies. Although she mentions gender and sexuality, she primarily focuses on perceptions of race and class and how they are informed by the lived social experience, as is evident in her (2004) title "The significance of race and social class for self-study and the professional knowledge of teacher education."

More recently some studies have addressed the complexities of gender identity. Conrad, Conrad, Misra, Pinard, and Youngblood (2010), in examining their identities as teachers of color at a rural university, primarily focus on race but acknowledge that "the complex interactions between age, class, ethnicity and race, gender and sexuality, religion, language, geography, education, ability/disability, social affiliations, and academic successes and challenges have all been related to aspects of identity" (p. 143). Tamdgidi (2009) also argues for the importance of recognizing the heterogeneity of diversity, including gender. He notes for example that when thinking about gender "one could be masculine and feminine at the same time" (p. 180). Expanding on this idea, Mulholland and Longman (2009) stress the importance of acknowledging that "the social construction of subjectivity includes trying on new roles within the contexts of gender, social class, and race among other discourses" (p. 208). Khau ably expresses the epistemological tensions that can arise from this complex position in a self-study she conducted collaboratively with Pithouse (2008) when she addresses the dilemmas she faces as a woman science teacher:

> The position I occupy is surrounded with conflicting social constructions of masculinity and femininity. As a Mosotho woman, I am expected to be submissive, unquestioning, and sexually innocent. However, as a science teacher, I am expected to be knowledgeable, powerful, and able to make decisions in any situation.... I believe the only way forward is to disturb and challenge the assumptions that my society has regarding these two seemingly conflicting positions. (pp. 6-7)

In conclusion we can say that although gender is addressed as an identifier for the purpose of a self-study, it is in general not problematized and is used in conjunction with other socially constructed self-identifiers. However, some recent studies show that this situation may be changing with more attention being given to the complexity of gender construction and its impact on teacher education practices.

Examining Gender as Part of a Larger Lens on Social Justice

From its inception, S-STEP has always had a significant commitment to exploring equity and social justice (LaBoskey, 2004; Schulte, 2006, 2009; Tidwell, Heston & Fitzgerald, 2006). For example, Griffiths, Bass, Johnston, and Perselli (2004) define social justice as "paying attention to individual perspectives at the same time as dealing with issues of discrimination, exclusions, and recognition, especially on the grounds of (any or all of) race, gender, sexuality, special needs, and social class" (p. 660). They continue, explaining that self-study can "show how the grand narratives of social justice can be disrupted, queered, deepened, given a fine grain and re-shaped, by little stories that pay attention to race, gender, dis(abilities), sexuality and social class, that pay attention to power, perspective, voice and self-respect" (p. 685).

Thinking about the intersections of gender and race in terms of social justice, both Schulte (2006) and Brown (2000) discuss how gender has the potential to help one understand the othering of race. In her study Schulte (2006) discusses the experience of attending a feminist course with a focus on gender that helped her to understand racial discrimination. In Brown's (2000) initial self-study, she discusses how her pre-service teachers used their experiences of being discriminated against as women to begin to think about othering and in particular being othered based on race.

Intentionally similar, Zeichner, in his self-study (1995), examines the discrepancy between his beliefs about teaching for social justice, including issues of race, gender, and culture, and his teacher education practices. He describes attempting to find a balance between giving voice to his mostly White students and encouraging them to take a critical stance towards these issues. Rodriguez (1998) too examines teaching about diversity to preservice teachers and concludes that although he presents a broad, inclusive lens of social justice, his students mostly defined diversity in terms of race and ethnicity. Again gender is referred to as a necessary component of a social justice approach but is not addressed specifically. We end this section by looking at a fairly recent development that shows how gender and sexuality intersect in self-studies that are explicitly focused on social action.

Emphasizing the importance of a gendered lens, some recent self-studies (Khau, 2009; Khau & Pithouse, 2008; Masinga, 2009; Wood, 2009) from South Africa address the teaching of sexuality education and in particular HIV and AIDS awareness. Although these studies focus on sexuality, the lens of gender is essential because all of the teachers are aware of their marginalization as women. As Khau (2009) reflects, "it became apparent that even among ourselves as friends, women, adults, teachers, and mothers, we were not able to freely talk about issues of sexuality" (p. 70). She notes how women teachers with whom she worked began to become aware of the "pervasive male gaze" (Dentieth, as cited in Khau, 2009) and male control over female sexuality. In a similar study, Masinga (2009, 2013) investigates how she interprets sexuality and its influence on her teaching of sexuality education in her sixth grade class. She reflects, "My self-study journey required me to first acknowledge that as a teacher, woman, and researcher, I have my own 'demons' that prevent me from talking openly about sexual matters to younger children" (p. 246). Her self-study is essentially the hard work of connecting her life as a woman to the decisions she is making about curriculum and pedagogy.

Narrowly Focusing on Gender Stereotypes

Besides including gender as either a self-identifier or part of a larger social justice lens, multiple self-studies focus on concerns about gender stereotyping of students in schools, of themselves as teacher educators, or of their preservice teachers. For example, Perselli (1998) conducts a self-study of her action research that examines the underachievement of middle school boys and the implications of gender difference. McGinnis and Pearsall (1998), on the other hand, look at gender stereotypes perpetuated in their own teaching of science methods showing how a male professor and his female graduate student can develop more gender inclusive practices. In a study that addresses another common gendered experience Bair, Bair, Mader, Hipp & Hakim (2010) focus on how faculty emotions impact teaching. In particular they explore how they are perceived by their teacher education students in light of the emotions they exhibit. The authors identify their own gender as a factor that encourages stereotypic expectations. For example, female faculty are expected to act emotionally but then if they do, they are perceived as lacking authority. One of the researchers who is White and male reflected that he had more permission to show

15

emotion in class because it would not "lessen" his authority. They conclude there are differences in emotional labor based on gender, among other identity markers such as race and sexuality.

Shifting the focus to preservice teachers, Wilcox, Watson, and Paterson (2004) explore how to help their teacher candidates become more aware of gender stereotyping and learn to avoid these tendencies when they become teachers. In a related fashion, Brown, Wiggins, and Secord (2008) explore how "preservice teachers' religious dogma could impact their gendered expectations of students" (p. 37). Pennington, Brock, Abernathy, Bingham, Major, Wiest, and Ndura (2012), likewise, use critical autoethnography to examine their own dispositions toward their preservice teachers through a social justice lens. Illustrating some frustrations in trying to get students to think differently, Wiest provides an example that focuses on her concerns about preservice teachers acknowledging gender stereotypes in mathematics. She writes: "I want them to acknowledge that people have different experiences in this world based on sex" (p. 74). Recognizing the importance of knowing students' gender and social class, James (2008) highlights some of the challenges of online teaching where these identity markers are not clear. Continuing the emphasis on problematizing stereotypes, Weber and Mitchell (2000), in their self-study, examine the ways in which dress influences perceptions about difference. In all of these studies, the authors show how self-study of our teaching practice can be used to resist and challenge gendered norms and stereotypes.

Gender and Agency

Finally, through a variety of self-studies, the relationship between gender, power, and agency emerges as a significant finding. Thomas and Beauchamp (2010) in their examination of agency in their professional lives, and its impact on their work as teacher educators, point out that their gender has an effect on the way they perceive the world. Khan (2012), in her self-study dissertation that uses a personal history methodology, shows the impact of gender on her self-esteem and agency, especially when she began teaching. Perselli (2004), using a Marxist framework, suggests studying gender and social class as a means "to think about the varying circumstances of women's lives and the constructs of power and economy that define us" (p. 700). Cole and Knowles (2004) also pay attention to the inequities faced by women in teacher education. Recognizing the status quo of academia and the ways in which women academics are marginalized, they discuss how the methodology of self-study could impact these inequities and potentially increase agency for women teacher educators.

As we can see from this literature review, there are a variety of studies that address gender from many perspectives. This is in line with the modus operandi of the field, where the focus is on individual practice but can be conceptualized in multiple ways. We see interest in the larger social justice issues involved in being a teacher educator as well as addressing our students as gendered from the perspective of being gendered. This takes us to the consideration of feminism.

FEMINISM

Throughout the S-STEP literature, there are examples of researchers who draw on a feminist perspective. The Arizona Group (2000), for example, explicitly self-identifies as feminist when they write "all of us are qualitative researchers, whose work is informed by feminist pedagogy, critical theory, and a constructivist view of learning, teaching, and researching" (p. 20). In a later study (2004), they are drawn to a feminist perspective in order to explore other epistemologies they used to "know things" about their practice as teacher educators (p. 1149). They embrace Ellsworth's (1992) feminist understanding that "all knowings are partial, that there are fundamental things each of us cannot know - a situation alleviated only in part by the pooling of partially, socially constructed knowledges in classrooms" (as cited in the Arizona Group, 2004, p. 1149).

Griffiths (1998) similarly points to the value of adopting a feminist epistemology in exploring collaboration in self-study. She therefore is convinced that "the knower is epistemologically significant" (p. 226). As self-study researchers, we also self-identify as feminists in multiple co/autoethnographies (Coia & Taylor, 2013; Taylor & Coia, 2006, 2009). In our latest piece (2013) we demonstrate the feminist nature of co/autoethnography as a methodology. In short, as Cochran-Smith and Lytle (2004) show, there are various ways in which feminist research has influenced practitioner research and self-study.

Feminist Perspectives on Self-Study

On occasion, self-studies are designed to explore pedagogy or practice through a feminist point of view. For example, Hamilton and Guilfoyle (1998) explore their tenure process through a feminist lens and Manke (2000) uses the same approach to problematize her leadership as an academic dean. Other times, specific feminist theories, like positioning theory (Davies & Harré, 1990), are the framework for a self-study. This is the case for Masinga (2013) in her self-study dissertation that explores her work with women teachers teaching sexuality education. Wood (2009) discusses the influence of patriarchy, addressing in some detail how it "contribute[s] to the reproduction of the status quo that places women in an inferior position to men in terms of sexual choices and freedom" (p. 286). She examines how gender normative attitudes and beliefs impact teaching HIV prevention through exploration of the question: "How can I influence the adoption of more gender equitable beliefs and practices among teachers?" (p. 286). But in the majority of instances, self-study researchers use a feminist poststructural or postmodern approach. This has been used to examine the following: teaching (McNeil, 2011); issues of power around race and language in teaching practices (Johnston, 2000; Johnston, Summers-Eskridge, Thomas & Lee, 2002); notions of identity and being a teacher educator (Abrams et al, 2012, Strom & Martin, 2013); self-study in general (Sandretto, 2009; Taylor & Coia, 2010); the collaborative nature of self-study (Taylor et al, 2006); reflexivity (Kirk, 2005); the paradoxes of praxis (Perselli, 2006); and emotions (Kelchtermans & Hamilton, 2004). Narrowing the focus, adopting a feminist stance can often lead to studying the self.

Studying the Self

Samaras, Hicks, and Berger (2004), in their discussion of personal history methodology as one stance for self-study, emphasize that their focus on the personal comes from a feminist perspective. Kirk (2005) who studies her work with women teachers in Pakistan, states, "I can only start to understand the multiple subjectivities of other women teachers if I can relate them to my own" (p. 232). She justifies starting with the self by citing Grumet (1988), Walkerdine (1990) and Steedman (1987) who draw on their experiences of mothering, teaching, and being a girl in school as lenses to understand and explore educational theories and practices. She observes in her study that "the position of a feminist researcher" is "at times a powerful one, but at others a marginal one" (p. 117). Galman, Lassonde, and Kosnik (2010) also draw parallels between self-study and feminist pedagogy, writing "research in both the self-study of teacher education practices and feminist pedagogy have long acknowledged the difficulties of merging boundaries between public and private and emphasized that quality collaboration can involve intellectual and emotional connectedness" (p. 89). They remind us that self-study facilitates the exploration of feminist issues. It enables us to "address relationships, question or even relinquish our ties to traditional ways of being scholars and teachers and emphasize, rather than bracket, the personal/private sphere" (p. 89).

Another perspective, provided by Feldman, Paugh, and Mills (2004) and Feldman (2006), uses Harding's (1989) question "Is there a feminist method?" to argue that like feminism, there are no distinctive methods in self-study. What is distinctive is how the methodology is characterized. In feminism gender is problematized; in self-study "the focus is on one's own self, and it is the role of the self in practice that is made problematic" (Feldman, 2006, p. 38).

Exploring Power and Authority

Echoing some of the important tenets of poststructural feminism, Kuzmic (2002) points out that self-study invites the researcher to examine self in relation to others, and discuss issues of power and authority, especially the relation between teacher educator and teacher education student. Similarly LaBoskey (2004) emphasizes the need for self-study research to address issues of power and examine the relationships between knowledge, power, and research in self-study. Not surprisingly, therefore, there are multiple self-studies that use a feminist or feminist poststructural theoretical approach to examine authority or power in the classroom. Chronologically, these include self-studies of the Arizona Group (1996), MacGillivray (1997), Johnston (2000), Johnston, Summer-Eskridge, Thomas, and Lee (2002), Coia and Taylor (2004), Taylor and Coia (2006), and Skerrett (2007).

18

Maintaining Complexity

More specifically, many self-study researchers clearly draw connections between the political issues that feminism raises and the potential of self-study. For example, LaBoskey (2004) refers to the influence of feminist, postmodern, and postcolonial scholars on self-study who encourage us to accept multiple epistemologies. She goes on to argue that "we have to find ways to maintain the complexity, include more voices, detect bias, and disrupt our own ways of knowing" (p. 824). This orientation to self-study resonates with several researchers. For example, Fitzgerald, Farstad, and Deemer (2002) discuss how adopting feminist and qualitative stances on inquiry in their self-study helps them to challenge "lingering, dominant views of what it means to provide evidence of one's competence" (p. 214). Ham and Kane (2004) too, in exploring when research is self-study, suggest that feminist and postmodern research methodologies are useful ways to problematize text, voice, and the crisis of representation. They see these frameworks as ways to help us move away from a positivist notion of "high" research and become more open to methodologies like self-study and practitioner research. Gamelin (2005) takes this way of thinking a step further when she points out how self-study can serve the needs of feminism by "transgressing the traditional boundaries of expression in academia" (p. 191). Moreover, she argues that "[s]elf-study is how the political arm of feminism reveals itself in the personal and daily. It is the manifestation of feminist principles in academia" (p. 191).

Using Feminist Research Methods in Self-Study

Besides examining practice through a feminist theoretical lens or focusing on feminist issues, numerous self-studies clearly incorporate feminist research methods as their primary mode of investigation. These are not always explicitly identified as feminist but they align with feminist criteria. For example, multiple self-studies use a variety of narrative strategies. Abt-Perkins, Dale, and Hauschildt (1998) use letter writing to examine how their personal and social backgrounds influence their teaching. Another example would be our work involving teachers and teacher educators telling narratives within an autobiographical group (Coia & Taylor, 2002). Weber and Mitchell (2002) use readers' theater to discuss the ways in which dress and shoes can either maintain gender and sexuality norms or disrupt them. Mitchell (2006) also uses diaries and journals as memory work texts in self-study. Other examples showing the variety of techniques include Butler-Kisber's (2005) incorporation of found poetry, Seaton's (2004) use of narrative inquiry to examine authentic experiences, and Strong-Wilson's (2005) construction of female travel narratives or "feminitopias." Although many embrace the value of narrative inquiry, Khau (2009) points out some of the challenges of this approach. She shows how using her own personal narratives to self-reveal to the participants in her study is complex and fraught with difficulty. The issues of vulnerability associated with self-revelation are common to self-study and very much associated with feminist work in general.

Besides narrative inquiry, a feminist lens often encourages self-study researchers to adopt innovative research methods that originate in other academic fields including the arts and psychology. Examples include Richards' (1996) study using self-portraits; the memory work that O'Reilly-Scanlon (2002) conducts; Perselli's (2002) radical arts based approach; and Guilfoyle, Placier, Hamilton and Pinnegar's (2002; Arizona Group, 2006) reliance on and exploration of dialogue.

QUEER THEORY

It is only in the last decade or so that teacher educators have more readily used queer theory as a means to conceptualize and question the field of teacher education. This is true within the self-study community as well. In the self-studies we examined, for the most part, queer is not used as a self-identifier with race, class, and gender. Instead, some self-study researchers use the term sexuality to refer to sexual orientation but do not employ a queer orientation. For example, in her research on the implications of race and social class for self-study, Brown (2004) mentions gender and sexuality as other identity factors that are influenced by the social experience. In this section, we discuss self-studies that address both sexuality and queer theory.

Addressing Issues of Sexuality

Although not necessarily explicitly queer oriented, there are several self-studies that have focused on issues of sexuality in teacher education courses with preservice teachers. This approach is illustrated by two studies that look at sexuality issues in teaching multicultural education courses. Mulhern and Martinez (1999) focus on confronting homophobia, and Ressler (2000) reflects on teaching about race and sexual orientation. In other studies, issues of sexuality emerge even though they are not the primary center of inquiry. Thus in Heston's (2008) study of building meaningful relationships, she describes the difficulty around discussing sexuality discrimination with her students. In doing so she highlights the role of the teacher educator, saying "I also try to be sensitive to times when I might trigger a wound that students may have learned to hide well. For example . . . during a discussion of the harassment experienced by gay, lesbian, bisexual, and transgender youth, I drew a parallel between kids calling each other 'gay,' and kids calling each other 'nigger'" (p. 176). Brown, Wiggins, and Secord (2008) in their self-study on the influence of religion in teacher education programs, consider how religion may influence the extent to which preservice teachers are receptive to teaching LGBT students. They comment that these religious preservice teachers may "reject students with alternative lifestyles" (p. 37). Finally, Kitchen and Bellini (2012) examine the teaching of a LGBT workshop informed by a queer framework that they offer to preservice teachers. Their hope is that this LGBT work encourages preservice teachers to create safe spaces for all students.

Influence of Sexuality on Teacher Educator Identity

Other self-studies focus on examining teacher educators' sexuality and the ways they influence teaching practices. Weber and Mitchell (2000) explore how dress can either confirm or disrupt gender and sexuality stereotypes. Biddulph (2005) uses mural making as a means to investigate his identity as an out gay teacher. He suggests the need to create queer spaces for gay teacher educators. Similarly, Conrad, Conrad, Misra, Pinard, and Youngblood (2010) in examining the influences of their identities on their pedagogy, question whether or not they need to limit discussion of sensitive issues dealing with race, gender, and sexuality because of their students' strong responses to these sorts of topics. Bair, Bair, Mader, Hipp, and Hakim (2010) examine faculty emotions and their impact on teaching. They observe that gay/lesbian faculty suffer more emotional stress than straight faculty. For example one of the researchers, a lesbian teacher educator, talked about the difficulties of self-disclosing her sexuality to her students. Although she thought it was important, her students interpreted this "outing" as over discussing issues of sexuality.

Queer Theory as an Analytical Lens for Self-Study

As we mentioned earlier, paralleling the wider field of teacher education, queer theory has become more prevalent as both a lens for analysis as well as a focus of self-study over the past decade. Pinar's book, *Queer Theory in Education,* was published in 1998 and the Queer SIG of AERA was only founded in 2002. Queer theory is an approach that disrupts normalized categories and binaries such as gay/ straight, masculine/feminine, and student/teacher (Meyer, 2012). Perselli (2002), for example, mentions queer pedagogies and in particular the work of Britzman (1998) and Sedgwick (1990) to support her radical arts approach. In a similar vein, Griffiths, Bass, Johnston, and Perselli (2004) describe the potential of self-study to challenge the status quo of social justice research. Adopting a queer perspective on self-study, Manke (2005) notes that both have been marginalized in their respective spheres, pointing out that "queerness is not a direction, but an option… queerness is tied to a psychology of constructivism" (p. 196). Thompson (2006) also uses queer theory as a way to rethink teaching inclusive education. In her work she shows how a queer perspective in problematizing the very idea of authentic categories can address the deeply ingrained positivism of some educational practices such as inclusive teacher education.

CONCLUSION

Our review of the literature shows that issues of gender have had a consistent presence in self-study from the beginning of the movement. There has always been interest in the impact of gender on our selves, our pedagogy, and our students' teaching. Gender, feminism, and queer theory are all looked at broadly in the self-study community with the focus emerging from the situated inquiry of the researcher in context. This is as one would expect in a field focused on knowledge of practice generated by educators engaged in that practice. One of the benefits of self-study is that it opens exploratory spaces and thus invites the use of multiple theoretical stances and methods (Samaras & Freese, 2006). As our review of the literature shows, these are often informed by gender, feminism, and queer theory in ways that enrich individual researchers' understanding of their practice.

The self-study community as a whole has paralleled the wider teacher education community in its interest and understanding of gender. Thus, in the earliest days of S-STEP we see researchers positioning themselves in terms of gender identity echoing trends in the feminist movement, along with a more general concern with social justice mirroring the rising interest in diversity in teacher education. These findings are not surprising given the deep commitment to prepare teachers who are caring and able to deal with social inequities in their classrooms.

We also see self-study researchers aligned with the wider teacher education community in adopting theoretical frameworks such as feminism, feminist poststructuralism, positioning, and queer theory to inform their work. These frameworks are used to problematize and understand the self in its relation to others. This is particularly apparent as we look at self-studies from the late 1990's onwards.

One of the great strengths of the self-study community is that it is international. This is reflected in our literature review where we found self-studies that address issues of gender, feminism, and queer theory from countries in Europe, North America, Africa, and Australasia. It is to this work that we now turn as we consider directions for future work. In thinking about how self-study might further interact with gender, feminism, and queer theory we see certain inspiring trends, particularly in the work being done in South Africa around urgent issues of social justice. These self-studies remind us of the potential of our work as teacher educators to engage in social action. If we are committed to nurturing our teacher candidates to become change agents who address issues of inequity around gender and sexuality, as Guilfoyle, Hamilton, Pinnegar, and Placier reminded us in 1995, we have to ask the same of ourselves. Today when our professionalism is questioned by increasing calls for accountability (Craig, 2008), there is an opportunity for S-STEP to use its unique stance on educational research to suggest alternatives as it has in the past when addressing the dominant positivist paradigm (Cole & Knowles, 2004). Acknowledging our identities as gendered and hetero-normed provides a perspective from which to critique the current reduction of our identities to economic units, a process through which our power and authority as teachers are taken away. Self-study methodology lends itself to social action that promotes change but as LaBoskey (2009) heeds, "the connection is not automatic... We need to ask the hard questions about equity of ourselves, our programs, and our students" (p. 81).

REFERENCES

Abrams, L., Abi-Hanna, R., Bess, N., Collucci, M., Dacey, C., Dauplaise, J., Mastellone, S., Strom, K. & Taylor, M. (2012). "I am what I am not yet": Becoming teacher educators and change agents. In L. B. Erickson, J. R. Young, S. Pinnegar (Eds.), *Extending inquiry communities: Illuminating teacher education through self-study. Proceedings of the 9th International Conference on Self Study of Teacher Education Practices* (pp. 17–20). Provo, UT: Brigham Young University.

Abt-Perkins, D., Dale, H., & Hauschildt, P. (1998). Letters of intent: Collaborative self-study as reform in teacher education. In A. Cole, R. Elijah, & J. Knowles (Eds.), *The heart of the matter* (pp. 81–100). San Francisco, CA: Caddo Gap Press.

Arizona Group. (1996). Navigating through a maze of contraindications: A conversation on self-study and teacher education reform. In J. Richards & T. L. Russell (Eds.), *Empowering our future in teacher education. Proceedings of the 1st International Conference on Self-Study of Teacher Education Practices* (pp. 96–101). Kingston, Ontario: Queen's University.

Arizona Group. (2000). Myths and legends of teacher education reform in the 1990s: A collaborative self-study of four programs. In J. J. Loughran & T. L. Russell (Eds.), *Exploring myths and legends of teacher education. Proceedings of the 3rd International Conference on Self-Study of Teacher Education Practices* (pp. 20–24). Kingston, Ontario: Queen's University.

Arizona Group, Guilfoyle, K., Hamilton, M. L., Pinnegar, S., & Placier, P. (2004). The epistemological dimensions and dynamics of professional dialogue in self -study. In J. J. Loughran, M. L. Hamilton, V. K. LaBoskey, & T. L. Russell (Eds.), *International handbook of self-study of teaching and teacher education practices* (pp. 1109–1168). Dordrecht, Netherlands: Kluwer Academic Publishers.

Arizona Group, Placier, P., Pinnegar, S., Hamilton, M. L., & Guilfoyle, K. (2006). Exploring the concept of dialogue in the self-study of teaching practices. In C. Kosnik, C. Beck, A. Freese, & A. Samaras (Eds.), *Making a difference in teacher education through self-study* (pp. 51–64). Dordrecht, Netherlands: Kluwer Academic Publishers.

Bair, M. A., Bair, D. E., Mader, C. E., Hipp, S., & Hakim, I. (2010). Faculty emotions: A self-study of teacher educators. *Studying Teacher Education* 6(1), 95–111.

Biddulph, M. (2005). The monochrome frame: Mural-making as a methodology understanding 'self.' In C. Mitchell, S. Weber, & K. O'Reilly-Scanlon (Eds.), *Just who do we think we are? Methodologies for autobiography and self-study in teaching* (pp. 49–57). New York, NY: RoutledgeFalmer.

Britzman, D. P. (1998). *Lost subjects, contested objects: Towards a psychoanalytic inquiry of learning.* New York, NY: Suny Press.

Brown, E. R. (2000). Identity, education, and the social order: The myth of racelessness. In J. J. Loughran & T. L. Russell (Eds.), *Exploring myths and legends of teacher education. Proceedings of the 3rd International Conference on Self-Study of Teacher Education Practices* (pp. 30–35). Kingston, Ontario: Queen's University.

Brown, E. R. (2004). The significance of race and social class for self-study and the professional knowledge base of teacher education. In J. J. Loughran, M. L. Hamilton, V. K. LaBoskey, & T. L. Russell (Eds.) *International handbook of self-study of teaching and teacher education practices* (pp. 517–524). Dordrecht, Netherlands: Kluwer Academic Publishers.

Brown, N., Wiggins, R., & Secord, D. (2008). And God sits next to me: The role of religion in teacher education programs. In M. L. Heston, D. L. Tidwell, K. K. East, & L. M. Fitzgerald (Eds.), *Pathways to change in teacher education: Dialogue, diversity and self-study. Proceedings for the 7th International Conference on Self-Study of Teacher Education Practices* (pp. 36–40). Cedar Falls, IA: University of Northern Iowa.

Butler-Kisber, L. (2005). Inquiry through poetry: The genesis of self-study. In C. Mitchell, S. Weber, & K. O'Reilly-Scanlon, (Eds.), *Just who do we think we are? Methodologies for autobiography and self-study in teaching* (pp. 95–110). New York, NY: RoutledgeFalmer.

Cochran-Smith, M., & Lytle, S. (2004). Practitioner inquiry, knowledge, and university culture. In J. J. Loughran, M. L. Hamilton, V. K. LaBoskey, & T. L. Russell (Eds.), *International handbook of self study of teaching and teacher education practices* (pp. 601–649). Dordrecht, Netherlands: Kluwer Academic Publishers.

Coia, L., & Taylor, M. (2002). Autobiography and community: An exploration of the use of autobiographical reflection by and with teachers. In C. Kosnik, A. Samaras, A. Freese (Eds), *Making a difference in teacher education through self-study. Proceedings of the 4th International Conference on Self-Study of Teacher Education Practices* (pp. 48–52). Toronto, Canada: OISE, University of Toronto.

Coia, L., & Taylor, M. (2004). What is at risk here? Recasting feminist authority through the lens of the past. In D. L. Tidwell, L. M. Fitzgerald, & M. L. Heston (Eds.), *Journeys of hope: Risking self study in a diverse world. Proceedings of the 5th International Conference on Self-Study of Teacher Education Practices* (pp. 59–62). Cedar Falls, IA: University of Northern Iowa.

Coia, L., & Taylor, M. (2013). Uncovering our feminist pedagogy: A co/autoethnography. *Studying Teacher Education, 9*(1) 3–17.

Cole, A. L., & Knowles, J. G. (2004). Research, practice, and academia in North America. In J. J. Loughran, M. L. Hamilton, V. K. LaBoskey, & T. Russell (Eds.), *International handbook of self study of teaching and teacher education practices* (pp. 451–482). Dordrecht, The Netherlands: Kluwer.

Conrad, D., Conrad, D., Misra, A., Pinard, M., & Youngblood, J. (2010). Studying the I in our teaching and learning: Influences of identity on pedagogy for faculty of color at a rural university. *Studying Teacher Education 6*(2), 143–159.

Craig, C. (2008). Change, changing, and being changed: A study of self in the throes of multiple accountability demands. In M. L. Heston, D. L. Tidwell, K. K. East, & L. M. Fitzgerald (Eds.), *Pathways to change in teacher education: Dialogue, diversity and self-study. Proceedings for the 7th International Conference on Self-Study of Teacher Education Practices* (pp. 87–90). Cedar Falls, IA: University of Northern Iowa.

Davies, B., & Harré, R. (1990). Positioning: The discursive production of selves. *Journal for the Theory of Social Behavior, 20*(1), 43–63.

Elliott, A. (2001). *Concepts of self.* Malden, MA: Polity Press.

Feldman, A., Paugh, P., & Mills, G. (2004). Self-study through action research. In J. J. Loughran, M. L. Hamilton, V. K. LaBoskey, & T. Russell (Eds.), *International handbook of self-study of teaching and teacher education practices* (pp. 943–978). Dordrecht, The Netherlands: Kluwer.

Feldman, A. (2006). Using an existential form of reflection to understand my transformation as a teacher educator. In C. Kosnik, C. Beck, A. R. Freese & A. P. Samaras (Eds.), *Making a difference in teacher education through self-study: Studies of personal, professional, and program renewal* (pp. 35–50). Dordrecht, The Netherlands: Springer Press.

Fitzgerald, L. M., Farstad, J. E., & Deemer, D. (2002). What get's "mythed" in the student evaluations of their teacher education professors. In J. Loughran & T. Russell (Eds.), *Improving teacher education practices through self-study* (pp. 208–221). New York, NY: RoutledgeFalmer.

Galman, S., Lassonde, C., & Kosnik, C. (2010). Teacher educators negotiate public and private selves and work: A collaborative epistolary romance in three acts. In L. B. Erickson, J. R. Young, & S. Pinnegar (Eds.), *Navigating the public and private: Negotiating the diverse landscape of teacher education. Proceedings of the 8th International Conference on Self-Study of Teacher Education Practices* (pp. 89–92). Provo, UT: Brigham Young University.

Gamelin, A. K. (2005). Visions, vulnerability and self-study. In C. Mitchell, S. Weber, & K. O'Reilly Scanlon, (Eds.), *Just who do we think we are? Methodologies for autobiography and self-study in teaching* (pp. 183–192). New York, NY: RoutledgeFalmer.

Glaser, B. G., & Strauss, A. L. (1967). *The discovery of grounded theory: Strategies for qualitative research.* Chicago, IL: Aldine.

Griffiths, M. (1998). Telling stories about collaboration: Secrets and lies? In A. L. Cole & S. Finley (Eds.), *Conversations in community. Proceedings of the 2nd International Conference on Self-study of Teacher Education Practices* (pp. 225–228). Kingston, Ontario: Queen's University.

Griffiths, M., Bass, L., Johnston, M., & Perselli, V. (2004). Knowledge, social justice and self-study. In J. J. Loughran, M. L. Hamilton, V. K. LaBoskey, & T. Russell (Eds.), *International handbook of self-study of teaching and teacher education practices* (pp. 651–707). Dordrecht, The Netherlands: Kluwer.

Guilfoyle, K., Hamilton, M. L., Pinnegar, S., & Placier, M. (1995). Becoming teachers of teachers: The paths of four beginners. In T. Russell & F. Korthagen (Eds.), *Teachers who teach teachers* (pp. 35–55). London, UK: Falmer Press.

Guilfoyle, K., Placier, P., Hamilton, M. L., & Pinnegar, S. (2002). Exploring the concept of dialogue in the self-study of teaching practices. In C. Kosnik, A. Freese, A. P. Samaras (Eds.), *Making a difference in teacher education through self-study. Proceedings of the 4th International Conference on Self-Study of Teacher Education Practices* (pp. 96–102). Toronto, Ontario: OISE, University of Toronto.

Grumet,M. (1988). *Bitter milk: Women and teaching*. Amherst: University of Massachusetts Press.

Ham, V., & Kane, R. (2004). In J. J. Loughran, M. L. Hamilton, V. K. LaBoskey, & T. Russell (Eds.), *International handbook of self-study of teaching and teacher education practices* (pp. 103–150). Dordrecht, The Netherlands: Kluwer.

Harding, S. (1989). Is there a feminist method? In N. Tuana (Ed.), *Feminism and science* (pp. 18–32). Bloomington, IN: Indiana University Press.

Harré, R., & van Langenhove, L. (1998). *Positioning theory: Moral contexts of international action*. Oxford, England: Wiley-Blackwell Publishing.

Hamilton, M. L. (Ed.). (1998). *Reconceptualizing teaching practice: Self-study in teacher education*. London, UK: FalmerPress.

Hamilton, M. L., & Guilfoyle, K. (1998). The tyrannies of tenure: A longitudinal self-study of women at a border crossing. In A. L. Cole & S. Finley (Eds.), *Conversations in community. Proceedings of the 2nd International Conference on Self-study of Teacher Education Practices* (pp. 17–20). Kingston, Ontario: Queen's University.

Hamilton, M. L., & Pinnegar, S. (1998). Conclusion: The value and promise of self-study. In M. L. Hamilton (Ed.), *Reconceptualizing teaching practice: Self-study in teacher education* (pp. 235–246). London, UK: FalmerPress.

Heston, M. L. (2008). Professional change through personal growth: Tools for reframing relationships with students and colleagues. In M. L. Heston, D. L. Tidwell, K. K. East, & L. M. Fitzgerald (Eds.), *Pathways to change in teacher education: Dialogue, diversity and self-study. Proceedings for the 7th International Conference on Self-Study of Teacher Education Practices* (pp. 173–176). Cedar Falls, IA: University of Northern Iowa.

James, E. A. (2008). Studying and improving connection and inclusion in online professorship dealing with the dark side. In M. L. Heston, D. L. Tidwell, K. K. East, & L. M. Fitzgerald (Eds.), *Pathways to change in teacher education: Dialogue, diversity and self-study. Proceedings for the 7th International Conference on Self-Study of Teacher Education Practices* (pp. 182–186). Cedar Falls, IA: University of Northern Iowa.

Johnston, M. (2000). Students of color as cultural consultants: A self-study. In J. Loughran & T. Russell (Eds.), *Exploring myths and legends of teacher education. Proceedings of the 3rd International Conference on Self-Study of Teacher Education Practices* (pp. 122–125). Kingston, Ontario: Queen's University.

Johnston, M., Summers-Eskridge, L., Thomas, M., & Lee, Y. A. (2002). Students of color as cultural consultants: A self-study with multiple theoretical re readings. In C. Kosnik, A. Freese, A. P. Samaras (Eds.), *Making a difference in teacher education through self-study. Proceedings of the 4th International Conference on Self-Study of Teacher Education Practices* (pp. 24–30). Toronto, Ontario: OISE, University of Toronto.

Kelchtermans, G., & Hamilton, M. L. (2004). The dialects of passion and theory: Exploring the relation between self-study and emotion. In J. J. Loughran, M. L. Hamilton, V. K. LaBoskey, & T. Russell (Eds.), *International handbook of self-study of teaching and teacher education practices* (pp. 785–810). Dordrecht, The Netherlands: Kluwer.

Khan, R. B. (2012). *Supporting foundation phase professional development: A self-study of a head of department*. (Unpublished masters dissertation). University of Kwazulu-Natal, Durban South Africa.

Khau, M. (2009). Journeys into the hidden self: Reflections on a collaborative inquiry into women teachers' memories of adolescent sexuality. In K. Pithouse, C. Mitchell, & R. Moletsane (Eds.), *Making connections: Self-study and social action* (pp. 59–76). New York, NY: Peter Lang.

Khau, M., & Pithouse, K. (2008). Studying ourselves as scholars-teachers in the age of HIV and AIDS in South Africa. *Human Architecture: Journal of the Sociology of Self-Knowledge, 1*(2), 39–48.

Kitchen, J., & Bellini, C. (2012). Making it better for Lesbian, Gay, Bisexual, and Transgender Students through teacher education: A collaborative self-study. *Studying Teacher Education, 8*(3), 209–226.

Kirk, J. (2005). Starting with the self: Reflexivity in studying women teachers' lives in development. In C. Mitchell, S. Weber, & K. O'Reilly-Scanlon (Eds.), *Just who do we think we are? Methodologies for autobiography and self-study in teaching* (pp. 231–241). New York, NY: RoutledgeFalmer.

Kuzmic, J. J. (2002). Research as a way of knowing and seeing. In J. Loughran & T. Russell (Eds.), *Improving teacher education practices through self-study* (pp. 222–235). New York, NY: RoutledgeFalmer.

LaBoskey, V. K. (2004). The methodology of self-study and its theoretical underpinnings. In J. J. Loughran, M. L. Hamilton, V. K. LaBoskey, & T. Russell (Eds.), *International handbook of self-study of teacher education practices* (pp. 817–869). Dordrecht, The Netherlands: Kluwer Academic Publishers.

LaBoskey, V. K. (2009). "Name it and claim it": The methodology of self-study as social justice teacher education. In D. L. Tidwell, M. L. Heston, & L. M. Fitzgerald (Eds.), *Research methods for the self-study of practice* (pp. 73–82). Rotterdam: The Netherlands: Springer.

Loughran, J. J. (2004). Learning through self-study: The influence of purpose, participants and contexts. In J. J. Loughran, M. L. Hamilton, V. K. LaBoskey, & T. Russell (Eds.), *International handbook of self-study of teacher education practices* (pp. 151–192). Dordrecht, The Netherlands: Kluwer Academic Publishers.

MacGillivray, L. (1997). Do what I say, not what I do: An instructor rethinks her own teaching and research. *Curriculum Inquiry, 27*(4), 469–488.

Manke, M. P. (2000). Power relations and how they work: Weaving threads of meaning. In J. Loughran & T. Russell (Eds.), *Exploring myths and legends of teacher education. Proceedings of the 3rd International Conference on Self-Study of Teacher Education Practices* (pp. 69–72). Kingston, Ontario: Queen's University.

Manke, M. P. (2005). A queer path across the straight furrows of my field: a series of reflections. In C. Mitchell, S. Weber, & K. O'Reilly-Scanlon (Eds.), *Just who do we think we are? Methodologies for autobiography and self-study in teaching* (pp. 193–204). New York, NY: RoutledgeFalmer.

Masinga, L. (2009). An African teacher's journey to self-knowledge through teaching sexuality education. In K. Pithouse, C. Mitchell, & R. Moletsane (Eds.), *Making connections: Self-study and social action* (pp. 237–252). New York, NY: Peter Lang.

Masinga, L. (2013). *Journeys to self-knowledge: A participatory study of teachers as sexuality educators.* (Unpublished doctoral dissertation.) University of Kwazulu-Natal. Durban, South Africa.

McGinnis, J. R., & Pearsall, M. (1998). Teaching elementary science methods to women: A male professor's experience from two perspectives. *Journal of Research in Science Teaching, 5*(8), 919–949.

McNeil, B. (2011). Charting a way forward: Intersections of race and space in establishing identity as an African-Canadian teacher educator. *Studying Teacher Education, 8*(1), 69–85.

Meyer, L. J. (2012). From here to queer: Mapping sexualities in education. In E. R. Meiners & T. Quinn (Eds.), *Sexualities in education: A reader* (pp. 9–17). New York, NY: Peter Lang.

Mitchell, C. (2006). In my own handwriting: Textual evidence and self-study. In C. Kosnik, C. Beck, A. R. Freese & A. P. Samaras (Eds.), *Making a difference in teacher education through self-study: Studies of personal, professional, and program renewal* (pp. 117–130). Dordrecht, The Netherlands: Springer Press.

Mulhern, M., & Martinez, G. (1999). Confronting homophobia in a multicultural education course. In W. Letts & J. Sears (Eds), *Queering elementary education: Advancing the dialogue about sexuality in schooling* (pp. 247–256). Lanham, MD: Rowman & Littlefield.

Mulholland, V., & Longman, S. (2009). Reframing autobiography in teacher education from a first nation's perspective. In K. Pithouse, C. Mitchell, & R. Moletsane (Eds.), *Making connections: Self-study and social action* (pp. 207–222). New York, NY: Peter Lang.

O'Reilly-Scanlon, K. (2002). Muted echoes and lavender shadows: Memory work and self-study. In C. Kosnik, A. Freese, A. P. Samaras (Eds.), *Making a difference in teacher education through self study. Proceedings of the 4th International Conference on Self-Study of Teacher Education Practices* (pp. 74–78). Toronto, Ontario: OISE, University of Toronto.

Pennington, J. L., Brock, C. H., Abernathy, T. V., Bingham, A., Major, E. M., Wiest, L. R., & Ndura, E. (2012). Teacher educators' dispositions: Footnoting the present with stories from our past. *Studying Teacher Education, 8*(1), 69–85.

Perselli, V. (1998). The political Is personal: An action researcher investigates issues of sex and gender in a Junior School. In A. L. Cole & S. Finley (Eds.), *Conversations in community. Proceedings of the 2nd International Conference on Self-study of Teacher Education Practices* (pp. 66–69). Kingston, Ontario: Queen's University.

Perselli, V. (2002). The importance of being an artist. In C. Kosnik, A. Freese, A. P. Samaras (Eds.), *Making a difference in teacher education through self-study. Proceedings of the 4th International Conference on Self-Study of Teacher Education Practices* (pp. 81–83). Toronto, Ontario: OISE, University of Toronto.

Perselli, V. (2004). Marx and education: Exploring the teachings of Marx in the context of my role as a school experience liaison tutor in initial teacher education. In D. L. Tidwell, L. M. Fitzgerald, & M. Heston (Eds.), *Journeys of hope: Risking self-study in a diverse world. Proceedings of the 5th International Conference on Self-Study of Teacher Education Practices* (pp. 198–201). Cedar Falls, IA: University of Northern Iowa.

Perselli, V. (2006). A Marxian approach in education: Paradoxes of praxis: Thinking about aspects of social justice in the context of school visiting. In D. Tidwell & L. Fitzgerald (Eds.), *Self-study and diversity* (pp. 71–88). Rotterdam, The Netherlands: SensePublisher.

Ressler, P. (2000). Race and sexual orientation in multicultural feminist teacher education. In K. Kumashiro (Ed.), *Troubling intersections of race and sexuality* (pp. 179–194). Lanham, MD: Rowman and Littlefield.

Richards, J. C. (1996). Turning to the artistic: Developing an enlightened eye by creating teaching self-portraits. In J. Richards & T. Russell (Eds.), *Empowering our future in teacher education. Proceedings of the 1st International Conference on Self-Study of Teacher Education Practices* (pp. 190–194). Kingston, Ontario: Queen's University.

Rodriguez, A. J. (1998). Strategies for counterresistance: Toward a sociotransformative constructivism and learning to teach science for diversity and for understanding. *Journal of Research in Science Teaching, 35*(6), 589–622.

Samaras, A. P., & Freese, A. R. (2006). *Self-study of teaching practices.* New York, NY: Peter Lang.

Samaras, A. P., Hicks, M. A., & Berger, J. G. (2004). Self-study through personal history. In J. J. Loughran, M. L. Hamilton, V. K. LaBoskey, & T. L. Russell (Eds.), *International handbook of self-study of teaching and teacher education practices* (pp. 905–942). Dordrecht, Netherlands: Kluwer Academic Publishers.

Sandretto, S. (2009). Theoretical and methodological tensions in a poststructural, collaborative self study research project. *Studying Teacher Education, 5*(1), 89–101.

Schulte, A. (2006). Assuming my transformation: Transforming my assumptions. *Studying Teacher Education, 1*(1), 31–42.

Schulte, A. (2009). *Seeking integrity in teacher education: Transforming student teachers, transforming my self.* Dordrecht, The Netherlands: Springer Press.

Seaton, L. (2004). Learning to be a gender equity consultant: Listening to teachers. In D. L. Tidwell, L. M. Fitzgerald, & M. Heston (Eds.), *Journeys of hope: Risking self-study in a diverse world. Proceedings of the 5th International Conference on Self-Study of Teacher Education Practices* (pp. 217–220). Cedar Falls, IA: University of Northern Iowa.

Sedgwick, E. K. (1990). *Epistemology of the closet.* Hammondsworth: Penguin.

Skerrett, A. (2007). Looking inward: The impact of race, ethnicity, gender, and social class background on teaching sociocultural theory in education. *Studying Teacher Education, 2*(2), 183–200.

Steedman, C. (1987). Prisonhouses. In M. Lawn & G. Grace (Eds.), *Teachers: The culture and politics of work* (pp. 117–129). London, England: Palmer Press.

Strom, K. J., & Martin, A. D. (2013). Putting philosophy to work in the classroom: Using rhizomatics to deterritorialize neoliberal thought and practice. *Studying Teacher Education, 9*(3), 219–235.

Strong-Wilson, T. (2005). 'White female teacher arrives in native community with trunk and cat': Using self-study to investigate tales of traveling White teachers. In C. Mitchell, S. Weber, & K. O'Reilly

Scanlon (Eds.), *Just who do we think we are? Methodologies for autobiography and self-study in teaching* (pp. 218–230). New York, NY: RoutledgeFalmer.

Tamdgidi, M. H. (2009). Rethinking diversity amid pedagogical flexibility: Fostering the scholarships of learning and teaching of the sociological imagination. In K. Pithouse, C. Mitchell, & R. Moletsane (Eds.), *Making connections: Self-study and social action* (pp. 169–186). New York, NY: Peter Lang.

Taylor, M., & Coia, L. (2006). Revisiting feminist authority through a co/autoethnographic lens. In D. Tidwell & L. Fitzgerald (Eds.), *Self-study research and issues of diversity* (pp. 51–70). Rotterdam, The Netherlands: SensePublishers.

Taylor, M., & Coia, L. (2009). Co/autoethnography: Investigating teachers in relation. In C. Lassonde, S. Gallman & C. Kosnik (Eds.), *Self-Study research methodologies for teacher educators* (pp. 169–186). Rotterdam, The Netherlands: SensePublishers.

Taylor, M., & Coia, L. (2010). Beyond classroom walls: Using self-study to understand our roles as educational researchers in schools. In L. B. Erickson, J. R. Young, S. Pinnegar (Eds.), *Navigating the public and private: Negotiating the diverse landscape of teacher education. Proceedings of the 8th International Conference on Self-Study of Teacher Education Practices* (pp. 253–256). Provo, UT: Brigham Young University.

Taylor, M., Coia, L., Hopper, T., Sanford, K., Smolin, L., & Crafton, L. (2006). Making collaboration explicit in self-study research in teacher education. In L. M. Fitzgerald, M. L. Heston, D. L. Tidwell (Eds.), *Collaboration and community: Pushing boundaries through self-study. Proceedings of the 6th International Conference on Self-Study of Teacher Education Practices* (pp. 247–251). Cedar Falls, IA: University of Northern Iowa.

Thomas, L., & Beauchamp, C. (2010). Understanding agency: A collaborative self-study exploring tensions in teacher education practice and research. In L. B. Erickson, J. R. Young, & S. Pinnegar (Eds.), *Navigating the public and private: Negotiating the diverse landscape of teacher education. Proceedings of the 8th International Conference on Self-Study of Teacher Education Practices* (pp. 257–260). Provo, UT: Brigham Young University.

Thompson, S. A. (2006). Brother, can you spare a 'digm? A self-study of the comfort of the insipient practical in inclusive/special education and teacher education. In L. M. Fitzgerald, M. L. Heston, & D. L. Tidwell (Eds.), *Collaboration and community: Pushing boundaries through self-study. Proceedings of the 6th International Conference on Self-Study of Teacher Education Practices* (pp. 252–256). Cedar Falls, IA: University of Northern Iowa.

Tidwell, D. L., Heston, M. L., & Fitzgerald, L. M. (Eds.) (2006). *Self-study research and issues of diversity*. Rotterdam, The Netherlands: SensePublishers.

Walkerdine, V. (1990). *Schoolgirl fictions*. New York, NY and London, UK: Verso.

Weber, S. A., & Mitchell, C. A. (2000). Prom dresses are us? Excerpts from collective memory work. In J. J. Loughran & T. Russell (Eds.), *Exploring myths and legends of teacher education. Proceedings of the 3rd International Conference on Self-Study of Teacher Education Practices* (pp. 248–251). Kingston, Ontario: Queen's University.

Weber, S., & Mitchell, C. (2002). Academic literary performance, embodiment, and self-study: When the shoe doesn't fit: Death of a salesman. In C. Kosnik, A. Freese, A. P. Samaras (Eds.), *Making a difference in teacher education through self-study. Proceedings of the 4th International Conference on Self-Study of Teacher Education Practices* (pp. 121–124). Toronto, Ontario: OISE, University of Toronto.

Wilcox, S., Watson, J., & Paterson, M. (2004). Self-study in professional practice. In J. J. Loughran, M. L. Hamilton, V. K. LaBoskey, & T. L. Russell (Eds.), *International handbook of self-study of teaching and teacher education practices* (pp. 273–312). Dordrecht, Netherlands: Kluwer Academic Publishers.

Wood, L. (2009). Teachers' self-exploration of gender constructs: A values-based approach to HIV prevention. In K. Pithouse, C. Mitchell, & R. Moletsane (Eds.), *Making connections: Self-study and social action* (pp. 285–300). New York, NY: Peter Lang.

Zeichner, K. M. (1995). Reflections of a teacher educator working for school change. In T. L. Russell & F. Korthagen (Eds.), *Teachers who teach teachers* (pp. 198–207). London, UK: Falmer Press.

AFFILIATIONS

Lesley Coia
Department of Education,
Agnes Scott College,
Decatur, Georgia

Monica Taylor
Department of Secondary and Special Education,
Montclair State University,
Montclair, New Jersey

KATHRYN STROM, RABAB ABI-HANNA, LINDA ABRAMS,
CHARITY DACEY & JACQUELINE DAUPLAISE

EXPLORING AND CONNECTING LINES OF FLIGHT IN A SELF-STUDY COMMUNITY

PROLOGUE

A small group of doctoral students and a professor faced each other around a narrow oval conference table during the final few moments of an intensive summer class where we had started to explore our individual capacities and identities as change agents. Although the class itself was at an end, we knew our work together was not done. We were just beginning to negotiate our identities as doctoral students and teacher educators, while examining and re-negotiating our identities as women, endeavors that were facilitated by our group process. That evening, nine of us made a commitment to continue reading, writing, and engaging in dialogue as a self-study group so that we could explore questions about our place in the world and the intersections of our multiple roles. Each of us had different motives for joining the self-study group, which later came to be known as "Wicked Smart Women." For some of us, the readings and discussions during the summer class struck chords that went far deeper than the scholarly content and we wanted to find ways to link theories that were new to us with our personal and shared experiences. Other members of the group craved the connections of a community and joined out of a need to belong. No matter our original intent, we have since realized that rather than meeting at the conclusion, or at the beginning, we met in the middle and became an assemblage—a multiplicity—that enabled collective growth.

CONTEXT

We are a group of doctoral students who came together because of a shared sense of dissatisfaction and disequilibrium in our various roles as students, teachers, and professionals. In our quest to explore who we were becoming in the context of our work and personal lives, we gravitated toward self-study methodology, which seemed a natural fit, as it "focuses on the nexus between public and private, theory and practice, research and pedagogy, self and other" (LaBoskey, 2004, p. 818). In the fall of 2011, we embarked on a self-study project to identify who we were becoming, the pedagogical beliefs that ground our practices in our new roles as doctoral students, and the ongoing evolution and reinvention of ourselves as teacher educators and

M. Taylor and L. Coia (Eds.), Gender, Feminism, and Queer Theory in the Self-Study of Teacher Education Practices, 31–43.

change agents (Abrams, Abi-Hanna, Bess, Collucci, Dacey, Dauplaise, Mastellone, Strom, & Taylor, 2012). Using a methodology of co/autoethnography to "write into each other's lives" (Taylor & Coia, 2006, p. 61), our challenge was to look to the past, while considering the present, and identify how our various identities affected who we were becoming.

As we pursued our self-study research together, we experienced deep growth as agents of change and were transformed collectively and individually (Tidwell, Farrell, Brown, Taylor, Coia, Abi-Hanna, Abrams, Dacey, Dauplaise, & Strom, 2012). Our transformation was not planned, but occurred through an authentic process of writing and dialogue. By carving out the space and time to reflect together on what we were each experiencing independently, it became clear that common themes were emerging for us as a group, including that of struggle, becoming, finding a feminist identity, and negotiating power in our roles as women. These themes became the centerpiece of our first collaborative self-study project, which was presented by five of the original nine members of our group at the Ninth International Conference on the Self-Study of Teacher Education Practices (Abrams, et al., 2012).

While we acknowledge our past growth and the lasting power of our collaboration, today we (the five authors of this chapter) find ourselves curious about how the transformation process occurred during that first year together. Like Butler (1995), we wonder "[h]ow is it that we became available to a transformation of who we are, a contestation which compels us to rethink ourselves, a reconfiguration of our place and our ground?" (p. 131). One of us had begun to engage with the concepts of rhizomatics (Deleuze & Guattari, 1987), and brought her work to the group, proposing that particular rhizomatic concepts offered the possibility of thinking differently about our work and generating thinking about our collective and individual processes of transformation. The Deleuzo-Guattarian notions of assemblages and lines of flight resonated with us as productive ways to theorize our work together. Therefore, the purpose of the present study is to explore the process of our growth by identifying the "lines of flight" that allowed our transformation to take place. We recognize lines of flight as opportunities to break away from our individual static identities and to collectively become a unique "assemblage" that produced new ways of thinking and looking at the world.

RHIZOMATICS

Our study is grounded in poststructural feminism, drawing from Deleuze & Guattari's (1987) notion of rhizomatics. Although not specifically a feminist theory, our use of this perspective follows in the footsteps of poststructural feminists (e.g., Braidotti, 2005; Lather, 1997; Ringrose, 2011; Ringrose & Coleman, 2013; St. Pierre, 2004) who see feminism and rhizomatics as complementary lenses that both emphasize non-hierarchical, relational ways of viewing the world and characterize thought/life as constantly becoming. The "rhizome" is scientifically defined as a tuber that is made of multiple lines that connect in unpredictable ways, growing every which way. Deleuze & Guattari (1987) explain that the rhizome is an "antidote" to the tree, or "arborescent thinking," which represents the linear, hierarchical, process-product, rationalist, male thinking that dominates social structures and society at large (Belenky, Clinchy, Goldberger & Tarule, 1997). Rather than emphasizing the individual as isolated in the world (and as such an autonomous actor with complete agency and control of her surroundings) the rhizome emphasizes multiplicities, or "assemblages," that come together for a particular function (Livesey, 2005).

Rhizomes are composed of two types of lines. *Molar lines* are rigid lines, macro-level forces that bind us to the status quo. These societal or institutional forces present themselves as hegemonic structures or discourses that reinforce asymmetrical power relations. In a classroom, the "grammar of schooling" (Tyack & Cuban, 1995)—the separation of subjects and grades, structures such as tracking, and traditional discourses of teacher as teller and student as passive receivers of knowledge—are examples of molar lines. However, molar lines rely on *molecular lines* for expression at the micro-level of society. Molecular lines are supple and flexible. These can carry out the work of the molar, but also have the potential to break away from the molar and disrupt the norm, thus becoming a *line of flight*. Lines of flight are lines of becoming-different—in other words, lines of change, or momentary breaks from the status quo. Too often, teacher educators are forced to play a part in the reproductive nature of schooling, reinforcing the status quo through institutional structures in which they have no say—such as the courses they are assigned to teach, allotted class times and schedules to which they are limited, and programmatic foci or emphases to which they must adhere. These are examples of the molecular work of the teacher educator that carries out molar lines. Alternately, moments may occur where the students and teacher break from their static roles or temporarily escape traditional educational norms. A student may ask an unexpected question, taking the class into a different direction than intended; a teacher educator might have a frank conversation with students about the skewed nature of standardized testing or discuss the very political nature of education with future teachers. These are lines of flight, interruptions of the norm. Although they are always recaptured by the molar—class ends, the teacher or professor has to return to the planned structure of a lesson—in that moment of escape, micro-changes occur that have the potential to shift the system as a whole. The work of mapping the rhizome, Deleuze and Guattari (1987) contend, is to follow lines of flight, for these are what contribute to larger changes in our social system. Because of its focus on collectives and the lines of flight they produce together, rhizomatics is an ideal frame for us as we explore the question of processes of becoming in a self-study learning community.

The theory of rhizomatics posits that we are in perpetual motion. We are always evolving, changing, becoming, in a perpetual middle—never at the beginning or end. Viewed through this lens, then, the purpose of research is not to describe what *is*, because that is a useless endeavor. By the time we write about it, we have already become something else. Therefore, research, in a Deleuzo-Guattarian sense, should focus on doing, functioning, and producing, on identifying lines of flight that lead to new possibilities. In our lives as practitioners, this attention to productive processes is also quite complementary as we refine and apply a new level of awareness. In keeping with this frame, our purpose was not to name or say what is, but to describe processes and functions—to ask, "How does our assemblage work? How does it function to create new potentialities?" To explore this question, we revisited our process during our first year as a self-study group—where we experienced a period of collective and intense growth—to produce thinking about the process of becoming-feminists, becoming-scholars, becoming-community, and becoming-who-we-are-not-yet.

MAPPING LINES OF FLIGHT

Our methodology is post-qualitative, seeking to create thinking around processes of becoming and growth while resisting traditional, positivistic research methods that code data/ideas and put them into separate boxes, thus closing them off from possible connections (St. Pierre, 2004, 2011). "Despite all our desperate, eternal attempts to separate, contain and mend, categories always leak" (Minh-ha, 1989, p. 94), defying the artificial neatness of traditional approaches to qualitative research, which often mimic the structures of quantitative methods. To treat our data as fluid and allow for linkages and blending, we turned to rhizoanalysis (Alvermann, 2000; Bowles, 2001; Honan & Sellers, 2008; Sellers, 2010) and rhizomatic cartography (Hagood, 2002; Waterhouse, 2011), "emergent" methods that map becomings by making connections and creating thinking around topics and processes.

These constructed maps of connections and becomings are not intended to represent "reality," but rather create thinking and express possibilities. Further, our maps are not products, but rather analytic tools. To analyze our collective becomings, we first individually brought evidence of "lines of flight"—places where we recognized an escape from the status quo, or some sort of micro-transformation—in our own narratives from the past year's project. We recorded these pieces of evidence on multicolored post-it notes and created maps of our individual journeys. We then brought our evidence together and, as a group, arranged our post-it notes into a collective map by theorizing connections to create emergent themes or ideas. These connections were both "productive and dangerous" (Albrecht-Crane & Slack, 2003, p. 196), creating a sense of uncertainty and disequilibrium. Yet, in trying to make sense of how our lines of flight connected to our practices, to each other, and to the world, we generated a "cartography" of our process of becoming, which is detailed next.

BECOMINGS

In this endeavor, we have decided to present *becomings*, rather than findings, as we recognized lines of flight as opportunities to become-who-we-are-not-yet, rather than truths we "found" in our narratives. As an assemblage, we identified several becomings: working as a group; raising consciousness; claiming power; enacting agency; and transforming self. We have chosen to express our becomings as transitive verb phrases in order to convey their nature as ongoing processes that are continuously evolving as they inform our work and lives. Thus, they are not presented as the ends or results of our work together, but as perpetual processes we experience individually and together. In the sections that follow, descriptions of becomings are blended with italicized narratives written by each of our group members, contextualizing the theme to personal experience. These personal stories serve as exemplars of the lines of flight constructed over the course of our time together.

Working as a Group

Group work brought us together, enabling us to recognize opportunities for lines of flight and to recharge our batteries. The group itself became a safe place where we were encouraged to tell our stories and find commonalities despite the diversity of our backgrounds and experiences. Reviewing our individual narratives, we noticed that working as a group created a support system and provided a sense of belonging and feeling valued. We became stronger together and individually when we shared our experiences, reflected on each other's narratives, and made sense of our problems and struggles. Growth occurred as we collectively and recursively engaged in a dialectical process of questioning and rethinking so that we were pushed to new levels of awareness.

I joined the group looking for a challenge. I had completed my coursework and did not want to be isolated from the discussion scene. I wanted to learn and evolve, but I was not expecting the outcome. The dynamics of the group members allowed the creation of a safety zone, where I felt encouraged to look inside myself and share without ever fearing that I would be judged. I was offered support and belonging. As an adjunct faculty member, I am made to feel expendable. I found myself constantly engaged in an internal battle questioning my beliefs, awaiting external approval to grant me validity. I wanted to provide my students with a safe environment where they can take ownership of their learning, and I wanted to give a voice to all who were silenced in a math classroom. I did not realize I was stifling myself in the process. Through the group's embrace, I was able to reclaim myself, repossess my voice. I find myself reinvigorated, energized and open to all the possibilities.

Consciousness Raising

A large part of our work, especially in the beginning, was reflecting on our past experiences and reframing them with the new concepts and vocabulary we were learning as we began our foray into feminist and self-study literature. Through our cycles of writing and reflection as individuals and then as a collective, we began to focus more sharply on issues of self through a feminist lens. This process of *bringing-into-focus* contributed to a collective consciousness-raising on the part of the group, although our explorations varied. Much of our work centered on identity, exploring questions of *Who am I? Who have I been, and Who am I becoming?* For some of us, consciousness-raising meant gaining awareness of the contradictions within, making space for new ideas, acknowledging the interweaving, shifting parts of our identities, and realizing the criticality of self-trust. For others, it meant recognizing that we bring our whole selves to our work, or seeing the importance of becoming comfortable with ambiguity.

As a younger scholar, I had never thought much about the idea of feminism. I was extremely committed to issues of social justice in education, but I framed these in terms of racism, classism, and language. I would have been quick to condemn a teacher that adopted a "colorblind" approach to teaching, but I now realize that I brought a "genderblind" lens to my life. I simply never thought about how my gender has shaped my experiences. As we began our self-study group, I was reading Women's Ways of Knowing *(1983), and I brought my learning to our discussions. As we talked about hierarchical, linear ways of being and knowing as privileged, I suddenly made connections between male knowledges and knowing and the oppressive structures of the academy, of research, of the new brand of corporate reform. After our discussion, I went home and wrote about how gender and patriarchy had shaped my life to that point. I felt as if I had been violently awakened, as if my eyes had been duct-taped shut and someone had just ripped the strip of silver off. For the first time, I put pen to paper (or rather, fingers to the keyboard) and I wrote about my nearly two-decades long struggle with bulimia. I wrote about the pudgy little girl who was inundated by messages about what female beauty should look like, and described how, in trying to bridge between my actual body and those impossible standards, I had developed a "coping strategy" that would follow me my entire life. For the first time, I had a place to bring this story and these awakenings, seen through a feminist lens.*

Claiming Power

We came together as individuals with personal stories that we carried on our backs the way turtles carry their shells. Our stories protected us from harm and frankly, from each other. We soon learned that left unexamined, our stories restricted our individual growth and limited possibilities for becoming-who-we-were-not-yet (Pinar, 1998, citing Maxine Greene). Through the process of storytelling, each of us re-discovered the significance of our life experiences and the strength we gained from them. By acknowledging injustices, addressing internal struggles, and recognizing our accomplishments together, our stories took on a new power and purpose as a platform for launching our work together.

I started my doctoral studies after a full teaching career because I wanted to become a legitimate voice in the conversation about education. At the time, it seemed that being a career educator did not qualify me to speak as an authority about my profession. I felt impotent in defense of my life's work. Researchers, scholars, administrators, politicians, union leaders, and pundits spoke for teachers. I believed that in the academy, however, I would find my voice—my power to speak for myself. Yet, once there, I was asked to detach myself from my own lived experience so that I could examine teaching with a more critical eye. Scientifically-based research methodologies that de-personalized, de-humanized, and separated story from truth split me, the doctoral student, from me, the teacher. I turned to this group to support me in pursuing a different kind of truth, one grounded in individual experiences and multiple ways of knowing. I discovered that each of us had experienced some kind of fracturing in our lives--sexual violence, broken marriages, uprooted lives--but in telling our stories, we were able to begin to mend our broken pieces. For me, this means folding together what I learned as a teacher with what I am discovering as a doctoral student and recognizing that my unique experience is my power.

Enacting Agency

One of the key linkages that we have shared has been a growing comfort with our active selves—starting to take action for change. Claiming our power began with each individual having the courage to articulate our struggles and clarify our aspirations. As we questioned our places in the world, re-examined our gendered experiences, and reflected upon our shifts in beliefs, a renewed sense of activism emerged in each of us. As each woman has spoken up for herself and her experiences, our connecting lines of flight have dovetailed. Our active selves are collectively unified around two major commitments to change: continuing to engage in transformative personal growth and re-directing current priorities and approaches in public education. We are all teachers at heart. In K-12 schools, in higher education, in our families, and in our communities, enacting agency is about our renewed commitment to *be* the change we want to see happen in the world.

Enacting agency has been very personal for me. It translates into the daily practice of not only listening to myself and to those around me more acutely, but also hearing what I, and those around me, have to say. I have taken great comfort in our feminist postmodern groundings. When we began together, I was struggling to reconcile my many identities: personally as a mother, sister, wife, and friend, while adding student and scholar to the list of often competing professional identities as teacher, mentor, colleague, and supervisor. I realized that whenever I am overwhelmed with many responsibilities, I run the risk of being consumed by the desire to please others, rather than to stay centered within. Through our reflections, I have learned that identities should not be compartmentalized. Their interrelatedness can be helpful. I cannot turn off my identity as a mother at work—I can better connect this identity by nurturing others' growth in our shared work. What needs to come first, however, is nurturing myself. I asked myself, "Why is slowing down and giving myself time to reflect something I used to perceive as selfish?" I see now that we each deserve self-awareness, respect, trust, and acceptance. I am worthy of my own time and attention and have given myself permission to attend to this work. Slowing down and being still, practices that are so seemingly simple, have emerged as the key to my growth. Only by shattering the myth of these acts as "being selfish" have I been transformed. By prioritizing myself, I also better serve those in my life.

Transforming Self

Each of these processes—group work, consciousness raising, claiming power, and enacting agency—happened alongside, while contributing to, transforming of self. As we re-evaluated our situations, refocused our attention, and questioned our assumptions and beliefs, we shifted our habits of mind (Schulte, 2008). Yet, to return to our initial wondering: *how* did we become available to such a transformation? Through our dialogues, we have come to a consensus that a confluence of initial conditions for productivity existed when we began our journey over a year ago. We were a group of women with open minds, who embraced self-study, and believed in the validity of personally generated knowledge. However, these initial conditions by themselves did not result in our transformations. When we were "liberated" from our class, free of the hierarchy of the professor/student binary, we were just women who each brought a story and the aforementioned qualities. As we connected, over time, we began to blur the personal and professional parts of our lives in discussions. Although we were building trust, we were still "colleagues," still shielding part of ourselves.

In August of 2012, the five of us authoring this paper traveled to England to present our original study at the S-STEP Castle conference (Abrams et al., 2012). We left our families, our jobs, and our other responsibilities back in the United States, journeying to a seventeenth century castle to talk about self-study research for four days. The castle itself was a nurturing environment. We stayed in dorms together, ate our meals with people who wanted to exchange ideas and dialogue about research, and bonded over an impromptu piano sing-along. During our time there, we coined our name—"Wicked Smart Women"—recognizing that we loved *being smart* together. In other words, we could enjoy our mutual intellectual engagement with educational theory and practice—something that was not a positive in our lives outside our group. Since our return last summer, and over the past several months, we have developed relationships with each other, becoming not just colleagues and self-study group members, but friends. We have developed a collective identity, which became a thing unto itself—an assemblage. This evolution of relationship, alongside the processes previously noted, contributed to our transformation as a group, which in turn facilitated our individual transformations.

Initially, I became a member of this study group to understand the role that my identities played in defining who I am as an educator, student, and mother. Reflection helped me understand that I have many identities and they affect the way I perceive a situation. One of these identities is not more important than another.

Yet through examination of my narratives, I realized that my writings reflected an internal struggle of questioning my beliefs as a mathematics educator and my place within the hierarchy of the educational system. The pressures faced by myself as a mathematics teacher in order to meet both personal and state/district expectations can, at times, be overwhelming. My narratives reflected an overall questioning of norms in and out of the classroom. I wondered, "Do teachers and administrators share the same goals?" I felt that we were at odds. Participating in the study group with those who were administrators, and developing relationships with them, helped me understand that administrators and teachers are not at odds, but are connected fibers that hold the educational system together. Through group discussion and self-reflection, I was able to transform my understanding of the dynamics that exist between teachers and administrators, realizing that while there may be a hierarchy that exists within the education system, it does not mean that teachers are of a lesser value. We are equally important.

DISCUSSION

Our project offers several implications for the practice of self-study, including the promise of "thinking with theory" (Mazzei & Youngblood Jackson, 2012) in self-study research and the potential of co/autoethnography in processes of transformation. We used poststructural theoretical concepts, specifically from rhizomatics, to *think differently* about collaborative self-study and collective processes of change. While we do not suggest rhizomatics is "the answer" or a "solution," we do posit that this particular frame provided tools, which produced new thoughts that may not have been available to us with a different lens. This idea of *thinking with theory* (ibid.) helped us theorize our specific processes. Conceptualizing our self-study group as an "assemblage" facilitated interrupting notions of subject and identity, and has brought our attention to our ongoing processes of fitting together for particular functions. This theoretical lens also led us to conceptualize our work as multiplicitous, the product of heterogeneous connections (i.e., each member of the study group) coming together in productive ways.

In this way, we have been able to escape normative conditions of the academy, such as the isolation of doctoral work. We interrupted the binary categories of personal/professional, student/teacher, teacher/teacher educator. We defied—albeit temporarily—the very individualized nature of our society. Over time, these lines of flight have been reconstructed through our meetings and opportunities to write together. We have changed together as we developed our sense of community while persisting in our efforts to grow as individuals. This process has challenged the "fixities of identity politics" (Goldberger, Tarule, Clinchy, & Belenky, 1996, p. 156), confirming that identities are multiple, not only within and between groups, but also between and within an individual. "Rather than being composed of any fixed essence or individual identity," (Maher & Tetreault, 1996, p. 163), we as individuals interacted with the assemblage as a whole, moving recursively between our group work and our individual teaching, projects, and lives. This is, as Strom and Pires (2013) describe:

> An ongoing, recursive process of folding in, refolding, and unfolding, connecting at particular points, and then going out to plug ourselves into our own ... work or other projects. We then looped back, bringing new ideas and happenings to our meetings and folding them into our conversations to make new connections, which then produced new affects and becomings to take and fold back into our individual work. (p. 9)

This continuous folding opens possibilities for pushing the limits of self-study in collaborative contexts, such as those offered by co-autoethnography (Taylor & Coia, 2006, 2009). Our experience affirms that just as "the fabric of the rhizome is the conjunction 'and...and...and'" (Deleuze & Guattari, 1987, p. 25) our process has been productive of "and" conditions for change, always expanding outward. Our meetings, like the rhizome, created "and" spaces and possibilities for us to become an assemblage that produced and explored new terrains, constructed new lines of flight, and produced new wonderings and wanderings. These "ands" happen *despite* and *because of* the molar lines—lines of stratification—that we faced in our daily lives. As we encountered these normalizing forces, the act of hitting up against them created friction and presented occasions for deeper analysis of problems, which in turn generated change. This stood in contrast to our previous binary or "tree" thinking (Deleuze & Guattari, 1987) about our conditions as "either/or," "black/white," "man/woman." Understanding that "tree" thinking—linear, positivistic, rational thought and structures—is always implicated in our work has turned our attention from *transcending* the tree to, instead, our daily work of navigating challenging circumstances and finding ways to break from the status quo. Like Edwards (2006), we look to replace our roots with routes.

Each of us has experienced a shift in the way we interact with/in the world. Once stifled and silenced, we now find ourselves with increasing confidence, speaking without apology and claiming our power. "Hearing" and "being heard" in our meetings and through our writing created lines of flight that were reconstructed over and over again, contributing to this transformation. We feel empowered by our experiences together and have extended what we have learned into our professional lives. Jacky and Rabab have radically changed the ways they teach mathematics, courageously negotiating more feminist, egalitarian, and power-conscious teaching practices with their students. Katie also brought democratic methods and self-study to her first undergraduate teaching experience, attempting to emphasize the importance of both shared power and privileging personal knowledge. These moments of transformational praxis were not mere application of ideas from our research, but were co-constructed in the specific contexts of the different learning spaces and negotiated differently with each teacher-student assemblage.

There are also those of us who are in positions where our learning is not easily transferred to our practices. Charity has navigated the challenges of completing her doctoral work without financial support from her employer by teaching a class at the university, thus creating both a financial benefit and an opportunity for professional growth out of an institutional roadblock (a molar line). Our work together gave Linda the confidence to make space in her busy schedule as a full-time doctoral student so that she could care for her terminally ill sister. Negotiating conflicting loyalties to her personal and professional commitments was challenging, but ultimately she found a way to be "and/also" rather than occupying a binary category—"either" a sister "or" a student. These instances of changing our professional practices demonstrate our commitment to taking risks and knowingly pushing ourselves. We understand that we always have to navigate molar lines—forces in our lives that seek to bind us to the status quo—which means we have to face them in order to transform ourselves and our practice.

EPILOGUE: WHERE DO WE GO NEXT?

Considering the lines of flight of our self-study group process has allowed us to recognize where we have been able to make change in our lives—changes we consider "micro-transgressions" or "micro-transformations" spurred by our collective work this past year. This group has provided the opportunity for us to celebrate those micro-transformations amid the traditionally isolated space of doctoral work and the academy. As we make those mini-breakthroughs, our group has become a space to be able to celebrate with individuals who understand each other's histories, who have written into each other's lives and experienced transformation alongside one another. We find that each group meeting turns into a form of rejuvenation. Our discussions and connections sustain us, push us, energize us, fortify us, and liberate us.

We have explored *who we are not yet* and our processes of transforming our practices and ourselves. We now find ourselves continuing to make productive connections with both material and non-material bodies, understanding how we come into composition with both other human actors and non-human elements, spaces, and ideas—in other words, expanding our "ands." We look to connect with other doctoral students, inviting them to enter into composition with our self-study community assemblage or form their own. We also see that bringing self-study, feminism, rhizomatics, and education into dialogue has allowed us to think differently about our processes and our work, providing new perspectives focusing on future lines of flight and potentialities not yet realized.

REFERENCES

Abrams, L. W., Abi-Hanna, R., Bess, N., Collucci, M., Dacey, C., Dauplaise, J., Mastellone, S., Strom, K., & Taylor, M. (2012). I am what I am not yet: Becoming Teacher Educators and Change Agents. In L. B. Erickson, J. R. Young, S. Pinnegar (Eds.), *Extending inquiry communities: Illuminating teacher education through self-study. Proceedings of the 9th International Conference on Self Study of Teacher Education Practices*, East Sussex, England (pp. 17–20). Provo, UT: Brigham Young University.

Albrecht-Crane, C., & Slack, J. (2003). Toward a pedagogy of affect. In J. Slack (Ed.), *Animations of Deleuze & Guattari* (pp. 191–216). New York, NY: Peter Lang.

Alvermann, D. E. (2000). Researching libraries, literacies, and lives: A rhizoanalysis. In E. St. Pierre, & W. Pillow (Eds.), *Working the ruins: Feminist poststructural theory and methods in education* (pp. 114–128). New York, NY: Routledge.

Belenky, M., Clinchy, B., Goldberger, N., & Tarule, J. (1997). *Women's ways of knowing: Development of voice, self, and mind, 10th anniversary edition.* New York, NY: Basic Books.

Bowles, S. N. (2001). *Deconstructing disability and (special) education: A rhizoanalysis.* (Unpublished doctoral dissertation.) University of Georgia, Athens, Georgia.

Braidotti, R. (2005). A critical cartography of feminist postmodernism. *Australian Feminist Studies, 20*(47), 169–180.

Butler, J. (1995). For a careful reading. In S. Benhabib, J. Butler, & D. Cornell (Eds.), *Feminist contentions: A philosophical exchange* (pp. 127–144). New York, NY: Routledge.

Deleuze, G., & Guattari, F. (1987). *Capitalism and schizophrenia: A thousand plateaus.* Minneapolis: University of Minnesota Press.

Edwards, R. (2006). A sticky business? Exploring the "and" in teaching and learning. *Discourse: Studies in the Cultural Politics of Education, 27*(1), 121–133.

Goldberger, R., Tarule, J. M., Clenchy, B. M., & Belenky, M. F. (1996). *Knowledge, difference, and power: Essays inspired by women's ways of knowing.* New York, NY: Basic Books.

Hagood, M. (2002). *Troubling identity and literacy: Young adolescents' subjectivities and literacies using popular culture texts.* (Unpublished doctoral dissertation). University of Georgia, Athens, Georgia.

Honan, E., & Sellers, M. (2008). (E)merging methodologies: Putting rhizomes to work. In I. Semetsky (Ed.), *Nomadic education: Variations on a theme by Deleuze and Guattari* (pp. 111–128). Rotterdam: Sense Publishers.

Jackson, Y.A., & Mazzei, L. (2012). *Thinking with theory in qualitative research: Viewing data across multiple perspectives.* New York, NY: Routledge.

LaBoskey, V. K. (2004). The methodology of self-study and its theoretical underpinnings. In J. J. Loughran, M. L. Hamilton, V. K. LaBoskey, & T. Russell (Eds.), *International handbook of self study of teaching and teacher education practices* (pp. 817–869). Dordrecht, The Netherlands: Kluwer.

Livesey, G. (2005). Assemblage. In A. Parr (Ed.), *The Deleuze dictionary* (pp. 18–19). Edinburgh, UK: Edinburgh University Press.

Maher, F., & Tetreault, M. K. (1996). Women's ways of knowing in women's studies, feminist pedagogies, and feminist theory. In R. Goldberger, J. M. Tarule, B. M. Clenchy, & M. F. Belenky (Eds.), *Knowledge, difference, and power: Essays inspired by Women's Ways of Knowing* (pp. 178–174). New York, NY: Basic Books.

Minh-ha, T. (1989). *Woman, native, other: Writing postcolonialism and feminism.* Bloomington, IN: Indiana University Press.

Pinar, W. (1998). *The passionate mind of Maxine Greene: 'I am what I am not yet.'* New York, NY: Routledge.

Ringrose, J. (2011). Beyond discourse? Using Deleuze & Guattari's schizoanalysis to explore affective assemblages, heterosexually striated space, and lines of flight online and at school. *Educational Philosophy & Theory, 43*(6), 598–618.

Ringrose, J., & Coleman, R. (2013). Looking and desiring machines: A feminist Deleuzian mapping of bodies and affects. In J. Ringrose & R. Coleman (Eds.), *Deleuze & research methodologies* (pp. 125–144). Edinburgh, UK: Edinburgh University Press.

Schulte, A. (2008). *Seeking integrity in teacher education: Transforming student teachers, transforming my self.* Dordrecht, Netherlands: Springer.

Sellers, M. (2010). Re(con)ceiving young children's curricular performativity. *International Journal of Qualitative Studies in Education, 23*(5), 557–577.

St. Pierre, E. (2004). Deleuzian concepts for education: The subject undone. *Educational Philosophy & Theory, 36*(3), 283–296.

St. Pierre, E. (2011). Post-qualitative research: The critique and the coming after. In N. Denzin & Y. Lincoln (Eds.), *The Sage handbook of qualitative research,* (4th ed. pp. 611–626). Thousand Oaks, CA: Sage.

Strom, K., & Pires, M. (2013). *Rhizomatics as a methodology of hope and transformation.* Paper presented at the American Educational Research Association Annual Meeting in San Francisco, CA.

Taylor, M., & Coia, L. (2006). Revisiting feminist authority through a co/autoethnographic lens. In D. Tidwell, & L. Fitzgerald (Eds.), *Self-study and diversity* (pp. 51–70). Rotterdam, Netherlands: Sense.

Taylor, M., & Coia, L. (2009). Co/autoethnography: Investigating teachers in relation. In C. A. Lassonde, S. C. Galman, & C. M. Kosnik (Eds.), *Self-study research methodologies for teacher educators* (pp. 169–186). Rotterdam, NL: Sense.

Tidwell, D., Farrell, J., Brown, N., Taylor, M., Coia, L., Abi-Hanna, R., Abrams, L., Dacey, C., Dauplaise, J., & Strom, K. (2012). *The transformative nature of self-study.* In L. B. Erickson, J. R. Young, S. Pinnegar (Eds.), *Proceedings of the 9th International Conference on Self Study of Teacher Education Practices* (pp. 15–16). East Sussex, England. Provo, UT: Brigham Young University.

Tyack, D., & Cuban, L. (1995). *Tinkering toward utopia: A century of school reform.* Cambridge, MA: Harvard College.

Waterhouse, M. (2011). *Experiences of multiple literacies and peace: A rhizoanalysis of becoming in immigrant language classrooms.* (Unpublished doctoral dissertation). University of Ottawa, Ottawa, Ontario, Canada.

AFFILIATIONS

Kathryn Strom
Teacher Education and Teacher Development,
Montclair State University,
Montclair, New Jersey

Rabab Abi-Hanna
Mathematics Education,
Montclair State University,
Montclair, New Jersey

Linda Abrams
Teacher Education and Teacher Development,
Montclair State University,
Montclair, New Jersey

Charity Dacey
Teacher Education and Teacher Development,
Montclair State University,
Montclair, New Jersey

Jacqueline Dauplaise
Mathematics Education,
Montclair State University,
Montclair, New Jersey

MARY LYNN HAMILTON & STEFINEE PINNEGAR

INTERPRETATION AND GENDER WITHIN THE ZONE OF INCONCLUSIVITY

In this chapter, we focus on how gender, feminism, and queer theory can influence and inform the Self-Study of Teaching and Teacher Education Practices (S-STTEP) methodology with particular attention to interpretation. Drawing from previously published work we explore interpretation and analyze the interpretive process within this methodology. This leaves open the contributions of gender, privilege, ethnicity and power and demonstrates how interpretation is an open, on-going process. In the next few pages we hope to demonstrate what it means to grapple with data. We do not abandon or deny the trustworthiness of our first reading and interpretation, but make visible interpretation as ongoing, utilizing additional lenses to trouble and destabilize it. For S-STTEP researchers our teaching, teacher education and research practice always exist in a zone of inconclusivity (Pinnegar & Hamilton, 2009). We arrive at points where we make evidence based assertions for action and understanding but even as we finalize research texts (e.g., Coia & Taylor, 2013), S-STTEP research studies never quite arrive at a final static point (e.g., Arizona Group, 2004). Our purpose is to make visible this shifting ontological space and the processes of dialogue and interpretation involved, thus, demonstrating the value of the fundamental qualities of openness and inconclusivity evident in S-STTEP research.

In this chapter, we explore our interpretive turns from a feminist perspective to positioning theory to queer theory. From the beginning of our academic work we have been named as feminists and we have used feminist theory, but we have struggled with the conception of our work as exclusively feminist since in such characterization we felt an absence in the application of this theoretical frame. We struggled to identify what that absence was. After the original publication of the work we present here, we returned to it wondering how we might push theoretical perspectives and therefore deepen understanding. These experiences led us to an awareness of the interpretive process as open, not static. We looked then to positioning theory as a way to explore identity formation (e.g. Harré & van Langenhove, 1998; Pinnegar & Murphy, 2011). Still, we felt an absence. This led us to explorations of the ideas of performativity resident in queer theory (e.g. Butler, 1999). Notice these turns in our demonstration of interpretation wherein we use past publications coupled with analysis guided by the application of additional interpretive lenses (e.g. positioning theory and queer theory). In this way we show how openness and inconclusivity foster a deepening of the interpretive process.

M. Taylor and L. Coia (Eds.), Gender, Feminism, and Queer Theory in the Self-Study of Teacher Education Practices, 45–60.

We begin our explanation of interpretation as open and inconclusive by summarizing the theoretical frames as well as present our understandings of S-STTEP research methodology. We then demonstrate the interpretive process using text fragments and commentary. As a thread throughout, we address the tension between trustworthiness and openness, responding to questions like: How is it that you can keep interpretation open yet present research findings that are trustworthy? How can you not avoid causing consternation in readers if the fluidity in your understandings is evident in your findings?

THEORETICAL FRAMES

Within this text, we use an historical view of feminism where women's understandings pushed against the boundaries set by the male-dominated world. Our understanding of feminism included a view that people advanced through merit and would simply be recognized for their good work (Aisenberg & Harrison, 1988). We recognized that women desire connection and pursue growth (Gilligan, 1982). Within our understanding of feminism, there were binaries – women/men – and conventional definitions of gender (Belenky, Clinchy, Goldberger, & Tarule, 1986). Upon reading the works of Foucault and others (e.g. Foucault, 1980; Sarup, 1993), we came to see that language was fluid, meaning was socially constructed, and affected perspectives and action. Our identity as female teacher educators emerged as we positioned others and were positioned by them. In this way gender was socially constructed and what constituted gender emerged as we enacted our pedagogy, interacted with others, wrote texts and took action (e.g., Pinnegar & Murphy, 2011). This led us to queer theory and consideration of gender as non-biologic and non-permanent (Butler, 1999).

Feminist and Queer Theories

In the 1980's some feminist theorists attended primarily to differences between women and men without addressing the social or political processes that established those differences (Belenky, Clinchy, Goldberger & Tarule, 1986). Other feminist theorists focused on oppression without considering ways to dislodge it (Code, 1991; Gappa & Uehling, 1979). In developing as teacher educators, we came to see how speech could also be considered action (Hymes, 1972) and the meaning of language and action emerged as we enacted or rejected the roles others cast for us (Harré & van Langenhove, 1998). As we came to understand more clearly the overlooked gendered nature of teaching and teacher education, we turned to queer theory which emerged from questions about sexual definitions and from cultural assumptions about gender including a rejection of static gender identity (e.g. Butler, 1999). By widening and overlapping concepts of gender, it opened a way of approaching gender identity and interrogating binary thinking, pushing against stereotypes and confronting labels. Gender identity became organic and performed rather than biologic and stationary. Queer theory destabilizes gender. Butler (1990) theorizes that there, "is no gender identity behind the expressions of gender" (p. 33). Rather than biological, gender is expressed through actions. She asserts that the "heterosexualization of desire requires and institutes the production of discrete and asymmetrical oppositions between 'feminine' and 'masculine' where these are understood as expressive attributes of 'male' and 'female'" (p. 23). As we suggested earlier, feminism presented gender in many ways as a non-negotiable presence and teaching and teacher education as fundamentally gendered. Queer theory opens space for reconsideration of gender within this context allowing for critique of heterosexist assumptions, consideration of identity and positioning of self in other than binary terms that some feminist theoretical perspectives may contain.

While both feminist and queer theories work to problematize the relations between sex, gender, and sexuality, S-STTEP researchers should remember, as Butler (1999) suggests, to accept our duty to work in contradiction. Recognizing that, "the gendered body is performative suggests that it has no ontological status apart from the various acts which constitute its reality. This also suggests that if that reality is fabricated as an interior essence, that very interiority is an effect and the function of a decidedly public and social discourse" (p. 363). As Butler points out:

> [Gender]…ought not be construed as a stable identity or locus of agency from which various acts follow…The effect of gender is produced through the stylization of the body and hence, must be understood as the mundane way in which bodily gestures, movements, and styles of various kinds constitute the illusion of the abiding gendered self. (p. 365)

This means that using queer theory as an interpretive lens pushes our thinking and calls us to re-open for consideration the ways we view ourselves: reconsideration of what gendered notions of our actions as teachers and teacher educators contributed to our interpretation of our selves in relationship to our practice.

Positioning Theory

While it might seem that as feminists we could shift easily from feminist to queer theory as an interpretive lens, in fact, we moved from feminist theory to considerations of identity formation through positioning theory based on work by Harré and van Langenhove (1998). Positioning theory articulates the ways in which identities emerge as we position Others and are positioned by them. Identity is developed not because we are positioned in particular ways but as we take up positions and embrace and enact the rights, responsibilities and duties entailed in one position rather than another. As an interpretive lens, positioning theory guides examination of what we say, how we enact practices, and the meaning we make of this as we position and are positioned by students, our institutions, or our colleagues. As Davies and Harré (1990) explain, when individuals discuss,

> 'sexism' or 'ageism' in the use of language, [they are]... highlighting...certain past conversations as...unacceptable exemplars... [These]...conversations can be deemed...objectionable as exemplars for speaking now,...not whether the speakers in the past or present intended...to be derogatory...[rather]...An individual emerges through the processes of social interaction, not as a...fixed end product but as one who is constituted and reconstituted through...various discursive practices...Accordingly, who one is is always an open question... (p. 44-45)

Positioning theory provides a framework and a set of analytic tools that support researchers in analyzing text, conversations and actions to examine how we, as gendered, white, educated professors, interact with students, colleagues, and institutions at given times and in specific places through which we and they build understanding.

SELF-STUDY OF TEACHING AND TEACHER EDUCATION PRACTICES RESEARCH

S-STTEP as a genre of qualitative research explores practice, the self-in-relation-to-practice and the self-in-relation-to-Other. Interpretation in S-STTEP research emerges in the process of dialogue and is based in an ontological stance toward research (Pinnegar & Hamilton, 2009). Since we are determined to produce authentic, rigorous, trustworthy accounts of situations that are problematic, troubling, and curious, we need to attend carefully to the accounts of practice we capture. Consideration of dialogue as a process of meaning-making and ontology are essential to the research design (Hamilton & Pinnegar, 2013). This means researchers focus on providing an accurate account of learning about and understanding practice while working to shape it to conform more closely with what is valued.

Dialogue

Dialogue holds a central role in the analytic/interpretive process, which includes reflection, reframing, analysis, and critique. Dialogue, as we have argued (Pinnegar & Hamilton, 2009), is an important facet of analysis in S-STTEP research with cycles of personal reflection, professional interchanges and public analysis, followed by private analysis (Arizona Group, 2006). Once an idea is put forward, it is met with reflection, critique, supportive anecdote and analysis that raises questions about insights expressed and a basis for meaning-making emerges (e.g. Arizona Group, 2004). Practice, theory, and experience are intertwined. Since the investigation focuses on human interaction, the *findings* or *results* that emerge and the inquiry itself exist in an inconclusive state where understandings are solidified but consideration of the ideas may continue. Through rigorous interrogation of both data and meanings and explanations arrived at we develop understandings that allow confident action: physical, mental, or explanatory. Indeed, dialogue is the process for coming-to-know and the procedure for ensuring the authenticity and veracity of data and claims of S-STTEP research. Through dialogue ideas that researchers have about things and their relationships to practice become established as findings and legitimized as claims about the ontological aspects of researchers' practice. In this way, dialogue becomes a crucible in which knowledge is shaped, becomes linked to evidence and gains authority.

Ontology As Stance

Because in S-STTEP research is our practice, "researching" increased skepticism concerning interpretation and trustworthiness is required. The consideration of ontology, of one's being in and toward the world, is a central feature. As Bullough & Pinnegar (2004) argue:

> [S-STTEP] understood as a matter of ontology, a stance, rather than a settling on a truth, requires of its practitioners involvement in an ongoing quest for greater goods, more productive ideas, more interesting and enlivening relationships, better forms of communication, a purer sense of one's obligations and a richer sense of one's own and others' possibilities. And, there is a moral imperative – to become increasingly open to contrary data. (p. 328)

Indeed, S-STTEP, as a methodology, dictates that we engage in inquiries, which entail ethical and relational obligations oriented toward contribution to the larger research conversation and improvement of our own practice (Pinnegar & Hamilton, 2009).

Interpretation

Interpretation is seldom a straightforward matter. It develops in the data collection-data analysis-data interpretation spiral. When we connect a piece of data with an assertion, we should make the connection clear so that readers can see in the presented interpretation how the researcher arrived at that point. As researchers we expand upon general qualitative research practice. The significant difference between a general qualitative research and the S-STTEP approach to data analysis and interpretation centers on the self-in-relation-to-Other. Within this methodology, we complicate the role of the self (since the researcher is positioned as both researcher and researched), and we situate the self in relation to the Other (e.g., Lunenberg & Hamilton, 2008; Guðjónsdóttir & Dalmau, 2002). An orientation toward developing ontological understandings of our practice and the utilization of dialogue extends through the iterative collection-analysis-interpretation process and shapes it (Pinnegar & Hamilton, 2012).

Bakhtin's Zones of Maximum Contact and Inconclusivity

Utilization of dialogue and an orientation to ontology deliberately locates our work in a zone of inconclusivity. This zone exists at a point of maximal contact between past, present, and future, making the boundaries of time permeable (Bakhtin, 1981). In analysis in S-STTEP research there is an intentional orientation toward shifting across dimensions of time – remembering past experience, anticipating where our thinking is heading (projecting our past/current understandings into the future) and thinking of our response in terms of what did or does constrain us. In inquiring into our experience and our practice, this shifting across dimensions of time reveals both our understandings and misunderstandings of practice and opens possibilities for understanding practice both differently and more deeply. This intentional shifting can free us from limitations and constraints on our thinking about experience leading to reconsideration of what we thought of as static or permanent or unalterable as permeable, shifting and emerging.

S-STTEP research is conducted on shifting terrain—the work seeks to examine practice and the understanding of it that shifts as it is enacted because the study and the practice emerges in the space between self and Other. We track what is revealed in our action, our thinking, our interaction with others and the shaping and constraining influences of context. Our research methodology is grounded in an orientation to ontology with projection into future contexts. There is uncertainty about the future trajectory of an idea. We have discussed how S-STTEP research and interpretative practices in it exist in Bakhtin's zone of maximal contact which is simultaneously a zone of inconclusivity—spaces of uncertainty and tentativeness. Projecting a course of action from within the zone of inconclusivity may destabilize or regenerate a theory, assertion or idea. While expressed in terms of the self, studies exist and are conducted in the spaces between the self and the Other – the self and practice – yet, as ideas survive and thrive in this zone, they become clearer and stronger as well as more valuable as assertions for action and understanding.

METHODOLOGY

We began by revisiting our work and identifying settled, published interpretations of experience constructed from a feminist perspective. We selected Arizona Group (1994) because unique features of that text allowed us to explore more fully the act of interpretation in relationship to a feminist perspective and to demonstrate the way in which in S-STTEP research interpretation always remains unsettled. We used L and K to indicate the author of the text fragments in order to maintain anonymity. The article emerged out of a particular ontological stance that attended to feminist, critical theory, and sociocultural orientations. The themes explicated represent themes reflective of these orientations. We then identified a published reinterpretation of this work (Arizona Group, 2007). We realized that in the second article our original interpretation shifted and we positioned ourselves differently in relation to the original texts as well as within our community. This demonstrated how even well-interpreted findings anchored in trustworthiness can be reopened and reconsidered. The second interpretation expands and exists in tension to the first but does not read over it. We then engaged in a careful analysis of the text using positioning theory (Harré & van Langenhove, 1998) to demonstrate again the inconclusive nature of interpretation. Like the tension between the concepts of being and becoming in work on identity formation in teacher education (Erickson, Young & Pinnegar, 2011), interpretation can be made and presented (a moment of recognition of being) and simultaneously exist in a context of inconclusivity (an ongoing situation of becoming) (e.g. Pinnegar & Murphy, 2011; Rice, 2011).

To demonstrate interpretation within a zone of maximal contact that engages not only the author or the work but readers as well, we began by reviewing this text. To more clearly explicate our understanding of interpretation we identified some considerations of the text as a whole. Next, we re-read this work and identified two text fragments to represent feminist theory as an interpretive lens. In turn, we revisited the 2007 piece identifying the ways in which these fragments were taken up. Then, we used analytic tools from positioning theory to reopen the texts and present an interpretation based in identity formation. We worked together discussing the text fragments and the reconsideration of them against feminist theory. In particular, we utilized a piece from Hamilton (1992) that provided a clear articulation of our stance in relationship to both pieces. One of us then constructed the analysis of the texts. Together we engaged in dialogue and considered, reconsidered, shaped and reshaped the interpretation. We ended by reopening the interpretive process pulling forward the three explications of interpretation as a whole into a zone of inconclusivity considering them in relationship to queer theory particularly the work by Butler.

INTERPRETIVE PROCESS

Interpretation played a key role in the design of the 1994 text. It was constructed so that it intentionally thrusts readers into the zone of maximal contact (Bakhtin, 1981). Rather than offering a static interpretation of the Arizona Group's experiences, it invites readers to interweave experiences with that of the authors as new faculty. In this study we each analyzed our correspondence and uncovered themes of balancing commitments, negotiating power, and struggling for survival. We introduce our process of interpretation by stating our theoretical orientation as being, "informed by feminist pedagogy, critical theory, and a constructivist view of teaching/learning/researching" (p. 71); notifying readers of the interpretive lenses we brought to our analysis.

In structuring the chapter, we did not use a traditional strategy for presenting data analysis wherein the author presents a theme, explicates it using examples from the data and makes visible the connection between example and interpretation. Instead we edited the letters to present an unfolding, chronologically arranged account of our experiences as beginners in academia. We invited readers to participate as interpreters. We constructed the text to communicate our interpretation of experience as embodied practical knowledge of that experience (Clandinin, 1985). We relied on the imagistic quality of the text to engage readers in experiencing our understanding not just reading about it (for another example, see Arizona Group, 1995). In this way we sought to engage the use of image as a form of knowledge that is not conceptual but experiential as Clandinin (1985) explains:

> Images are within experience and are not only in the logically defined words that specify our conceptual status. Accordingly, for our work, images are embodied and enacted. Our embodiment entails emotionality, morality, and aesthetics and it is these affective, personally felt and believed, meanings that engender enactments. (p. 363)

We expected that as readers read the account, the edited texts would resonate in such a way that they would experience being a beginning professor in the academy through the constructed, imagistic interpretation and would come away with an embodied knowing of the experience and the themes of balancing commitments, negotiating power, and struggling for survival. In constructing the text, we strove to present the multi-vocal character of our experience so that readers would be aware of our individual as well as our collective voices. We wanted the text to provide disconfirming as well as confirming evidence of experience. As constructed, the text provides evidence of dialogue as our way of coming-to-know and further communicates an ontological stance toward research. Since the purpose in the design of the text was to communicate an experiential and embodied understanding, the original design of the text represents a gendered and feminist reading from a critical, sociocultural perspective. The themes are the issues we wished readers to uncover and experience and they represent the theoretical orientation we brought to the interpretive act involved in the analysis of the data and the construction of the research text.

As readers take up the text, they are invited in as an interpreter and are thus repeatedly thrust into the zone of maximal contact wherein, according to Bakhtin (1981) the past is brought forward into the present of the readers' experience forcing a reinterpretation of the past, a shifting of the ground of the present and a reorientation of the future experience of readers. In engaging with the text, the readers' understanding of past experience, our present understanding and our own future being and becoming are disrupted. As researchers when we attempt to provide objective accounts, the experiences we choose, the words we use to describe and label the experience, and the things we leave unsaid are all interpretive acts. Therefore, the process of interpretation begins long before we take-up the act of data analysis. Interpretation is present in the problem we choose, the way we phrase and structure that examination, the literature we choose to review, as well as in our presentation of the literature.

Text Fragment One: November 1st

> Often when I, as a new professor, question the system, the reply is, "We do it because it's tradition."... Will the system ever make sense to me? I wonder...

as I walk down the corridor which houses the various chancellor's offices. I enter what I call Famous Men's Hallway. On the walls there you will find a series of photos of the people who have made intellectual contributions to this institution. They are all male. Actually all white male with one exception, an Asian male. I have no idea if there was ever a famous female on this campus. Some days I don't notice these kinds of messages. Other days they are so blatant.

The problem with being a new academic is that the work is so, so male and so, so alien that no matter how I develop my skills they do not seem to fit. L (p. 75)

In this fragment, L posts a query and then provides an interpretation or reading of a hallway within her context. The reading is based in our taking-up of the feminist perspective at that time and the data are read from a feminist perspective making more visible the power negotiations. It is oriented toward an assumption that the world is male-dominated and that this affects our experience of the academy (Gilligan, 1982; Tannen, 1990), hence Famous Men's Hallway. The question the fragment begins with and the sentence at the end asserts feminine ways of knowing (we are all female) and understanding as distinctive and dissimilar from the traditional perspectives on knowledge and academia (Belenky, Clinchy, Goldberger, & Tarule, 1986). The orientation, in line with feminist theory of the era, focused on power differentials and how the institution communicated messages of what was valued and valuable in ways that were oriented toward male-domination and action in the world.

The image of Famous Men's Hallway can be considered a labyrinth—the path through life with the ultimate goal earning a place in Famous Men's Hallway. The hallway connects the chancellor's offices to each other. As one walks down the hallway, toward or away from the leadership of the institution, it is adorned with representations of what it takes to be valued in this institution. All the representations are of males who have made intellectual contributions valued by the institution. The implicit message, which L labels as "blatant", is that no women have made such contributions. The image is that of an alien landscape that is unwelcoming. Our response is one of recognition of it as an image of male-dominance, an alien space, and is reminiscent of feminist orientations where women take up positions in places like the academy to change them (Aisenberg & Harrington, 1988).

Reinterpretation 1

In 2007, we reconsidered our experiences in academia in an analysis and critique of the 1994 piece. In this article we revisited our earlier interpretations, and one of the fragments we chose to reconsider was this one. We discuss this event saying:

While eleven years later the drama of the statement of our Otherness brings a smile, we each still feel that we struggle to make a place for ourselves… It continues simply as an artifact of university life that revealed us as living contradictions…we can identify places at our institutions that continue to represent Famous Men's Hallways and against which we define our Otherness as women, as scholars, as educators. In fact these experiences do not call us to support or acquiesce but to resist participation. (p. 56)

In this discussion we present a more nuanced view. We recognize that our scholarly orientation to highly subjective qualitative methodology, our position as teacher educators closely connected to practice and developing a new generation of practitioners, as well as our status as women contribute to our on-going struggle to "fit" and our alienation from places such as Famous Men's Hallway. L's reading and representation of the text of the hallway as "Famous" captures our sense of being under surveillance (Foucault, 1995) by a group of people both male and female who found us wanting (even though we did reach tenure). It also reveals our resistance to the oppression of that hallway. The trustworthiness of this interpretation of the context is heightened since the authors articulate Famous Men's Hallway as an archetypal image and mention identifying such places at other institutions.

Establishing Trustworthiness

We argued earlier that interpretation exists in all aspects of the research. We explored how in data analysis we uncovered themes that resonate with feminist theory—imposition of power. We recognized that one strategy for developing interpretations is the use of a theoretical lens since it provides a framework for determining what might be negative case examples—crucial in establishing the trustworthiness of interpretation. In this case the naming of the theme as negotiations rather than impositions of power implied our struggle with whether a uni-dimensional application of feminist theoretical orientations seeking to reveal impositions of male power truly captured our experience. This questioning led to consideration of power negotiations rather than merely imposition.

At this point in our discussion, interpretation seems settled. The 2007 piece expands the interpretation but only slightly disrupts it. In establishing it as a trustworthy interpretation of institutionalized male-dominance, in using other examples of events from our letters that support the identified theme of negotiating power, in characterizing the image as archetypal and our assertion of our ability to identify Famous Men's Hallways in other academic contexts, we build the trustworthiness of our interpretation. In communicating an interpretation, we often attribute a settled and stable quality to it. However, as S-STTEP researchers we continually study our practice to develop deeper understandings of it and potentially improve it leaving no interpretation done once-and-for-all.

Recent work by Coia and Taylor (2013) represent a current example of how this works. In this study, they revisit what they thought were settled understandings of feminist theory and uncovered the ways in which their original understandings were present and had also transformed in their current work. Our point here is that establishing trustworthiness of interpretation at one point in time does not bind meaning of experience or pin it down. We have the potential to re-open interpretation and understanding of gendered experience within the academy. Part of why we labeled our theme "negotiation of power" was our sense that just as we felt the imposition of male-oriented power in our lives, we also recognized that as professors we held positions of power in relationship to our own students as well as secretaries and student workers. There were indeed power differentials in many of the relationships we had.

SHIFT TO POSITIONING THEORY

We return to the text fragment and use an alternative theory making visible positioning of self and Other within a context—re-interpreting the fragment revealing a different reading of the text. Positioning theory (Harré & van Langenhove, 1998) and the analytic matrix with self and Other positioning on one axis and performative and accountive positioning on the other provided new insights, as did examining the fragment in terms of the positioning theory triad (position, storyline, and illocutionary force). Positioning theory allowed us to look at identity formation as we negotiated our experience. We intentionally re-enter the zone of inconclusivity drawing forward experience from the past into the present and reconceptualizing past, present and future experience and interpretation of it.

When we reconsider this fragment using the triad, we are struck anew by the labyrinth as a life pathway. Famous Men's Hallway becomes emblematic of the revered plotline for academics. It is a plotline gaining value and power through making intellectual contributions. L positions herself standing on that pathway in relationship to the Hallway, but the illocutionary force of her text is one of defining herself not as a person taking-up the valued path but a person standing in opposition. She is not cowed by the portraits and presents herself in resistance to those images. She positions not only herself, but also other women as people taking up alternative plotlines. She does not undercut the importance of enacting a plotline of intellectual contribution but opens other pathways for contributions. She points out that there seem to be no "famous" women on this campus or in its history. Thus, in this interpretive act she presents our pathway as alien and resisting the positioning of Famous Men's Hallway rather than submitting to it.

When we consider the fragment from the perspective of the two axes of the positioning theory matrix, we gain deeper insight into L's identify formation as a teacher educator. The first axis calls attention to whether others are positioning the person or whether, in response to such positioning, the person positions him/herself. The second axis explores whether the positioning is performative or whether it is accountive. Famous Men's Hallway has the potential to represent an accountive positioning of L. The portraits and the hallway represent the valued male-dominant orientation that L identifies as the way in which the institution would orient her identity formation. The Hallway imposes a life path in which one would emulate the paths of the men staring down along the hallway. If L submits to this positioning, she would be forced to evaluate her work—her scholarship and teaching—from this orientation. Yet, in her somewhat silly name for the hallway, she undercuts the positioning the institution communicates through this image. In her labeling the hallway as "alien" and her reporting that women are absent from it, L is enacting a performative self-positioning in which she asserts Famous Men's Hallway as an alien pathway and declares the pathway as one not open to women. She performs this positioning from a perspective of redefinition of the pathway to participation in the institution.

This interpretation of the fragment using positioning theory asserts L and her co-authors as women who are not merely oppositional or oppressed by male-dominance, but as women who take up an identity of teacher educator. We position ourselves as academics who propose an identity plot or story line that diverges from the prescribe pathway of Famous Men's Hallway. This is not merely an act of resistance but is an act of redefinition of what is and should be valued and valuable. It is a rejection of the notion of fitting-in and an assertion of a forging of a new identity pathway. It pushes interpretation beyond a traditional static feminist reading of male oppression and institutional sexism reopening the text and inviting a reimagining of the plotline, position and action of teacher educators forging their identity within male-dominated institutions.

Text Fragment 2: December 8th

> I love you all so much and your letters have been so healing for me. Merry Christmas—to new traditions for our children and ourselves. When my children sing DECK THE HALLS, they'll think of academic halls and coloring in mom's office as she works on grades while students and faculty pop in to say hello and I want that to be as beautiful a memory for them as my own memories of Christmas are for me. K (p. 80)

Absent in this text fragment is a feminist orientation toward uncovering male-dominance, power and oppression and instead it represents a feminist ethic-of-care. This feminist ethic-of-care emerged at this time represented by Gilligan's (1982) assertion of a feminist moral reasoning centered in care and connectedness. In addition, Noddings' (1984) work which focused on the relationship of giving-care and being-cared-for emerged. This text fragment represents a feminist orientation toward care and connectedness. By placing personal commitments to mothering and family life within the context of academic responsibility, the fragment presents an image of balance of academic and personal obligation and represents balancing commitments by linking both spheres.

Reinterpretation 2

In the 2007 text, we articulate the connection between the two themes:

> The image of Famous Men's Hallway represents the running of the gauntlet that might initiate members into the community. Hopefully by surviving a

walk through the hallway emotionally, physically, intellectually, we would arrive at community. (p. 54)

This quote highlights the dissonance rather than resonance found in the 1994 work emphasizing the contrast between the image of community and the gauntlet of Famous Men's Hallway. We (2007) asserted that the earlier view represented a modernist orientation and a dichotomous view of the world contrasting male-dominance and power and female connectedness. The juxtaposition of the two text fragments makes evident that in the 1994 interpretation the stance represented was resistance, struggle, and survival as the only pathway. However, resonant in this passage is a deeper understanding that what feels like male oppression may indeed result from institutional dynamics. Taking up a feminist ethic of care recasts the academic community in a hopeful way uniting and balancing community, familial, and academic commitments. Yet, this later interpretation still suggests resistance to the gauntlet of Famous Men's Hallway and a skepticism that such a walk would lead to a valued community. In the 2007 reinterpretation, we pose this view of what constitutes an academic community: "Our strongest community connections remain with academic friends across the country and around the world rather than in the office next door" (Arizona Group, 2007, p. 63).

Shift to Positioning Theory

When we consider this fragment through the lens of positioning theory, we examine the juxtaposition of the tradition of Famous Men's Hallway against the image of a different tradition of community than the one we inherited. In the first piece, the image of Famous Men's Hallway is one of forced accountive positioning wherein the novice is brought under the scrutiny of those in power and forced to walk the gauntlet her worthiness judged by the men in the portraits. In this piece, K (in an act of performative self-positioning and through the account's illocutionary force) repositions herself and her colleagues at the center of the universe with children coloring in her office as she attends to the responsibility of grading and as colleagues come by as friends with good wishes and kindness. Notice the imagistic change from linear path to a circle of community with family and academic obligations and responsibilities balanced and fulfilled in harmony. The ethical image of these two fragments and a reading that holds these two images in tension with each other shifts the landscape. It invites readers into a zone of maximal contact and offers promise for living out a balanced life and meeting competing obligations.

QUEER THEORY AS INTERPRETIVE LENS

Still, in 2013 we returned to explore what we might be missing in our analysis. We wondered if we had opened up the gendered aspects of our work to fully understand what might be happening. We wondered if our binary examination of gender – female-male – rightfully captured what we experienced or were we shackled by an historical view of gender. Furthermore, we wondered if our understanding of positioning theory was affected by our potentially binary views. With these wonders in mind, we turned to the work of Butler and others to once again open interpretation– this time taking up queer theory as a way to frame our gaze.

Like positioning theory, queer theory claims that identity is bounded by time and action. From Butler's perspective gender is a social construct, an identity bounded by time that remains amorphous until, through a repetition of acts, identity is consolidated. However, in that consolidation there is an ebb-and-flow with nothing held static by the consolidation. She sees that society marginalizes those who perform outside the essentials of socially-constructed notions of gender (Butler, 1988). Queer theory contests the traditional and the dominant and attempts to deconstruct the modern views of gender, sex and desire (Hutchinson, 2013; Presnell, 2013). Foucault (1990) challenges the simple binaries of female-male, heterosexual-homosexual and asserts that use of these terms and what they symbolize exerts power of one over another. Butler (1990) turns to feminist theorists challenging them to drop the binary since this contributes to the dominant paradigm. She points to performativity – the ways we act – as critical to challenging this reification of gender. According to Hutchinson (2013), an example of Butler's work would be, "'women' [who] behave in culturally defined ways to be considered women. She advocates performing acts that subvert the dominant cultural views that, in effect, mock defined cultural roles" (p. 13).

When we turn to our own works we can see that we operated within the gender binary. We did not question expectations that we behave in certain ways to define ourselves as an academic, a scholar, or a woman. Instead, we remained caught in the binaries of the time and our understandings. Even as we turned to positioning theory we still mired ourselves within a limited view of gender (power/race/class) binaries. It is queer theory that supports us in bursting open our interpretations to challenge our ways of thinking and organizing what we think we see.

CONCLUSIONS

We recognize that, as S-STTEP researchers, our work emanates from our ontology as we focus on the particular through dialogue as our coming-to-know process. In the chapter we made visible aspects of interpretation to illustrate for readers the zone of inclusivity that leads researchers to provide evidence of knowing yet leave it vibrant. We propose that interpretation, like gender, race, class, and culture is contested but never fully resolved. S-STTEP researchers attempt to build understanding while questioning self and Other. In our discussion of methodology we made more visible the ways in which interpretation in S-STTEP research is anchored in ontology, the process of coming-to-know through dialogue and the value of exemplar validation. We explored interpretation within the methodology of S-STTEP research making clear that while researchers must take the establishing of trustworthiness seriously, interpretation remains fundamentally contested. In teacher education research issues of gender are implicit. These are issues that we must not let settle and they cannot afford to be hidden.

REFERENCES

Aisenberg, N., & Harrington, M. (1988). *Women of academe: Outsiders in the sacred grove*. Amherst: University of Massachusetts Press.

Arizona Group, Guilfoyle, K., Hamilton, M. L., Pinnegar, S., & Placier, P. (1994). Letters from beginners: Negotiating the transition from graduate student to assistant professor. *The Journal, 8*(2), 71–82.

Arizona Group, Guilfoyle, K., Hamilton, M. L., Pinnegar, S., & Placier, P. (1995). Becoming teachers of teachers: Alternative paths expressed in beginners' voices. In F. Korthagen & T. Russell (Eds.). *Teachers who teach teachers: Reflections on teacher education* (pp. 35–55). London, UK: Falmer Press.

Arizona Group, Guilfoyle, K., Hamilton, M. L., Pinnegar, S., & Placier, P. (2004). The epistemological dimensions and dynamics of professional dialogue in self-study. In J. J. Loughran, M. L. Hamilton, V. K. LaBoskey, & T. L. Russell (Eds.), *International handbook of self-study of teaching and teacher education practices* (vol. 2, pp. 1109–1168). Dordrecht, Netherlands: Kluwer Academic Publishers.

Arizona Group, Guilfoyle, K., Hamilton, M. L., Pinnegar, S., & Placier, P. (2007). Reconsidering unanswered questions: Negotiating transitions from graduate student to assistant professor to associate professor. In R. Martin (Ed), *Transforming the academy: Struggles and strategies for women in higher education, Volume II* (pp. 53–66). Earlene, IA: Graymill Corporation.

Arizona Group: Placier, P., Pinnegar, S., Hamilton, M. L., & Guilfoyle, K. (2006). Exploring the concept of dialogue in the self-study of teaching practices. In C. Kosnik, C. Beck, A. Freese, & A. Samaras (Eds.), *Making a difference in teacher education through self-study* (pp. 51–64). Dordrecht, Netherlands: Kluwer Academic Publishers.

Bakhtin, M. (1981). *The dialogic imagination: Four essays*. Austin, TX: University of Texas Press.

Belenky, M., Clinchy, B., Goldberger, N., & Tarule, J. (1986). *Women's ways of knowing*. New York, NY: Basic Books.

Bullough, R. V. Jr., & Pinnegar, S. E. (2004). Thinking about thinking about self-study. In J. J. Loughran, M. L. Hamilton, V. K. LaBoskey, & T. L. Russell (Eds.) *International handbook of self-study of teaching and teacher education practices* (pp. 313–342). Dordrecht, Netherlands: Kluwer Academic Publishers.

Butler, J. (1988). Performative acts and gender constitution: An essay in phenomenology and feminist theory. *Theatre Journal, 40*(4), 519–531.

Butler, J. (1990). *Gender trouble: Feminism and the subversion of identity*. London, NY: Routledge.

Butler, J. (1999). From interiority to gender performatives. In Fabio Cleto (Ed.), *Camp: Queer aesthetics and the performing subject: A reader* (pp. 361–368). Ann Arbor, MI: The University of Michigan Press.

Clandinin, D. J. (1985). Personal practical knowledge: A study of teachers' classroom images. *Curriculum Inquiry, 15*, 361–385.

Code, L. (1991). *What can she know: Feminist theory and the construction of knowledge*. Ithaca, NY: Cornell University Press.

Coia, L., & Taylor, M. (2013). Uncovering our feminist pedagogy: A co/autoethnography. *Studying Teacher Education, 9*(1), 3–17.

Davies, B., & Harré, R. (1990). Positioning: The discursive production of selves. *Journal for the Theory of Social Behavior, 20*(1), 43–63.

Erickson, L., Young, J., & Pinnegar, S. (2011) Teacher Educator Identity: Emerging understandings of person, positioning, roles, and collaborations. *Studying Teacher Education, 7*, 105–107.

Foucault, M. (1980). *A history of sexuality, volume 1: An introduction*. In R. Hurley (Trans.). New York, NY: Vantage Books.

Foucault, M. (1995). *Disciple and punish: The birth of the prison. 1975*. New York, NY: Vintage.

Gappa, J. M., & Uehling, B. S. (1979). *Women in academe: Steps to greater equality. AAHE ERIC/Higher Education Research Report No. 1*. Washington DC: AAHE.

Gilligan, C. (1982). *In a different voice: Psychological theory and women's development.* Cambridge, MA: Harvard University Press.

Guðjónsdóttir, H., & Dalmau, M. C. (2002). Framing professional discourse with teachers: Professional working theory. In J. T. Loughran & T. Russell (Eds.), *Improving teacher education practices through self-study* (pp. 102–129). London, UK: Routledge/Falmer.

Hamilton, M. L. (1992). *Making public the private voice of a teacher educator.* Paper presented as a part of a Division K Symposium–Holding up the mirror: Teacher educators reflect on their own teaching - at the annual meeting of the American Educational Research Association, San Francisco.

Hamilton, M. L., & Pinnegar, S. (2013). *What's in a name? Exploring the edges of auto-ethnography, narrative, and self-study methodologies.* A paper presented at the annual meeting of American Educational Research Association in San Francisco, California.

Harré, R., & van Langenhove, L. (1998). *Positioning theory: Moral contexts of international action.* Oxford, England: Wiley-Blackwell Publishing.

Hutchinson, D. (2013). *Narrative defiance: Re-narrating beliefs through teacher blogs.* Unpublished paper.

Hymes, D. (1972). Models of the interaction of language and social life. In J. Gumperz & D. Hymes (Eds.), Directions in sociolinguistics: The ethnography of communication (pp. 35–71). New York, NY: Holt, Rinehart & Winston.

Lunenberg, M., & Hamilton, M. L. (2008). Threading a golden chain: An attempt to find our identities as teacher educators. *Teacher Education Quarterly, 35*(1), 185–205.

Noddings, N. (1984). *Caring: A feminine approach to ethics and moral education.* Berkeley: University of California Press.

Pinnegar, S., & Hamilton, M. L (2012). Openness and inconclusivity in interpretation in narrative inquiry: dimensions of the social/personal. In E. Chan, D. Keyes, & V. Ross (Eds.), *Narrative inquirers in the midst of meaning-making: Interpretive acts of teacher educators* (pp. 1–22). Bingley, UK: Emerald Group Publishing Limited.

Pinnegar, S., & Hamilton, M. L. (2009). *Self-study of practice as a genre of qualitative research: Theory, methodology, and Practice.* Dordrecht, Netherlands: Springer.

Pinnegar, S., & Murphy S. (2011). Commentary: Teacher educator identity emerging through positioning self and others. *Studying Teacher Education, 7,* 155–158.

Presnell, N. (2013). *The "Cool" blogger: Is she really as cool as she thinks she is?* Unpublished paper.

Rice, M. (2011). Competing and conflicting identity plotlines: Navigating personal narratives of entering teaching. *Studying teacher education: A journal of self-study of teacher education practices, 7*(2), 145–154.

Sarup, M. (1993). *An introductory guide to post-structuralism and postmodernism* (2nd ed.). Essex, England: Pearson Education Limited.

Tannen, D. (1990). *You just don't understand: Women and men in conversation.* New York, NY: William Morrow and Company. Inc.

AFFILIATIONS

Mary Lynn Hamilton
Curriculum and Teaching,
University of Kansas
Lawrence, Kansas

Stefinee Pinnegar
McKay School of Education,
Brigham Young University,
Provo, Utah

RACHEL FORGASZ & ALLIE CLEMANS

FEELING: FEMINIST? A SELF-STUDY OF EMOTION AS A FEMINIST EPISTEMOLOGY IN EDUCATION PRACTICE

We teach in the Education Faculty of an Australian university. Rachel teaches mainly in pre-service teacher education programs while Allie teaches in adult education programs. This chapter marks an evolution of our interest in, and attention to, emotions in our teaching practice across our different sites of practice. It was propelled by our earlier interests in examining how our sense of being present during our teaching allowed us to attend to particular dimensions and to improvise as a facet of our pedagogy. Like all good ideas, this one struggled to find a conceptual home, circling around various pedagogical concepts. It was with the gift of time that our eyes were drawn to emotion and feeling as an epistemological stance as much as a pedagogical one. This study marks our attempt to articulate this, and to examine our relationship to ways of knowing and doing and the significance of emotion in this process.

OUR PROVOCATION

In 2012 Rachel taught a unit on reflective practice for workplace learning as part of an undergraduate Adult Learning & Development course. Within it, she introduced a range of theories and approaches to reflection, including ideas about reflecting on the emotional – as well as the cognitive – dimensions of our human experiences, and ideas about embodied self-reflexivity (Forgasz, 2013). After their final class together, Rachel relayed to Allie her account of the following incident in which the extent of students' fears around the display and discussion of emotion played out.

During this class, students received feedback on their reflective narrative drafts. Having just read hers aloud, T listened to feedback from the group. Essentially, while T's narrative clearly told the story of what had happened, she had not provided any description of how she had felt.

T sat and listened silently for some time until a response erupted from within her: "I can't believe it! I'm always being told I'm too emotional and now the one time when I can include my emotions I left them out!" The eruption was full of feeling; T's voice was raised, and it shook. There were tears in her eyes. Rachel was worried that T was feeling criticized so she assured her of her excellent writing and encouraged her to add emotional responses to the paper. But Rachel also ventured into the emotion and asked T why she was about to cry.

M. Taylor and L. Coia (Eds.), Gender, Feminism, and Queer Theory in the Self-Study of Teacher Education Practices, 61–75.

T's tears overflowed. "I know," she replied, half laughing, half crying. She was apologetic to the group for crying, observing that she didn't mean to ruin their last class. Other class members were viscerally uncomfortable – shifting in their seats, some of them looking away. One class member raised her objection to the whole exercise. She accused Rachel of endangering the student, arguing that what was going on in the room was entirely inappropriate since Rachel did not have the qualifications or training to enter into this kind of dialogue with the student. Doing so was unprofessional, uncaring and unsafe.

This experience left questions unanswered. Why did T have to feel embarrassed by her excess of emotion? Why were her peers so uncomfortable in the face of T's tears? And why was Rachel's act of inquiring about her emotions ("why are you crying?") an act, that, in another context would be seen as caring and responsible, deemed unprofessional, inappropriate, and even dangerous?

Ultimately, while her tears were a source of discomfort, T also drew productively on her public outpouring of emotion. She wrote about it as part of her final assignment:

I remembered how I have been told many times in my work experience to be aware of my emotions however, this reflective exercise was calling on them to be used [which] overwhelmed and confused me … I was internally torn and in a sense hiding my natural, instinctive use of my emotions and feelings while at work and at university.

For T, connecting her emotional experience of crying in class to her workplace autobiography enabled the production of new knowledge and insight.

Her story provided the provocation for this chapter in which we present a self-study of what happened (for us and for our students) when we recast emotion in our teaching as a source and way of knowing, that is, as a legitimate epistemology.

EMOTION AND EPISTEMOLOGY

Buoyed by T's experience of the potential of emotion, we scoured the literature together in order to begin to theorize the positioning of emotion as a dimension of epistemology within our teaching practice. By the term emotion, we follow Zembylas' (2002) writing on emotions which calls on Williams' idea of "structures of feeling" to portray feelings as "the subjective dimensions of experience" (Williams, as cited in Zembylas, 2002, p. 193) which are neither spoken of nor recognized. Feelings are impulses in which thought is felt and feeling is thought. Zembylas (2002) thus describes emotion as "a form of mediation between experience and language" (p. 194) that comprises "'what is not fully articulated, all that comes through as disturbance, tension, blockage, emotional trouble'" (Williams, as cited in Zembylas, 2002, p. 194).

In the field of teacher research, we discovered examples of the repositioning of emotion as part of an approach to reflection and professional development. For example, Zembylas (2003) asserts the particular importance for teachers to "identify how their emotions expand or limit possibilities in their teaching, and how these emotions enable them to think and act differently" (p. 122). Akinbode (2013) is likewise committed to the exploration of teacher emotion as a fundamental dimension of teacher reflection. White (2009), too, suggests that emotions can be a tool for teacher learning. In this chapter, we are interested in considering emotion beyond its inclusion as a dimension of pedagogical practice or professional development. We propose positioning emotions as epistemological: that our emotions offer a legitimate way of knowing.

Specifically, we (re)consider emotions within a feminist sociological tradition that argues for a need to reorient those abstract and traditional knowledge forms that have tended to alienate women as subjects through a failure to attend to their local and embodied knowledge and material experiences (Smith, 1987; 1997). This means that we attend to emotions not just for the value they hold, but also for the political act they symbolize; for us, it is "a form of decolonization, making way for the liberation of subjugated knowledge" (Lawrence, 2012, p. 77).

One of the ways in which emotions have been subjugated as a form of knowledge is through various social constructions of emotions as undesirable. The provocation that began this chapter was especially provocative for us because of the student's accusation that Rachel's exploration of emotions was dangerous, threatening students' safety. Henry (2013) reports similar reservations being voiced by educators who "talk about not wanting to deal with students' feelings about subjects because they do not feel well trained to do so, nor do they want to be responsible for doing so" (p. 6). At the same time, she observes, there are many other ways in which teachers require students to be vulnerable: "to submit their writing to us for evaluation, to speak in class, to present their knowledge to us in multiple ways" (p. 6). In our experience, students are, by and large, unquestioning in their willingness to make themselves vulnerable by acquiescing to these traditional academic demands. Likewise, most educators are unquestioning in making such demands without considering the powerful emotional responses they might provoke. And yet, when it comes to traversing explicitly emotional terrain, both students and educators voice objections on the basis of feeling unsafe.

To make sense of the source of these perceptions of danger, we found Smith's (1987) feminist analysis of the rupture between local and abstract ways of knowing particularly helpful. First, if emotions are included as part of a feminist epistemological standpoint, they stand as a provocation and challenge to conventional (and abstract) ways of knowing, authority and power. In short, they are subversive and therefore potentially dangerous. Second, as localized knowledges, emotional knowing and embodied knowing are traditionally positioned in contrast to acceptable professional knowledges and practices that are considered balanced, reasonable and restrained (Carson & Templin, 2007). Emotional and embodied knowledges are labelled as irrational, indulgent, and potentially dangerous.

According to Smith's (1987) analysis, this preference for logical and scientific reasoning leads to suppression of the personal, and is reflected in the way criteria, standards and notions of professional performance are often constructed. Hargreaves (2000) accounts for the genesis of teacher professionalism in much the same way. Teacher professionalism, he argues, is, "defined according to a 'classical' masculine model" that encourages emotional distance and is indeed "prejudicial to feminine, 'caring' ethics of teaching" (p. 816). Within this masculine professional paradigm, emotions are seen to signal the uncontrollable and to contaminate reason and judgement. Emotions are therefore dismissed in the workplace as unprofessional and we are taught early on to associate professionalism with the control and suppression of emotion. In this way, too, emotions are seen to threaten the kinds of professional judgement and expertise which rationality is assumed to assure.

In teacher research, the complex interplay between the personal and the professional, and between emotion and cognition, is well documented (Day & Leitch, 2001; Shapiro, 2010). Research reveals that teachers often experience these relationships in tension. This is evident in Day & Leitch's description of teacher-participants' "inner debate[s] between the personal and the professional, the emotional and the cognitive" (p. 414), and in Shapiro's multiple examples of her own experience of controlling and restraining her expression of emotion as a teacher (p. 617) within the context of broader unspoken expectations to maintain social distance from her colleagues (p. 618).

In this study, we defy the tendency to position feeling and knowing in binary opposition. Instead, we draw on a feminist epistemological standpoint, which facilitates a legitimate study of our emotions as both a form of knowledge and a process of knowing. Such framing positions the emotions of everyday, embodied experience as significant and instructional. Focusing our study in this way creates multiple possibilities:

- it allows us to see the emotions that inevitably shape our supposedly objective forms and ways of contemporary knowing (Jaggar, 1989);
- it prompts us to feel and recognize the connections between our everyday experience and the larger social and economic relations of ruling (Smith, 1987);
- it invites us to "rethink the relation between knowledge and emotion and to construct conceptual models that demonstrate the mutually constitutive rather than oppositional relation between reason and emotion" (Jaggar, 1989, pp. 156-57).

Through studying our practice, we investigate the ways in which working with and through feeling and emotion in our teaching enabled such possibilities to be realized.

THE STUDY

In considering feelings and their articulation as emotions, we wondered: what happens (for us, for our students) when we recast emotion as a legitimate epistemological approach to knowledge and to knowledge production? In what ways does the experience of doing so alter our sense of our roles and our work as educators? In this regard, our starting point was, perhaps, unusual in the context of self-study, which can tend to focus on "dilemmas, tensions and disappointments" as contradictions are revealed between beliefs and practice (Loughran, 2004, p. 26). We began, rather, with the crystallization of our beliefs in relation to emotion and designed our study to see what would happen through our deliberate enactment of those beliefs in our practice.

We began our study where Henry (2013) ended hers; with the understanding that "the affective and intellectual, in fact, move together, not separately, in education" (p. 2). We were interested in what that this might look like in our practice. What would happen – for us, for our students - if we took up where Henry ended, and did "attend to the influence of emotion" (Henry, p. 2); if we did "incorporate into [our] educational philosophy the place for emotive risk-taking" (p. 2); if we did "reposition emotion alongside reason in the quest for education that engages the whole learner" (p. 5)?

Over a period of five months (Jan – May 2013) we each adopted some deliberate strategies to bring feelings to the fore in our individual teaching spaces. In this sense, our self-study collaboration was akin to the second of three collaborative self-study models described by Nicol, Novakowski, Ghaleb & Beairsto (2010). It involves "educators coming together to understand a particular event, concept or idea, moving into their respective classroom contexts to explore that idea and then returning to the group to share their experiences of self-study" (p. 238). This collaboration ensued within our respective teaching contexts. Allie gathered data over four full days of intensive teaching with a group of 18 first year adult education students. Rachel's data gathering spanned two 2-3 hour sessions in the United States in which she was a guest presenter and seven 3-4 hour workshops with 17 graduate level teacher education students over a 12 week semester.

As is often the case in self-study research, our purpose in studying our practice was connected to a desire that our teaching practices should positively impact student learning (Loughran, 2004). It was, therefore, important to capture and analyze data of our students' experiences of classroom interactions and practices around emotion. To that end, several data sources for our study took the form of student posts to online discussion forums. These posts were also part of students' regular coursework engagement. At the same time, however, we did not want to fall into the trap of distancing ourselves from our practice by examining it only through others' perceptions (Tidwell & Fitzgerald, 2004). As such, student data were counterbalanced with our own reflective writing to each other about our teaching, and our written responses to one another from a critical-friend perspective. This mix of data sources reflects the delicate balance that self-study research demands between "self in relation to practice and the others who share the practice setting" (Bullough & Pinnegar, 2001, p. 15).

For this chapter, we draw on data from four sources:

1. Rachel's & Allie's discussion posts: 12 posts over 16 weeks in which we recorded our perspectives on the use and impact of using these approaches through posting

our experiences and impressions to a shared online forum. We recorded both what we perceived to be happening to/for our students and how this work was affecting our own experiences and understanding of our work as educators.

2. Toolbox posts (TP): 58 posts over six weeks from Rachel's 17 students. This coursework task involved the students creating a conceptual toolbox as an archive of their learning about teaching which was generated by responding to the prompt: "consider a powerful experience you had as a learner in this week's class and what it helps you to consider/understand about teaching."

3. Emotion Reaction posts (ERP): 14 anonymous posts by Rachel's students in response to their experimentation with Henry's (2013) Emotion Reaction approach to reading. The approach invites the reader to record their emotional response to what they are reading and then consider how the emotion affected their critical interpretation. Specifically, the students' ERPs responded to the prompt: "how did you find the experience of using an Emotion Reaction approach to this week's reading?"

4. Feeling posts (FP): 14 posts by Allie's students in relation to the prompt: "have you noticed anything about you or your responses when you are asked how you *feel* about some academic content?"

We undertook a thematic content analysis to identify emergent themes in the data in order to see what happened when we took emotions seriously and presented emotion as a way through which students arrived at new knowledge. Data were analyzed and categorized in the qualitative tradition of iterative analysis, which we understand as an essential part of a "deeply reflexive process [which] is key to sparking insight and developing meaning" (Srivastava & Hopwood, 2009, p. 77). We coded the data for instances where we could see our understanding of emotion as epistemology coming to the surface. The categories that emerged were considered against key ideas from the literature in relation to the nature and dimensions of feminist epistemology. We present these below, according to the ways in which the data raised issues around three themes related to a feminist sociological framing of the knower, the known and the process of knowing (Sprague & Kobrynowicz, 1999):

1. What counts as knowledge? Repositioning feelings as a form of knowledge.
2. Who knows? The ways in which valuing emotion empowered students to position themselves as knowers.
3. How do we come to know through feeling? Features of a process to encourage drawing on emotion as a dimension of knowledge production.

These are discussed below.

What Counts as Knowledge: Repositioning Feeling as a Form of Knowledge

As researchers and educators working in higher education, we share the experience of having been taught to value reason, logic, and objectivity and to regard with caution personal, emotional, and subjective ways and forms of knowing. We have been encouraged to live our professional lives in "the 'rupture' between the lived, material and everyday world [of women] and the conceptual world which comprised socially organised practices and knowledge forms" (Campbell, 2003, p. 7). This was a position that we first challenged – within our teaching and within our research – during a 2011 self-study (Forgasz, Clemans & Berry, 2011). In one communication, Allie wrote about our collective anxieties about the decision to research our emotional experiences in the context of our work as educators:

> We appeared to experience the tension that neutral and disembodied knowing would be perceived by our peers as more valid and hard-edged than our embodied and affective research labour promised. As researchers we knew that there was validity in addressing emotions yet, at times, felt compelled to work hard to frame our focus so that it would be accepted as valid knowledge rather than personal indulgence. (Allie, ISATT notes 2011)

In some ways, the very subject of the current self-study evinces the evolution of our journey to embrace emotion as one of multiple ways of knowing. And yet, consideration of emotion as a legitimate epistemology required us to recast how we chose to notice our emotions within our teaching work. In the early stages of our study, while Rachel was willing and able to notice her feelings during teaching moments, she found it difficult to draw on them in epistemologically productive ways. This was evident in Rachel's writing to Allie about her teaching experience in the United States:

> I felt stressed and disappointed … I was paranoid … [and] when I was feeling all these negative feelings, I was less connected to the students … When I am worried about myself (how I look) I have less space to really focus on the students' experiences and their learning.

But with her drama education students, Rachel committed to a conscious and deliberate exploration of her emotions, as a dimension of her knowing which would contribute to determining her next pedagogical action. With this deliberate focus, Rachel's relationship to her feeling responses altered from one of individual judgment to one that allowed emotion to feed productively into knowing:

> …The thing that felt different to me today was this idea of noticing my feelings without judgement. Treating them as a site of 'knowing' e.g., … I am feeling the energy flagging = they may be overloaded. (Rachel, March 4)

In the US, Rachel noticed her negative feelings while teaching, but she stayed stuck in them, using them only as evidence of her teaching failures. Here, she began to draw on her feeling responses as a dimension of her pedagogical knowing. She not only noticed that she was "feeling the energy flagging," she drew on this feeling response as earnestly as any other information she might use to theorize what might be going on for learners and, consequently, what pedagogical action to take next.

Nevertheless, drawing on emotion as a dimension of epistemology continued to require an effort of mind. As Rachel wrote to Allie:

> Much less than my students, it was I who had to reframe emotion as a legitimate form and way of knowing because only in this reframing could I give myself permission to explore/allow/encourage emotion as a legitimate part of 'the work,' of 'the learning' rather than a deviation/aberration/caring tangent from the main event. (Rachel, May 18)

While she was personally convinced of the value of addressing emotion, Rachel struggled to allow and make space for emotion as epistemology. She had to undo her learned sidelining of it as a deviation, an irrational aberration, and, instead, to reposition emotion as a place from which to begin to know (Smith, 1997).

Who Knows? Feeling as a Way Into Knowledge Production Positions Students as Knowers

Our deliberate approach to using feelings as a way for students to find their way into academic knowledge forms was experienced in different ways. Allie asked students to reflect in their postings about how they had experienced her question: "have you noticed anything about you or your responses when you are asked how you feel about some academic content?" Their responses reveal various ways in which beginning with their personal/emotional responses to scholarly ideas enabled Allie's students to position themselves as producers of knowledge, rather than simply demonstrating a reproductive understanding of the ideas contained in the reading.

Working in these ways allowed students to start with, but also to push beyond, their everyday experience and expand on what they first thought they knew. J explained that: "I tend to relate my responses & how I feel about the things I am reading to my own experiences … as I start to expand my experiences through the reading & discussions" (FP/J).

Allie's invitation was significant for the way it invited students into knowing. Asking students how they *felt* about some academic content appeared not only to succeed in encouraging them to respond to the question, but it also tended to elicit a noteworthy depth of response. It prompted a fuller consideration, going beyond the ideas under discussion:

> Asking how you feel about it elicits a more holistic response about how you *feel* about the article overall and prompts you to relate to the author. If you were to ask me what I *think* about it I would be inclined to comment on smaller points within the article that drew my attention. (FP/A)

This invitation seemed to offer a way for students to reflect on the beliefs and values that influenced their thinking. Asking about their feelings compelled them to attend to themselves as knowers and, in this way, evoked stronger and more committed responses. G observed that "[w]hen asked how we felt, I too drew on my personal experiences and beliefs; whereas, if you would have asked what we thought, I would have tried to answer more specifically on elements mentioned in the article" (FP/G). Similarly, N understood that "asking what I feel instead of what I think elicits a stronger and more connected response from me that feels more authentic" (FP/N).

This commitment was experienced in the form of position-taking. While the students themselves experienced that feeling their way into scholarly ideas was easier than being asked to think their way through, we observed that it also encouraged them to engage with those ideas more deeply than purely cognitive responses demand. They felt obliged to adopt a position:

> What do you feel? The word 'feel', does make one respond in a fashion that is personal, based on one[']s values and beliefs, so it adds more emotions to it with a sense of commitment, whereas 'think' is more a non-committed/personal expression/response, where answers can be more objective. (FP/L)

Allie's invitation to her students to consider their feelings in relation to scholarly ideas (rather than their thoughts) appears to have repaired for them the "line of fault" that Smith describes as dividing the world "[as] directly experienced from oneself as center (in the body) on the one hand and world organized in the abstracted conceptual mode, external to the local and particular places of one's bodily existence" (p. 84) on the other. Repositioning their feelings, experiences and embodied knowing as legitimate knowledge forms allowed Allie's students to produce committed, personal responses to the scholarly ideas they encountered.

This notion of producing a committed, personal response was precisely what Rachel's students found so challenging about feeling their way into scholarly ideas. After assigning Henry's (2013) Emotion Reaction approach to a reading as homework, Rachel wrote to Allie that her students "found it difficult to imagine being asked to take their feeling responses as a starting point" (Rachel, March 4). Students' anonymous Emotion Reaction posts revealed the degree to which they (like us) had been acculturated through their higher education to adopt a view of subjectivity as the enemy of scholarship. Rachel's students struggled to unlearn analytical objectivity:

> I found it very difficult to make an emotional connection to a text assigned for uni [university]. This was because of the way I have approached uni [university] readings for the past three years ... Analysis of a more clinical nature was what came easier. (ERP 1)

Their responses indicated that Rachel's students valued the author of the text as knower, placing greater stock in being able to reproduce his position than in ascertaining their own responses to those ideas. One student wrote: "Unfortunately, I must admit that I probably missed 50% of what the author was saying, as I was so determined to find an emotional response from myself" (ERP/7). Another responded that: "I did not enjoy writing my emotional response as I felt that it took away from my concentration reading the chapter" (ERP/2). In both cases, the students described in deficit terms the experience of repositioning their focus on themselves as knowers.

Traditional scientific epistemologies teach that personal, emotional responses contaminate the knowledge produced through rational and objective thinking processes. But as one student revealed, maintaining objective distance sometimes resulted in a mindless abnegation of responsibility as a knower: "sometimes I just read but don't think" (ERP/14). In contrast, when required to focus on their personal response, this same student engaged in high order thinking at the level of critical evaluation: "by doing the emotion task it made me think about what I was reading and what I believed" (ERP/14).

As in the example of Allie's students whose sense of commitment deepened through the invitation to feel their way into ideas, some of Rachel's students also came to experience scholarly ideas at the level of beliefs and personal investment:

> … [it] enabled me to invest in the text in a more rounded way – on an emotional level first, then by connecting those emotional responses to concrete experiences and rational concepts. I felt I had experienced the text more fully. I absorbed more of the text and felt more connected to the author. (ERP/9)

Inviting students to begin with their personal, feeling responses to scholarly ideas was a way of responding to Smith's call to reposition the starting point of knowing from the abstract to the local, embodied, everyday world. Doing so enabled these students to make real connections between the world of scholarly abstraction and everyday experience. It constructed experience and embodied knowing as legitimate knowledge forms and, in this way, it positioned our students as knowers.

How Do We Come To Know Through Feeling? Processes For Working With Feeling

What became apparent to us in our study of feelings as a form of knowing was that working in these ways compelled us to work with, through and from feelings in particular ways. As Rachel worked with her students and brought feelings to the surface through her lectures and discussions with students, she was aware that she had to be involved too. In fact, her willingness to show vulnerability created: "a kind of trusting environment they needed later in order to take risks because I, too, had been willing to share myself" (Rachel, Post 4 March 2013). She continued later, "… And in that softer, more honest, more vulnerable space, what they are willing to say and where they are willing to go opens up even more" (Rachel, Post 18 May 2013).

Through encouraging and inhabiting such spaces, Allie noticed her "heightened awareness of life, spirit and the flow of life," which led her to what she perceived as a fine-grained stance of discernment and sensitivity to handling emotions with care:

> I have recognised through these constant conversions and transitions [for and with students around forms of knowledge], that the handling of emotions and

allowing for their expression goes hand in hand with their expression … It is part of an epistemological process because the expression [of feelings] or handling [feelings] is one of the things that encourages the elicitation of knowledge. (Allie Post, February 20)

Like Allie, Rachel saw that handling students with care was necessary in order to encourage sharing and drawing on feelings as a legitimate, appropriate and normal part of classroom culture. To that end, she modeled for her students a process of focusing on her feelings as a starting point for reflection: "[i]t's the fact that I feel so down now that has my attention. Driving home, I really felt flat and disheartened" (Rachel, TP March 11). Importantly, this modeling moved beyond just sharing her feelings to demonstrating how to draw on them to create new knowledge about her teaching practice: "I've left feeling really frustrated and disappointed with myself because of the way our discussion (of the reading) went today … I am disappointed because as the FACILITATOR my job was … So why didn't I do that? … So what have I learned?" (Rachel, TP March 11).

Leading by example in sharing her fears and feelings, Rachel routinely invited students to do the same. This opportunity to share their feelings eased anxieties: "Hearing that everyone else shared these same concerns eased my anxiety slightly and assured me that I was not alone" (TP/O March 12) and built a sense of community: "The fact that so many members of last week's class acknowledged their own feelings of incompetence and hesitation … made me feel part of a group or club" (TP/M May 20).

With a classroom culture of feeling established, Rachel's students were willing to share the fears and vulnerabilities which, unexpressed, might have prevented learning. This was powerfully evident in J's courageous post in which she shared her fears following a particularly challenging class:

"Far out! I am confused. Really confused. What's this stuff about Drama politics? It seems really important and I am just not getting it" - is what I thought on my long stroll back down to free parking yesterday afternoon. That night I was so overwhelmed with information I decided to treat myself and not do any study. Instead, I sat down with mum and watched the rest of The Great Gatsby… (TP/J April 9)

In her post, J went on to share the story of a late night revelation in a spirit of inquiry, humbly seeking clarification from her peers to assist her in creating new knowledge and understanding. J's willingness to make her fears public inspired A to share hers too: "I left class feeling pretty down on myself for not 100% understanding the topic. However your Gatsby insight has helped me somewhat, so thank you :)." And as in J's case, admitting her fears allowed A to push past them in order to test her new understanding of the content: "It reminded me of a very similar situation that I had in high school…" (TP/A April 9). J's post sparked a string of seven replies in which Rachel's students supported one another through the uncomfortable fears and feelings associated with not understanding, while simultaneously building a shared understanding of the content that deepened and enriched what they had only partially understood on their own.

Scholarly writing around teacher vulnerability tends to frame it in deficit terms, as a micropolitical dimension of teachers' work that must be dealt with or coped with or overcome in order to regain a sense of professional competence and composure (Kelchtermans, 1996; 2009). But our research takes a different view of teacher vulnerability and how to handle it. Like Akinbode (2013), Rachel found that in the context of teacher education, "there are aspects of modeling that involve demonstrating what it means to be a teacher, which involves emotion and revealing a teacher's vulnerability" (p. 71). Like White (2009), we saw the extent to which "the safe environment [of our classrooms] allowed emotion to surface and protected people's vulnerability" (p. 16). And in that safe space, neither vulnerability nor emotion was perceived to be disempowering, unprofessional, inappropriate or dangerous. They merely exposed another dimension from which to draw knowledge.

THINKING THROUGH IMPLICATIONS

Through this exploration, we have come to understand that our various interests and practices in relation to teaching with and through emotions are grounded on an epistemological premise. Our previous research in this field circled around the attention we paid to emotions for their own sake or our awareness that we had tended to jettison them on the grounds that they softened the work we did. In this study, however, we framed emotions as epistemology and this had profound effects. It clarified our purpose in drawing emotions into our teaching and revealed three particular aspects. First, it significantly repositioned our students and ourselves as knowing subjects. Second, by drawing from local and abstract contexts, it expanded the basis on which knowledge was constituted, and enabled students to develop awareness of the ways in which knowledge is influenced by their own, and others', values and beliefs. Third, framing emotions as epistemology influenced the teaching processes we adopted to elicit emotional responses and they, in turn, were deeply connected to the knowledge claims that were made possible. In short, purpose, process and outcome were interlinked.

Framing this work as epistemological as much as pedagogical is substantial in that it established the value of teaching through emotion and exposed moments when the significance of this was not sufficiently apprehended by us or by our students. For example, our intentions were never for students to stay in the realm of personal experience or to work through feelings in order to make learning easier. Without an understanding of emotions as an epistemology, it is conceivable that drawing in feelings as a way of knowing can too easily position feelings as the end of the scholarly journey rather than the beginning. As Bannerji et al. (1992) remind us:

> There is no better point of entry into a critique or reflection than one's own experience. It is not the end point, but the beginning of an exploration between the personal and the social and therefore the political. And this connection process, which is also a discovery, is the real pedagogic process... (p. 67)

Calling on feelings was intended as an approach to knowledge production of a particular kind. It legitimated personal and embodied feeling as sources of knowledge from which to make connections to broader and more abstract concepts; student postings reflect that process as having been both embraced and resisted. The postings also stand as a note of caution around the ease with which we can potentially use feelings to valorize particular knowledge forms over others and to fail to achieve the epistemological outcomes that emerge when, as Smith (1987) showed, local and abstract knowing are connected.

Contrary to being easy, teaching through emotions was hard. It enforced responsibility for that which we know, calling on the knower to stand apart from the authoritative text or teacher and to take a stand. It compelled a position and an articulation of what the knower believed. Working through feelings expanded insights, made them count and invited and led us into active knowing. A transmissive and passive orientation to teaching was overtaken by one of empathy and engagement. From Rachel's deliberately created "soft and vulnerable" space emerged the hard-edged work of knowledge production and critique. It seemed to take on a life of its own and fostered alternative standpoints.

Striking to us in the data was the orientation to knowing and knowledge production that surfaced. Students learned through and with each other. They attended with sensitivity to each other's emotions as well as taking in and, occasionally, acting on the emotions we shared with them. A sense of reciprocity between knowers was generated as much as a sense of interdependence was created between us. Curiously, this is what signaled our growth and autonomy rather than the traditional ways in which growth is attributed - as independence shown by an individual. Instead of fostering dependence and the reproduction of knowledge, starting with emotions led the way into autonomy for learners through interdependence – and into knowledge production (Eneau, 2008).

In conclusion, our working through and with emotion was not just about adding in another domain of knowing. Rather, it was a deliberate epistemological stand we took about what counts as knowledge, who knows and how this process unfolds. We have learned that constructing this approach as pedagogical alone is helpful as it contributes to caring, ethical and expert teaching and learning. Framing this approach as epistemological, however, is profound for the powerful messages it conveys to us as educators and to our students about the nature of what we learn, of where we stand in relation to it, and to the processes by which we come to know.

REFERENCES

Akinbode, A. (2013). Teaching as lived experience: the value of exploring the hidden and emotional side of teaching through reflective narratives. *Studying Teacher Education, 9*(1), 62–73.

Bannerji, H., Carty, L., Delhi, K., Heald, S., & McKenna, K. (1992). *Unsettling relations: The university as a site of feminist struggles.* Boston, USA: Southend Press.

Bullough, R. V., & Pinnegar, S. (2001). Guidelines for quality in autobiographical forms of self-study research. *Educational Researcher, 30*(13), 13–21.

Campbell, M. (2003). Dorothy Smith and knowing the world we live in. *Journal of Sociology & Social Welfare, 30*(1), 3–22.

Carson, R. L., & Templin, T. J. (2007). *Emotion regulation and teacher burnout: Who says that the management of emotional expression doesn't matter?* Paper presented at the Paper presented at the American Education Research Association Annual Convention, Chicago, IL.

Day, C., & Leitch, R. (2001). Teachers' and teacher educators' lives: The role of emotion. *Teaching and Teacher Education: An International Journal of Research and Studies, 17*, 403–414.

Eneau, J. (2008). From autonomy to reciprocity, or vice versa? French Personalism's contribution to a new perspective on self-directed learning. *Adult Education Quarterly, 58*(3), 229–248.

Forgasz, R., Clemans, A., & Berry, A. (2011). *The personal in the professional: teachers' professional vision.* Paper presented at the 15th Biennial of the International Study Association on Teachers and Teaching, ISATT, University of Minho, Braga, Portugal.

Forgasz, R. (2013). *Embodied reflection on the emotional dimension of learning to teach.* Manuscript submitted for publication.

Hargreaves, A. (2000). Mixed emotions: teachers' perceptions of their interactions with students. *Teacher & Teacher Education, 16*, 811–826.

Henry, S. E. (2013). Vulnerability and emotional risk in an educational philosophy. *Emotion, Space and Society, 8*, 11–17.

Jaggar, A. M. (1989). Love and knowledge: Emotion in feminist epistemology. In A. M. Jaggar & S. R. Bordo (Eds.), *Gender/body/knowledge: Feminist reconstructions of being and knowing* (pp. 145–171). New Brunswick, NJ: Rutgers University Press.

Kelchtermans, G. (1996). Teacher vulnerability: Understanding its moral and political roots *Cambridge Journal of Education, 26*(3), 307–323.

Kelchtermans, G. (2009). Who I am in how I teach is the message: Self-understanding, vulnerability and reflection. *Teachers and Teaching: Theory and Practice, 15*(2), 257–272.

Lawrence, R. L. (2012). Coming full circle: Reclaiming the body. *New Directions for Adult and Continuing Education, 134*(Summer), 71–78.

Loughran, J. J. (2004). A history and context of self-study of teaching and teacher education practices. In J. Loughran, M. L. Hamilton, V. K. LaBoskey & T. Russell (Eds.), *International Handbook of Self-study of Teaching and Teacher Education Practices* (Vol. 1, pp. 7–39). Dordrecht, The Netherland: Kluwer Academic Publishers.

Nicol, C., Novakowski, J., Ghaleb, F., & Beairsto, S. (2010). Interweaving pedagogies of care and inquiry: Tensions, dilemmas and possibilities. *Studying Teacher Education, 6*(3), 235–244.

Shapiro, S. (2010). Revisiting the teachers' lounge: Reflections on emotional experience and teacher identity. *Teaching and Teacher Education* (26), 616–621.

Smith, D. (1987). *The everyday world as problematic: A feminist sociology.* Boston, MA: Northeastern University Press.

Smith, D. (1997). Comment on Hekman's Truth and Method: Feminist standpoint theory revisited. *Signs, 22*(2), 392–399.

Sprague, J., & Kobrynowicz, D. (1999). A feminist epistemology. In J. S. Chafetz (Ed.), *Handbook of the sociology of gender* (pp. 25–43). New York, NY: Kluwer Academic/Plenum Publishers.

Strivastava, P., & Hopwood, N. (2009). A practical iterative framework for qualitative data analysis. *International Journal of Qualitative Methods, 8*(1), 76–84.

Tidwell, D., & Fitzgerald, L. (2004). Self study as teaching. In J. Loughran, M. L. Hamilton, V. K. LaBoskey & T. Russell (Eds.), *International Handbook of Self-study of Teaching and Teacher Education Practices* (Vol. 1, pp. 69–102). Dordrecht, The Netherland: Kluwer Academic Publishers.

White, K. R. (2009). Using preservice teaacher emotion to encourage critical engagement with diversity. *Studying Teacher Education, 5*(1), 5–20.

Zembylas, M. (2002). 'Structures of feeling' in curriculum and teaching: Theorizing the emotional rules. *Educational Theory, 52*(2), 187–208.

Zembylas, M. (2003). Interrogating 'teacher identity:' Emotion, resistance, and self-formation. *Educational Theory, 53*(1), 107–127.

AFFILIATIONS

Rachel Forgasz
Lecturer,
Faculty of Education,
Monash University,
Melbourne, Australia

Allie Clemans
Senior Lecturer,
Faculty of Education,
Monash University,
Melbourne, Australia

JEFFREY J. KUZMIC

DISTURBING MASCULINITIES: EPISTEMOLOGY, OUTLAW EMOTIONS, AND THE GENDERED SELF IN SELF-STUDY RESEARCH

As well as motivating critical research, outlaw emotions may also enable us to perceive the world differently from its portrayal in conventional descriptions. They may provide the first indications that something is wrong with the way alleged facts have been construed, with accepted understandings of how things are. (Jaggar, 1989, p. 161)

This chapter explores the epistemological significance of emotions as a component of researcher subjectivity and self-study research methodology. Focusing on my teaching of/in *Teaching as Research*—a course on doing teacher-research for beginning teachers—I explore how doing teacher-research (undertaken by the teachers in my class) and self-study (undertaken by me in this course) are epistemologically and ontologically situated (Guba & Lincoln, 1994) in ways that blur and even redefine the boundaries between subjectivity-objectivity, between personal-professional, and between private-public. Drawing on one student's emotional struggles with doing teacher-research I examine the challenges she and I experienced in dealing with several key emotions (particularly guilt and anger) as components of researcher subjectivity and how my efforts to deconstruct these contribute to my own epistemological understanding of outlaw emotions for/in self-study research.

This chapter is a retelling, a story if you will in three parts: "a thrice told tale" (Wolf, 1992). The first part was initially written as a paper and presented at the Castle Conference on Teacher Education Practices (Kuzmic, 2004). The second part was a presentation at the American Educational Research Association Conference the following year and emerged as I rethought that first paper, sketching out the ideas that sought to take it further (Kuzmic, 2005). The third part is this chapter, an extension of and an outgrowth of the first two.

Like its predecessors, this chapter is an examination of the relationship between epistemology and methodology both in self-study (Bullough & Pinnegar, 2001; Cole & Knowles, 1996; Kuzmic, 2002) and in teacher-research (Cochran-Smith & Lytle, 1993, Freeman, 1998). This chapter however, is an analysis of self in a way that the first two "tellings" were not. Specifically, I re-examine/re-think/re-visit this previous work in light of my own and Madison's (pseudonym) identities as gendered subjects.

M. Taylor and L. Coia (Eds.), Gender, Feminism, and Queer Theory in the Self-Study of Teacher Education Practices, 77–92.

Based on my own and Madison's experience in doing research I argue for the need to acknowledge what Luttrell (2003) refers to as an "irresolvable epistemological tension" in two ways of ethnographic knowing: analytic distance and emotional participation. My own emergent epistemological understandings here not only serve to acknowledge this tension, but also point to how the dominance of reason/ rationality is situated in and reproduced through what Hearn (1992) refers to as the taken-for-granted "malestream" of public and social science discourses.

EPISTEMOLOGY AND EMOTIONS

Are emotions simply physiological responses, feelings and as such pre-cognitive? As Solomon (2008) notes, current theories generally recognize the relationship between emotions and cognition. However, emerging primarily from scientific, biomedical, physiological, and psychological discourses, emotions have been viewed as individual not social/cultural constructs (Harré, 1986; Svašek, 2005; Zembylas, 2005). More recently, drawing on Burkitt (1997) and Lupton (1998), Hubbard, Backett-Miburn, and Kemmer (2001) define emotions as "simultaneously and inseparably as a sensuous, cognitive, and social/cultural experience" (p. 121). Williams (2001) states that "emotions, in other words, are *emergent* properties, located at the intersection of physiological *dispositions*, material *circumstances* and socio-cultural *elaboration*" (p. 750). These latter definitions recognize three fundamental epistemological realities. First, emotions are intimately connected to both the cognitive world and our social/culture experiences in/of the world (Ellis, 1991; Kleinman & Copp, 1993). Second, given these intimate relationships, emotions need to be understood as an important ontological dimension of our abilities to experience and understand the social world (Campbell, 2002; Davies, 2010; Jaggar, 1989; Luttrell, 2003; Stanley & Wise, 1993). And third, emotions and affect are not simply individually oriented, but relational, and as discursive practices, speak to relations of power (Zembylas, 2005).

While the importance and role of emotions in the human condition has been extensively explored in a variety of the social and natural science disciplines (e.g., Holland, 2007; Stearns, 2008; Stets & Turner, 2008; Williams, 2001; Zembylas, 2005), explorations of the role of emotions in qualitative research has a much more recent history (Campbell, 2002; Ellis, 1991; Kleinman, 1991; Kleinman & Copp, 1993; Luttrell, 2003; Zembylas, 2007). Van Maanen, Manning, & Miller (1993) argue that "anger, boredom, confusion, self-doubt, depression, lust, despair, frustration, and embarrassment are perhaps more than occasionally associated with fieldwork, but are not often discussed, at least not in print, because such sentiments violate the pleasure principle so often associated with model practice" (p. vii). Equally as important, field researchers, even qualitative researchers, as members of a larger discipline are socialized into and share a culture dominated by an ideology of professionalism and science embedded in an objective stance and rationality perpetuated through patriarchy, what Campbell (2002) refers to as "learning not to feel" (p. 16). Even when researcher subjectivity is validated, as in the case of qualitative research methodologies, emotions are suspect within this ideology; they contaminate research by impeding objectivity and as such should be avoided by conscientious researchers (Campbell, 2002; Davies, 2010; Kleinman & Copp, 1993; Luttrell, 2003).

I borrow Jaggar's (1989) use of the term outlaw in the title and throughout the chapter to emphasize the continued epistemological marginalization of emotions. As Jaggar and others (e.g., Bloom, 1998; Fonow & Cook, 1991; Harding, 1991; Lather, 1991; Weiler, 2001) have argued even with the paradigmatic challenges of naturalistic epistemologies and postmodern/post-structuralist critiques, the dominance of reason and rationality still serve as the epistemological foundation for research methodology. However, from the standpoint of feminist epistemology, this is not merely about the methodological relationship between rationality and emotion as ways of knowing, but how this is situated within a patriarchal epistemological hegemony.

ENGENDERING THE SELF: MASCULINITY AND METHODOLOGY

Drawing on Madison's work for the course (including her research journal, course assignments, written research report, interviews, and video recording of her research presentation), my field notes from the course, and my own struggle to work through her emotional engagement with her research, I examine how the process of doing teacher-research, for Madison, expressed itself in guilt and anxiety and led me to an epistemological abyss of sorts. Using what Fine (1994) has termed "working the hyphens" as a conceptual starting point, I analyze Madison's experiences as the renegotiation of her identity and the redefining of the boundaries between subjectivity and objectivity, between personal and professional, and between private and public. In this case, by examining the hyphen that separates and merges one's identity as a teacher and as a researcher, I reflect not only on the tensions inherent in doing teacher-research, but the meaning and possibilities of thinking about the hyphen that separates and merges my own gendered identity as a teacher educator with that of self-study researcher. Additionally, based on feminist critiques of science, objectivity, and reason (Alcoff, 1989; Grosz, 1993; Harding, 1991; Jaggar, 1989) I explore the different ways in which Madison and I initially, and then subsequently, dealt with her emotional struggle while doing research.

For Madison, anger, guilt, and anxiety were the terrain on which she struggled to redefine her professional identity to accommodate that of both teacher and researcher. While painful, the outcome overall was positive in the long, if not the short-term. Madison initially struggled with, sought to reject, and then embraced her emotions as she worked through what it means to do teacher-research, while I initially failed to "see", then ignored, and then examined why I ignored this aspect of her research. I interpret these responses from our situated perspectives as gendered subjects, as teachers, and as researchers that point to epistemological tensions inherent in research where study of self is central to one's inquiry. In exploring our experiences, I examine how my own identity as a male and as an instructor were epistemologically in conflict with my identity as a researcher in ways that document my epistemological embeddedness in a patriarchal world. While feminist and postmodern critiques have challenged the dominance of objectivity and reason as the foundation for social and educational research, I believe that situating the self as an object/subject of study highlights these tensions anew and affords new insights to these analyses.

COMING TO KNOW DIFFERENTLY: PATRIARCHY, EPISTEMOLOGY, AND THE GENDERED SELF

"You're such a guy." This is a statement my partner says every now and then, usually at the end of a conversation about something she is trying to get me to understand or listen to. And usually it comes after I have listened for a while, then asked her to look at the situation logically, and when this doesn't seem to work, I immediately jump in and try and fix things; find a solution, make things right. And then it comes, not in anger, perhaps in frustration, and certainly with the desire to help me understand: "You're such a guy. I don't want you to make things right, to fix it, or even to necessarily try and make me feel better. I want you to listen, to share, to feel with me." Initially, when I focused on the last two sentences I was somewhat befuddled, baffled, bewildered, and perhaps now as frustrated as she. Wasn't that what I was doing? However, it is the first sentence that really holds the clue for me. It was this sentence that had me thinking long afterward; thinking about my own reading and theoretical appreciation of feminist scholarship, how I have utilized this as a theoretical lens to interrogate and examine educational phenomena through my own research, and how difficult it was for this to ever penetrate my male sensibilities in the practice of my own life. My partner is a feminist because of how she has experienced a gendered world and a feminist scholar as a political response to patriarchy. While my own experience and exposure to this scholarship has brought the understanding that we live in a patriarchal world, I experience, navigate, and understand that world from a position of privilege and power; a position that often makes my own gendered identity and positionality invisible. I'm such a guy.

The more I thought about Madison, my paper, and the conversation that followed my AERA presentation, the more I felt the need to explore both the epistemology and pedagogy of my research from our perspectives as gendered subjects.

> Spoke to Madison about her meltdown in class tonight. I knew she was struggling with her research because she felt responsible in some way for Carrie's retention in 3rd grade- her 3rd grade, again. Still, I didn't recognize how powerful an impact this was having (maybe I should be reading their research journals more often). While she sounded less angry, she wasn't apologetic for

her behavior and obviously is still upset, but about Carrie, not what went on in class. I decided not to deal with the class situation, but her research. I told her that I think she needed to stop collecting data since we're so near the end of the quarter and step away from her project to get some distance and perspective in order to be able to complete her analysis and the final paper; that she was too close to things and it was obviously having an impact. She agreed and at least she seemed to have calmed down. (Fieldnotes)

This statement never found its way into the initial drafts because I was focusing on Madison and not on myself. Looking at this now I can only say "I am such a guy." I refer to what happened in class that night as a "meltdown." While I don't think I was thinking of this in a necessarily pejorative manner—I had then and still have an enormous amount of respect for Madison, she had taken the notion of teacher-research not only seriously, but with a seriousness that was rare among the beginning teachers who populate this course—it is obvious that I did not see her reaction as appropriate. What troubles me more, particularly in light of the previous arguments that I made with regard to the need to recognize emotions (based on her experiences) in our research, is that I dismissed these at the time. Again, this seems remarkable given that this is the incident that stayed with me and prompted me to further explore emotions and researcher subjectivity. My reading of this now is to question, or at least wonder, is this the way the "malestream" (Hearn, 1992) works? By that I mean, was my initial reaction to Madison to validate her research yet dismiss her reaction as a problem for her research, rather than see it as central to it, constitutive of a privileging of reason over emotion, a form of epistemological hegemony? And how do I think of this in light of the fact that I eventually came to see an epistemological significance to the role of emotions in her/our research?

The answers to these questions, I now believe, were wrapped up in an unexamined patriarchal epistemological stance where I privileged researcher rationality and made other ways of knowing, particularly those connected with emotions, decidedly problematic at best or invisible at worst. Madison too wrote in her research journal that evening:

I am so frustrated—I feel like I've officially gone off the deep end and I'm being swallowed up by this research project. Tonight in class I nearly broke down into tears when we analyzed my data analysis paper. It's as if I've become so depressed over the course of this and I haven't even noticed it. Each day that I collect data I'm immersed in Carrie's world—a world that is unstable and unhappy. I'm unbelievably protective of her—like a lioness with a cub. I feel like I want to shield her from any more trauma, any more pain. But I can't. Tonight I nearly bit Sarah's head off when she said "Do you think you're getting a little too emotional about this?" It felt like a sharp punch in the stomach. Too emotional? How can you not be emotional when everything you observe is upsetting, every article you read is pessimistic, and every bit of analysis you do makes you feel more and more helpless. I've no understanding of teachers who do not care deeply for their students. It must be possible, but I can't fathom how to do it. (Madison's Research Journal)

I am struck by the difference in tone between my own and Madison's journal entry. While I chose to view Madison's reaction to Sarah's comments as an emotional outburst, a reaction to rather than a central component of her teaching/research, Madison herself sought to both explain and validate her feelings within the context of doing research.

Looking back, what I find epistemological troubling is how little attention and how little merit I gave to this struggle at the time. My comments to her on her final paper seem to only begin to validate the latter and seem like an afterthought.

This is indeed impressive; incredible in terms of its depth, substance, and power. It speaks of the complexity of the relationship between teacher and student and how these are related to larger institutional policies and practices. It shows that understanding the latter is critical to understanding the former. It is the power of these voices (yours and Carrie's) that is oftentimes ignored as we try and think about the taken-for-granted character of policies directed at accountability. It is also where your story/research has much to say. It is a sad commentary when such policies cause thoughtful, creative, dedicated teachers like yourself to question their abilities. I know the strength of your own self-concept as a teacher will only allow you to take this so far, but it makes me worry for those who don't have this inner strength and confidence.

In effect, I was validating her analytic stance, but not her emotional participation. Since Madison's teacher-research project, this is a separation that I am less comfortable with, one I have come to question particularly in relation to teacher-research and self-study. Her project demonstrated how one's emotional self is intimately connected to one's professional self. Just because one adds the role of the researcher to that identity doesn't mean that we have to take up the traditional separation between analytic distance and emotional participation. In fact, as Krieger (1991) further articulates, to fail to do so limits our ability to understand social and educational phenomena.

I wish to suggest the self is not a contaminant, but rather it is the key to what we know, and that methodological discussions might fruitfully be revised to acknowledge the involvement of the self in a positive manner. The self is not something that can be disengaged from knowledge or from research processes. Rather, we need to understand the nature of our participation in what we know. The problem we need to worry about is not the effect of an observer's inner self on evidence from the outside world, but the ways that the traditional dismissal of the self may hinder the development of each individual's unique perspective. (pp. 29-30, cited in Campbell, 2002)

Drawing on Denzin and Lincoln (1994), Bullough and Pinnegar (2001) acknowledge that the Fifth Moment in educational research has situated questions of context, process, and relationship at the center of inquiry. "Who the researcher is," they argue, "is central to what the researcher does" (p. 13). In this next section, as a way of making an argument to honor and deal with the tension between the self as analytic observer and emotional participant, I explore how Madison's emotional involvement helped her frame her research project, supported its development, and ultimately had an impact that went beyond her classroom or her work with Carrie.

OUTLAW EMOTIONS

I don't know how teacher-research cannot have some level of emotion when it refers to your teaching and your students and your practices. I think it's there, it's inherent in it and we just have to deal with it. (Madison's Teacher-Research presentation to T&L 612)

For Madison, emotions played a central role in her teacher research project in a variety of ways. They informed the very topic for her project. Our class and my request to find a topic for a research project came very shortly after she learned that three of her students had been held back in 3rd grade. Not only did she disagree with this, she felt wronged because she hadn't been part of the decision, she felt helpless, and to a certain extent that it was her fault; she just hadn't been a good enough teacher for these students.

Did this have an impact on the fact that she chose to focus her teacher-research project on one of these students? I can't help but think that it did, and in positive ways. As Jaggar's (1989) quote at the outset suggests, it was Madison's emotional investment in this topic/focus that allowed her to see beyond an individual student failing the test and begin to examine how this could happen; how the larger context of educational policy impacted her and her students directly. Madison's emotional investment in the project not only forced her to examine her own role in this process, her relationship with the students involved, her response to the retention decision, and that she felt wronged, but it enabled her to challenge and change the policy in her school. Exploring and validating her emotions as part of the research process allowed her to better understand what Carrie was going through, while looking beyond merely fixing the problem in her classroom, to exploring the possibility of how to bring about change.

This year when the test scores came out and one student didn't pass, I was prepared. I had a portfolio of work and went to the principal to make a case that he shouldn't be retained. She agreed with me in this case. Other teachers have started doing the same. My research enabled me to have more confidence to be able to go to her (the principal) and say that we shouldn't be relying only on test scores as the basis for these decisions. I'm advocating that we use a variety of measures in evaluating the promotion or retention of students. (Madison's Teacher-Research presentation to T&L 612)

Zembylas (2007) suggests that some emotions, like anger and frustration, can motivate people to take action against injustice. I believe, that for Madison, validating or at least acknowledging her frustration and anger allowed, perhaps even necessitated, her to find a productive way to speak back to what she came to see/feel (because of her research and understanding of Carrie's experiences) was a flawed policy.

Madison and I reacted to her research and its emotional dimensions in different ways. I believe this was due in part to how our gendered selves are shaped by and defined differently within a patriarchal world. Whether we are conscious of it or not, we are influenced by social, cultural, political, and epistemological narratives that privilege certain perspectives and practices while marginalizing or making invisible others. We also experience and understand these narratives and practices in different ways based on the complexities of our identities as gendered, raced, classed, and sexualized beings depending on how we are situated in relation to these. Through Madison, I believe, I came to see my own epistemological understanding about why, how, and in what ways we undertake research, in particular self-study research, in a different light.

DISTURBING MASCULINITIES: EMOTIONS, EPISTEMOLOGIES, AND PATRIARCHY

And what about me? Can/should I take some solace in the fact that, because of Madison, because of self-study, I have come to understand my own complicity in the patriarchies that structure and give meaning to our social, pedagogical, epistemological, and methodological worlds and therefore am able to act in ways to challenge and/or change things? Perhaps. But that would be too easy, in spite of the fact that I believe my constructions and understandings of self-study, teacher-research, and my own pedagogy have been significantly altered. Before turning to that however, I would like to take up what I am referring to as "disturbing masculinities"; a rhetorical mechanism to explore the space that lies between the dangers and the possibilities, the visibility and invisibility, in our/my efforts to understand the epistemological impact of patriarchy. I use this term in a dual sense. In its first sense, I use the term "disturbing" to acknowledge an awakening of sorts to the power of my identity as a gendered subject, which shapes my understanding and experiences of the world in ways that make my complicity in the inequalities of patriarchy invisible. In the second sense, I use "disturbing" as a conscious political act intended to disrupt and redefine the ideological, social, epistemological, and methodological terrain that serves as the hegemonic foundation for patriarchy.

I believe my failure, and the failure/resistance of researchers more generally to take seriously the epistemological tension between rational and emotional ways of knowing in terms of thinking about the self of self-study research, is not only situated within a form of epistemological hegemony, but is supported in/through patriarchy. In order to explore this more fully, as this relates to my own emergent understandings, I draw on what Jaggar (1989) refers to as the "myth of dispassionate investigation," "emotional hegemony," "outlaw emotions," and the "epistemic potential of emotion."

Twenty-five years ago Jaggar (1989), exploring the relationship between emotion and feminist epistemology, approached the question of the role and place of emotion in Western research traditions (even qualitative ones) as not simply a methodological question, but fundamentally an epistemological and philosophical one, politically and socially situated. In short, it is about power and how knowledge is constructed. Taking as a starting point the fact that emotion has been construed as epistemologically subversive, she explores the emergence and solidification of the privileging of rationality over emotion, challenges (both philosophically and epistemologically) the empirical superiority of rationality, and demonstrates emotion as an equally valid means of both engaging and constructing our world. For Jaggar, the epistemological marginalization of emotion is not philosophically, epistemologically, biologically, or methodologically justified. Rather, this marginalization is fundamentally ideological and gendered, situated and maintained within/through the hegemony of patriarchy. And through the creation of an epistemology that supports this separation, has come not only the dichotimization of reason and emotion, but the separation of mind and body, and objectivity and subjectivity, within a masculinist world view that privileges the former and marginalizes, and even, demonizes the latter. Jaggar (1989), having exposed the marginalization of emotions as an ideological project based in patriarchy, argues for the necessity to rethink the epistemological relationship between reason and emotion "in order to construct conceptual models that demonstrate the mutually constitutive rather than oppositional relation between reason and emotion" (p. 163). One of the challenges in dealing with the concept of emotions, Jaggar argues, is that the boundaries between the social, political, psychological, and epistemological are not clear and are often confused. This is also one of its potential strengths. In rethinking the relationship between reason and emotion epistemologically, comes the potential to reexamine, perhaps even better understand, the taken for granted ways in which patriarchy is maintained and embedded in the complexity of the social, political, economic and psychological.

Where are we, twenty-five years after Jaggar's epistemological critique? I wish I could say that we have begun to construct epistemological models that demonstrate the mutually constitutive rather than oppositional relation between reason and emotion. Sadly, this is not the case. While researcher subjectivity has been validated within and through qualitative research traditions, emotions, it would appear, are still epistemological outlaws; subversive and detrimental to our ways of knowing (Ellis, 1991; Kleinman, 1991: Luttrell, 2003). Recognizing this epistemological tension, and validating it, seems all the more critical when considering forms of research where the type of research one is doing is embedded in the researcher's study of self and where the identity of one's self is embedded in a complex set of

85

socially constructed dimensions based on difference and differential power. How can we truly separate the inner life of the researcher, intimately connected as it is / has to be to the emotional side of who we are as teachers/teacher educators, from the analytic distance we are supposed to demonstrate as researchers?

The reflexive methodological turn in qualitative research has emerged as a result of a complex set of epistemological (a critical stance toward researcher subjectivity) and theoretical factors (a critical analysis of modernity based on postmodern discourses), and I believe, it is precisely this reflexive turn that opened the doors to both the emergence and solidification of self-study research (and other forms of qualitative research that acknowledge/problematize researcher subjectivity; feminist research and auto-ethnography) within the social sciences generally and the field of education specifically. While self-study research has pushed, both methodologically and epistemologically, the boundaries of the role of the researcher in the process of doing research, I believe the gendered nature of the latter needs to be further explored. There is a certain irony in this given the unique epistemological positioning of the researcher in self-study research. Through Madison's experiences in my class, I have been challenged to consider, epistemologically, how we, as self-study researchers, might contribute to pushing these epistemological dialogues. Building on feminist epistemological critiques that have laid the foundation to both recognize and problematize the privileging of rationality over emotions, a number of scholars have sought to provide a framework for thinking about the role of emotions in research. I turn to some of these outlaw epistemologies as a way of summarizing my own emergent epistemological understandings and to highlight the implications for self-study research.

GENDER, OUTLAW EMOTIONS, EPISTEMOLOGY, AND SELF-STUDY

What do I take away—and what might I offer by way of concluding thoughts—from this exercise in reexamining/rethinking/revisiting my research and the relationship between reason and emotions?

Emotional Matters: Deconstructing the Epistemological Hegemony of Patriarchy

For Madison, emotions were constitutive, but not determinative in terms of her engagement with her research. Toward this end it is important to reemphasize that emotions in research, like reason and rationality, are not unproblematic (Jaggar, 1989; Zembylas, 2007). I believe, like all conundrums, relationships, and dilemmas, and particularly in the case of reason/emotion it is probably not either/or, but both/and. In the case of my research, acknowledging this relationship has re/opened epistemological doors previously closed, or perhaps just forgotten or ignored, in the face of the dominance of the hegemonic forces that privilege rationality, marginalize emotional ways of knowing, and limit our ways of thinking about researcher subjectivity. As Williams (2001) suggests, emotions influence reason, providing it with meaning, direction, purpose, and thus, he argues, the relations between reason and emotion are more or less supportive if not constitutive of each other. It is only when we recognize these relations that we can begin to see and understand the epistemological implications and limitations of a modernist project that marginalizes emotions. The subversive focus on the self of self-study creates new ways of recognizing and exploring the methodological and epistemological relationship between emotions and reason in non-binary ways.

As with Madison, this suggests that the very choices that we make about what to research are influenced and indebted to the inseparability of reason and emotion. As Hubbard et.al. (2001) note, "knowledge is not something objective and removed from our bodies, experiences, and emotions but is created through our experiences of the world as sensuous and affective activity" (p. 126). What this means, I believe, is that we as researchers need to situate/understand our rationale for exploring a topic not only theoretically, but experientially/personally as well. Looking at my own self-study research and the work of other self-study researchers, I believe this is both inherent and implicit in both our methodological framing of our research and its epistemology. I would encourage us, in order to recognize the unique epistemological possibilities of self-study research, to explore these aspects of our research more explicitly.

The complexity of emotions and research, however, is not relegated to our decisions about what to research, but are equally embedded in our engagement in the field through both data collection and analysis (Hubbard et al., 2001; Kleinman & Copp, 1993). Hubbard et al. (2001) acknowledge that this can work in a number of different ways: "a respondent's emotions may be used as data", "the emotionality of one interview setting, may influence how a researcher manages emotion in the next", and "a researcher's own emotional response to the respondent's experiences can be used to interpret data and may indeed be part of the reflexive process" (p. 131). As a means of capturing the complexity of these relationships, Campbell (2002) refers to the possibilities of "emotionally engaged research" which seeks to acknowledge that emotions are an important resource and not a source of bias. In order to honor this in/through our research she argues, based on Nodding's (1984) notion of an ethic of care, that caring (itself an emotion) should serve as a foundation for how we approach our research and for creating a balance between thinking and feeling. I believe, as feminist epistemologists have acknowledged (Bloom, 1998; Lather & Smithies, 1997), that ethics is not merely a methodological response, but an epistemological one as well.

A final way in which emotions can impact our research (and probably the most challenging) is through our written reports and manuscripts submitted to scholarly journals (Tonkin, 2005). Given the hegemonic emphasis on reason and the marginalization of the emotional work of qualitative research, this is risky business (Campbell 2002: Kleinman & Copp, 1993). The field of self-study research (with its own conference, journal, and significant scholarship both within and outside the field) can provide both a forum and safe space to accomplish this.

Gender Matters: The Politics of Outlaw Emotions

Based on my own epistemological travels, it is important to recognize, methodologically and epistemologically, gender matters. What does this mean in terms of the self of self-study? Given the centrality of the self in self-study research, the complexity of our identities and their impact on our research, these need to be consciously, continually examined and critiqued. Both Madison's and my own engagement with research were framed by our socially constructed gendered identities. As feminist scholars (Butler, 1990; Lather, 2007, St. Pierre & Pillow, 2000) and other critical scholars (e.g., Apple, 1982; Delgado & Stefancic, 2001; Giroux, 2001; Seidman, 1996) have long asserted, scholarship and the inquiry upon which it is based has to both acknowledge the historical, social, political, cultural, and economic context of our educational world and seek to address the inequities that exist because of these. In short, critical scholarship and research is both personal and political. To the extent that the hegemony of rationality and the marginalization of emotions contributes to the maintenance of patriarchy, troubling our epistemological stance in a way that acknowledges the centrality of emotions in human understanding and inquiry is part of this critical engagement. As Zembylas (2007) points out, the demonization of emotion in critical inquiry in education reflects a carefully invented absence of affect as a political force through which hegemony (in all its forms) is, in part, maintained. In arguing for a "politization of emotion," Zembylas is not arguing for a privileging of emotion *per se*, but a validation of emotion as an important social, cultural, political and educational construct. While Madison's emotional response to one of her peers in class may have seemed inappropriate in term of its tone (from my perspective at the time), the underlying anger and frustration with a dehumanizing educational system and its impact on one of her students is not only understandable, but contributed to her desire to name her anger and to act. Zembylas (citing Lyman, 1981) further points out that while anger is oftentimes branded with negativity, anger can be defined as an "essential political emotion" because it motivates people to raise their voice against injustice and can be used to inspire transformation and social change (2007, p. xii).

Based on a second aspect of how gender matters, when we acknowledge one's emotional participation as a researcher, we epistemologically and methodologically speak back to the hegemony of patriarchy. Bloom (1998), drawing on Jaggar (1989), notes that within Western epistemology emotions have been contrasted with reason and rationality and as such have been associated with the irrational, the physical, the natural, the particular, the private, and the female, all of which are devalued. However, Bloom argues, there are other ways to frame how our understanding of emotions are constructed. Drawing on Lutz (1988), she notes that emotion is also contrasted with estrangement or disengagement. Emotion in this sense is associated with life, community, relationship, the subjective, the natural, the authentic, commitment, morality, and the female.

Emotion, then, is defined similarly in both sets of binaries, but is "evaluated" differently in Western epistemology. In the first set, when emotion is contrasted to reason, emotion is devalued; in the second set, when emotion is contrasted to disengagement, emotion is valued. Given that emotion is evaluated differently in these two binary constructs, it is important to recognize that emotion is always about someone or something; therefore the social context or personal relations in which emotions are expressed and lived are critical to an understanding of the discourse of emotions. (Bloom, 1998, pp. 114-15)

I think it is in this latter sense that emotions can contribute to our epistemological and methodological understanding of self-study. Like other aspects of researcher identity and subjectivity—race, class, gender, and sexuality—that have been both validated and problematized as a result of the postmodern turn, emotions are socially constructed and, as such, represent a way of linking the self and the social, situating our inquiry in a way that provides the researcher researching the self a means to avoid decontextualized, narcissistic, and individualistic traps and critiques. In this sense emotions reflect our ideologies (Hochschild, 1983). Exploring our emotions is a way of getting at the ideologies that frame, inform, and influence our work.

DISTURBING EPISTEMOLOGIES: CONCLUDING THOUGHTS

Emotions are but one aspect of any human experience, and we do violence to the complexity of lived experience when we make analytical cuts between emotion and thought, or emotion, the senses, thought and action. (Davies, 2010, p. 25)

As I contemplate the un/finishedness of this chapter, one thing has become clearer for me on this journey. Within a narrowed epistemological world framed by patriarchy and dominated by reason, the politics of one's research, the motivation behind one's research, is always suspect (Lather, 2004). Deemed too personal, too subjective, too ideologically driven, one's analytic stance is questioned because we live within an epistemological world that chooses to separate analytic and emotional ways of knowing. This not only bifurcates the self, but also denies the "why" of why we act and do research. Hage (2010) argues that it is in the space created by bringing together, acknowledging, and problematizing our analytical and emotional ways of knowing that we recognize a third way; the political. Recognizing this engenders an epistemological stance that not only allows us, as self-study researchers, to understand the complexity of lived experience (our own and others), but to act because of and based on this. It is in this way that self-study research, in a positive epistemological sense, can be both political and disturbing.

REFERENCES

Alcoff, L. (1989). Justifying feminist social science. In N. Tuana (Ed.), *Feminism & science* (pp. 85–103). Indianapolis, IN: Indiana University Press.

Apple, M. (1982). *Education and power.* Boston, MA: ARK.

Bloom, L. R. (1998). *Under the sign of hope: Feminist methodology and narrative interpretation.* Albany, NY: State University of New York Press.

Bullough, R. V., & Pinnegar, S. (2001). Guidelines for quality in autobiographical forms of self-study research. *Educational Researcher, 30*(3), 13-21.

Burkitt, I. (1997). Sociological relationships and emotions. *Sociology, 31*, 37–55.

Butler, J. (2006). *Gender trouble: Feminism and the subversion of gender.* New York, NY: Routledge.

Campbell, R. (2002). *Emotionally involved: The impact of researching rape.* New York, NY: Routledge.

Cochran-Smith, M., & Lytle, S. (1993). *Inside/outside: Teacher research and knowledge.* New York, NY: Teachers College Press.

Cole, A., & Knowles, G. L. (1996). *Self-study in teacher education: Empowering our future.* Paper presented at Herstmonceux I, First S-STEP International Conference, Herstmonceux Castle, East Sussex, United Kingdom, August 5–8.

Davies, J. (2010). Introduction: Emotions in the field. In J. Davies & D. Spenser (Eds.), *Emotions in the field: The psychology and anthropology of fieldwork experience* (pp. 1–34). Palo Alto, CA: Stanford Press.

Delgado, R., & Stefancic, J. (2001). *Critical race theory: An introduction.* New York, NY: NYU Press.

Ellis, C. (1991). Emotional sociology. *Studies in Symbolic Interaction, 12,* 123–145.

Fine, M. (1994). Working the hyphens: Reinventing self and other in qualitative research. In N. K. Denzin & Y. S. Lincoln (Eds.), *Handbook of qualitative research* (pp. 70–82). Thousand Oaks, CA: Sage.

Fonow, M., & Cook, J. (1991). Back to the future: A look at the second wave of feminist epistemology and methodology. In M. Fonow & J. Cook (Eds.), *Beyond methodology: Feminist scholarship as lived research* (pp. 1–15). Bloomington, IN: Indiana University Press.

Freeman, D. (1998). *Doing teacher research: From inquiry to understanding.* Boston, MA: Heinle and Heinle.

Grosz, E. (1993). Bodies and knowledges: Feminism and the crisis of reason. In L. Alcoff & E. Potter (Eds.), *Feminist epistemologies* (pp. 187–216). New York, NY: Routledge.

Guba, E. G., & Lincoln, Y. S. (1994). Competing paradigms of qualitative research. In N. K. Denzin & Y. S. Lincoln (Eds), *Handbook of qualitative research* (pp. 105–117). Thousand Oaks, CA: Sage.

Giroux, H. A. (2001) *Theory and resistance in education: Toward a pedagogy for the opposition.* Westport, CN: Bergin & Garvey.

Hage, G. (2010). Hating Israel in the field: On ethnography and political emotions. In J. Davies & D. Spenser (Eds.), *Emotions in the field: The psychology and anthropology of fieldwork experience* (pp. 129–154). Palo Alto, CA: Stanford Press.

Harding, S. (1991). *Whose science? Whose knowledge? Thinking from women's lives.* Ithaca, NY: Cornell University Press.

Harré, R. (1986). An outline of the social constructionist viewpoint. In R. Harré (Ed.), *The social construction of emotions* (pp. 2–14). New York, NY: Basil Blackwell.

Hearn, J. (1992). *Men in the public eye.* New York, NY: Routledge.

Hochschild, A. (1983). *The managed heart: Commercialization of human feeling.* Berkeley, CA: University of California Press.

Holland, J. (2007). Emotions and research. *International Journal of Social Research Methodology, 10*(3), 195–209.

Hubbard, G., Backett-Milburn, K., & Kemmer, D. (2001). Working with emotion: Issues for the researcher in fieldwork and teamwork. *International Journal of Social Research Methodology, 4*(2), 119–137.

Jaggar, A. M. (1989). Love and knowledge: Emotion in feminist epistemology. *Inquiry: An Interdisciplinary Journal of Philosophy, 32*(4), 151–76.

Kleinman, S. (1991) Field-workers' feelings: What we feel, who we are, how we analyze. In W. Shaffir & R. Stebbins (Eds.), *Experiencing fieldwork: An inside view of qualitative research* (pp. 184–195). Newbury Park, CA: Sage.

Kleinman, S., & Copp, M. (1993). *Emotions and fieldwork.* Newbury Park, CA: Sage.

Krieger, S. (1991). *Social science and the self: Personal essays on an art form.* New Brunswick, NJ: Rutgers University Press.

Kuzmic, J. (2002). Research as a way of knowing and seeing: Advocacy for the other. In J. Loughran & T. Russell (Eds.), *Improving teacher education practices through self-study* (pp. 222–236). London, UK: Routledge Falmer.

Kuzmic, J. (2004). "Working the hyphen" in teacher-research (and self-study): Exploring guilt, anxiety, and researcher subjectivity. In D. Tidwell, L. Fitzgerald & M. Heston (Eds.), *Journeys of hope: Risking self-study in a diverse world* (pp. 273–276). Cedar Falls, IA: Fifth International Conference on Self-Study of Teacher Education Practices.

Kuzmic, J. (2005). *Emotions, subjectivity and the reflexive self in self-study research: Disturbing masculinities.* Paper presented at the 2005 American Educational Research Association conference, Montreal, Canada, April 12–17.

Lather, P. (1991). *Getting smart: Feminist research and pedagogy with/in the postmodern.* New York, NY: Routledge.

Lather, P. (2004). This is your father's paradigm: Government intrusion and the case of qualitative research in education. *Qualitative Inquiry, 10*(1), 15–34.

Lather, P. (2007). *Getting lost: Feminist efforts toward a double(d) science.* Albany, NY: SUNY.

Lather, P. A., & Smithies, C. (1997) *Troubling the angels: Women living with HIV/AIDS.* Boulder, CO: Westview Press.

Lewis, M, Haviland-Jones, J. M., & Barrett, L.F. (Eds.) (2008). *Handbook of emotions.* New York, NY: Guilford Press.

Lupton, D. (1998). *The emotional self.* Newberry Park, CA: Sage.

Luttrell, W. (2003). *Pregnant bodies, fertile minds: Gender, race, and the schooling of pregnant teens.* New York, NY: Routledge.

Lutz, C. (1988). *Unnatural emotions: Everyday sentiments on a Micronesian atoll and their challenge to western theory.* Chicago, IL: University of Chicago Press.

Noddings, N. (1984). *Caring, a feminine approach to ethics & moral education.* Berkeley: University of California Press.

Seidman, S. (1996). Introduction. In S. Seidman (Ed.), *Queer theory/sociology* (pp. 1–30). Malden, MA: Wiley-Blackwell.

Solomon, R. C. (2008). The philosophy of emotions. In M. Lewis, J. M. Haviland-Jones, & L.F. Barrett (Eds.), *Handbook of emotions* (pp. 3–16). New York, NY: Guilford Press.

Stanley, L., & Wise, S. (1993). *Breaking out again: Feminist ontology and epistemology.* New York, NY: Routledge.

Stearns, P. (2008). History of emotions: Issues of change and impact. In M. Lewis, J. M. Haviland-Jones, & L. F. Barrett (Eds.), *Handbook of emotions* (pp. 17–31). New York, NY: Guilford Press.

Stets, J. E., & Turner, J. H. (2008). The sociology of emotions, In M. Lewis, J. M. Haviland-Jones, & L. F. Barrett (Eds.), *Handbook of emotions* (pp. 32–46). New York, NY: Guilford Press.

St. Pierre, E. A., & Pillow, W. A. (2000). Introduction: Inquiry among the ruins. In E. A. St.Pierre & W. A. Pillow (Eds.), *Working the ruins: Feminist and poststructural theory and methods in education* (pp. 1–24). New York, NY: Routledge.

Svašek, M. (2005). Introduction: Emotions in anthropology. In K. Milton & M. Svašek (Eds.), *Mixed emotions: Anthropological studies of feeling* (pp. 1–24). New York, NY: Berg.

Tonkin, E. (2005). Being there: Emotion and imagination in anthropologists' encounters. In K. Milton & M. Svašek (Eds.), *Mixed emotions: Anthropological studies of feeling* (pp. 55–70). New York, NY: Berg.

Van Maanen, J., Manning, P. K., & Miller, M. L. (1993). Editor's introduction. In S. Kleinman & M. A. Copp (Eds.), *Emotions and fieldwork* (pp. 7–8). London, UK: Sage.

Weiler, K (2001). Introduction. In K Weiler, (Ed.). (2001). *Feminist engagements: Reading, resisting, an revisioning male theorists in education and cultural studies* (pp. 1–13). New York, NY: Routledge.

Williams, S. (2001). *Emotion and social theory.* Thousand Oaks, CA: Sage.

Wolf, M. (1992). *A thrice-told tale: Feminism, postmodernism, and ethnographic responsibility.* Palo Alto, CA: Stanford University Press.

Zembylas, M. (2005). Discursive practices, genealogies, and emotional rules: A poststructuralist's view on emotion and identity in teaching. *Teaching and Teacher Education, 21,* 935–948.

Zembylas, M. (2007). *Five pedagogies, a thousand possibilities: Struggling for hope and transformation in education.* Rotterdam, Netherlands: Sense Publishers.

J. J. KUZMIC

AFFILIATIONS

Jeffrey Kuzmic
Associate Professor,
Department of Leadership, Language, and Curriculum,
College of Education,
DePaul University,
Chicago, Illinois

DEBORAH L. TIDWELL WITH PAMELA T.
SCHWARTZ & JANET T. DUNN

FAMILIAL REALITY ENGENDERING FEMINISM: THE IMPACT OF A MATRIARCHAL UPBRINGING ON THINKING ABOUT TEACHING AND LEARNING

Much of the literature on feminist pedagogy confronts the hierarchical values within a patriarchal society and subsequent institutional settings (Bardsley, 2006; Bauer, 2009). Within this argument and through this lens of thinking about teaching and learning, the focus is often on providing females access and opportunity for the same experiences and engagement within the learning environment that their male counterparts are provided (Buchman, Diprete, & McDaniel, 2007; Lynch & Feeley, 2009). Research has examined the ways in which educators approach males and females and the dichotomy found within cultures and across institutional systems (Dee, 2007). In addition, the roles of females in the home and the work place have been a focus of research, both in terms of traditional frames and in changes that have occurred over time in response to cultural change (Buchman, Diprete, & McDaniel, 2007; US Department of Labor, 2011). Yet matriarchal systems embedded within the overarching patriarchal culture have functioned in concert and in contrast to the pervading cultural structures. In this chapter, we address this often overlooked and under-researched area through a self-study that uses our own lived experiences within our family's matriarchal structure to examine the impact of matriarchy on ways of knowing and engaging.

Matriarchy by definition is a complex term, as it reflects different meanings within research on matriarchal systems and of matriarchy as a cultural structure (Gatson, 2007). Earlier research on the dynamics of a matriarchy connect the phenomenon to motherhood and how motherhood is defined through the manner in which social systems are arranged for distribution of resources (Hoskins, 2005). Some define matriarchy as matrilineal in nature, connecting one's heritage to female roots within the family/social community (Gough, 1961), or matrilocal where locations of families are determined by female location (Ember, 1974). Yet these two maternal connections are dismissed in some of the literature as not truly matriarchal as they do not represent political or economic power relations (Schneider, 1961). Engels ([1884] 1972) suggests that the materialistic nature of motherhood stems from the group marriage dynamic within early human societies where there was a lack of certainty of the paternal connection to the child. Thus lineage is more reliably connected to females and the matrilineal connections from generation to

M. Taylor and L. Coia (Eds.), Gender, Feminism, and Queer Theory in the Self-Study of Teacher Education Practices, 93–110.

generation. Engels finds that such matriarchal structures give power to women both politically and in economic terms, and sees matriarchy as an earlier cultural structure (mother right) which progresses toward patriarchy (father right) over time. Laquer (1992) takes a different view from Engels, arguing that matriarchy represents the material (child bearing), equating motherhood to a natural phenomenon whereas fatherhood/patriarchy reflects idea (factual) over matter (the body). In the mid-1900s, matriarchal structures are described by some as a dysfunctional dynamic due to socio-economic hardship and disruption of the family (Frazier, 1968; Moynihan, 1965). This deficit view of matriarchy grew out of research on African American families in the United States where the growth in the number of single mother families of lower socio-economic status was declared both dysfunctional and destructive to the overall culture. These varying views on matriarchy are not mutually exclusive, in that a matriarchy may include several dynamics that support a matriarchal structure. Additionally, a social structure may not be solely a matriarchy or a patriarchy, but may fluctuate depending upon the context or may reflect neither. More recent research on matriarchy (Goettner-Abendroth, 2004, 2005) argues that matriarchy is not only an historical structure, but can also be found today in some cultures.

While my sisters and I grew up in a macro culture in the United States during the mid-1950s through the 1970s that reflected an over-arching patriarchal system, our family culture was matriarchal in its structure. In defining our family as a matriarchy, we borrowed from different aspects of the diverse range of characterizations in the literature for matriarchy to describe how our family culture functioned. In our home the senior female held a position of high regard and deference, where economic and political (family) decisions were strongly influenced by her input. Using both personal history and family mythology as realized through story telling, this chapter examines the norms, values and experiences within a matriarchal upbringing that may have influenced our understanding of the world around us and, more specifically, my thinking and actions as an educator.

The use of personal history and narratives is not new as a method for self-study of practice (Bullough, 1994; Kitchen, 2009). What makes this self-study unique, however, are the processes in which my critical friends (my sisters) and I engaged in collaboratively creating scenarios through storytelling, and in examining those scenarios through the lens of our family matriarchy. Our focus was on understanding how our family matriarchy impacted our life experiences and our understandings about the world around us. As explained in the following section, the initial examination of my key personal history scenarios expanded into collaborative storytelling that resulted in multiple scenarios. Our use of collaborative personal history narratives closely resembled the process of collaborative autobiography (Lapadat, Black, Clark, Gremm, Karanja, Mieke, & Quinlan, 2010). Our collective understandings helped me as an educator in connecting my personal history to my professional work. The organization of this chapter represents that process of unfolding scenarios inherent in our methodology. The context of the self-study provides an initial methodological intent, followed by a description of the changes in method that led to an evolving scenario dynamic, culminating in discussions of exemplar scenarios that informed our thinking and understanding of the impact of our family matriarchy on our ways of knowing.

THE CONTEXT FOR THE SELF-STUDY

We began this self-study acknowledging, with support from the literature, that our family structure was indeed matriarchal. Through our discussions of the scenarios on family engagement, a parallel discussion emerged on the historical influences on this matriarchy. While the scenarios were the focus of our data, the historical overview provided a grounding of sorts for the various scenarios that emerged. My mother's parents both attended and graduated from a co-educational college in the South during the early part of the 1900s. While this was considered quite unusual for its time, in our family this set the norm for the expectations of females. My father grew up in a family where the female members played important roles in decision-making. His mother was widowed before he turned one, and they moved with his grandparents from Texas to a farm on the Colorado dry lands. During his childhood my father's grandmother, aunt and mother were strong influences on his upbringing. As my younger sister Jan described, my father's life experiences, coupled with his own personality and intelligence, led him to be a creative and bright male family member who was comfortable with a matriarchal structure and who was in many ways progressive. In addition to the historical influences on our family, the environment in which we grew up also played a role in informing us on how the world worked.

We were a nuclear family in that we lived in a home with a mother, a father, three children (all girls), a dog, a cat, and an occasional goldfish or parakeet. As a young girl growing up in northern California, I spent most of my childhood in what is commonly referred to as the Bay Area (the *bay* being the inlet of water by San Francisco, and the *area* being all the towns, small cities and burgs that surround the bay). I was exposed to different cultures and languages around me, mostly those of Mexican Americans, Chinese Americans, and Japanese Americans who lived and worked in the communities around the bay. While these cultures were ever present in my life, they were not an integral part of my family culture. Rather, we lived among a diverse population but not truly within a diverse population. What we shared culturally across the different groups related to the dynamics occurring in the Bay Area: a growing suburban life style, a vanishing farm community, an increase in the hustle and bustle of daily living (more traffic, more businesses emerging, more people moving in yearly). This fast moving and rapidly changing community influenced my understanding of the notions of change and difference. The changing political and social scenes in the 1960s across the country and in the Bay Area also impacted how I made sense of the world. In addition, this rich tapestry of different cultures seemed a norm to my growing understanding of how the world worked, especially the daily exposure to and common use of Spanish names and terms as part of the deep history of the area.

While the culture of the Bay Area influenced my overall thinking about how communities work and how one negotiates constant change, I saw my family culture as instrumental in influencing how I think and make sense of the world. This is not an uncommon phenomenon. Research on culture describes the family as its own micro culture, which is impacted by the macro culture(s) in which it resides (Banks, 2001; Kluckhohn, 1949; Kroeber, 1952). The daily interactions within that family culture influence how individuals make sense of the world around them. It is this impact of the family culture on an individual's negotiation of the world that is the focus of this self-study.

METHODOLOGY

In this self-study, I examine the impact of my family culture on my thinking (how the world works and how I approach the world around me). As a teacher educator I was interested in how my experiences growing up in a matriarchy may have influenced my thinking about my practice and shaped my actions within my teaching (LaBoskey & Hamilton, 2010). My initial research question was: How does the analysis of key scenarios of my life in a matriarchy inform my thinking about my teaching practice? I combined both narrative inquiry (Clandinin & Connelly, 2000; LaBoskey & Cline, 2000) with video analysis (Heath, Hindmarsh, & Luff, 2010) to examine specific scenarios representing exemplars of my life experiences. Initially, the three events highlighted from my life included two scenarios from my childhood and represented the memories of my engagement with my mother as the senior female in the family. One scenario depicted the protocol observed by my family during holiday meals. The second scenario depicted a familiar experience riding in the car as my mother drove in suburban/urban traffic. A third scenario depicted an early experience as a professor at university responding to research data analysis.

The self-study began with me, as the educator, contacting my older sister Pam and my younger sister Jan, to ask if they would serve as critical friends using narratives reflecting my personal history. As the focus of my self-study was on the influence of a matriarchy on my thinking about teaching, I viewed my sisters as culturally informed critical friends. The original design of the study was to provide my three specific scenarios to my critical friends who would then read these scenarios and provide feedback through their lens of shared cultural experience within a matriarchy (see the Appendix for the complete text of the three scenarios). They would provide oral responses that would be transcribed and used to analyze the language of my scenarios with the language of their responses.

I shared my written scenarios with each of my sisters (as critical friends) separately, with the intent of using these three scenarios as the key exemplars in which we would explicate the connections of my experiences to my thinking, and ultimately to my thinking about teaching and learning. The process of discussing the scenarios was facilitated using Zoom™, an internet video conferencing format that enables multiple speakers on line at the same time, allows for documents to be shared, and easily facilitates the recording of video meetings. We initially met one to one to discuss the three events. These online video sessions were recorded and used for further review of content provided.

During our online video conferences, we found that the initial scenarios brought to mind other scenarios that reflected similar contexts or dynamics. Over time we became intrigued by the contexts and meaning derived from the scenarios that emerged out of our discussions of childhood experiences in a matriarchy. The more we discussed the burgeoning number of scenarios the greater our interest became in how such data can inform our thinking about how we make sense of the world around us. Our research question evolved at this point into two research questions: How do scenarios about our experiences in a matriarchy inform our thinking about the world? How does the analysis of key scenarios from my life in a matriarchy inform my thinking about my teaching practice? To address this second question, I used what I termed *iconic* scenarios from my earlier experiences as a classroom teacher in the public schools. I labeled these teaching scenarios iconic as they represented generalized memories reflecting my perceptions of my teaching and classroom dynamics. Results from the examination of my family culture were used as a framework to more closely examine the iconic teaching memories.

MAKING MEANING FROM SCENARIOS

As we discussed my original three scenarios, we found my description of a holiday meal particularly evocative as a catalyst for a larger discussion on expectations, assumptions, and protocols. The initial meal scenario depicted our family collaborating to prepare the holiday meal with my mother serving as the lead and coordinator of the event. An important aspect of the meal was honoring her skills and efforts by waiting for her to be seated first before we all were seated at the table. From our discussion of the role and value placed on the senior female in this scenario, Pam provided an addendum where after we had all been served food, we waited for Mom to take the first bite before we began eating. As we continued discussing how this role of the lead female in our family influenced our lives, more and more scenarios began to unfold.

One of these unfolding scenarios from the holiday dinner analysis highlighted the concept of after dinner discussions. This post-dinner discussion scenario represented a daily protocol of engagement, where each daughter was expected to provide a verbal report on events she found important that day. Each of us was given full attention by our parents. And when we spoke, it was expected that all would listen, including the other two sisters. In our discussion of this scenario, an example from my own experience revealed how Mom provided clear guidance for engaging in storytelling and in responding to others' stories. When one of our stories was interrupted, Mom would lead the discussion back to the individual's story by recounting the events up to the point where the interruption occurred. We concurred that her ability to redirect by recalling what had been said (by the daughter who had been interrupted in her storytelling) would give that daughter a sense of being listened to and being valued – both for the content being shared and for the daughter's ability to tell a story. Mom would also provide a model for how to respond as a listener by asking questions, providing comments, and making personal connections to the story. While it was not expected that we respond to each other's stories, we were encouraged to do so and we often did. Within this after-dinner discussion scenario were inherent expectations that we would all have something important to say, and that what we had to offer would be valued. As we examined the process that occurred during these after-dinner discussions, we realized a third inherent expectation: Whatever was shared after dinner would be considered private, that what was discussed at the dinner table stayed at the dinner table and went no further. This notion of privacy represented what we recognized as trust, and was seen as a key element in being able to share our experiences, ideas and opinions. This provided an avenue for learning how to speak our mind and to share our opinions in earnest. We saw this storytelling dynamic in our daily family life as powerful in shaping our understanding of ourselves as females through the value placed on our individual experiences and interests.

Across many of the scenarios, the power dynamics of this senior female played out again and again within the family, receiving high respect and deference for her actions, opinions, and expectations. This power role is exemplified in Jan's tree planting scenario that emerged from our discussion of independent and individualized actions. Our family had moved to a new suburb in the Bay Area. As the town was adjusting to the new population and homes, the city council had made some decisions about planting trees along the sidewalk of our new subdivision. However, they had not contacted the new residents to let them know of their decision. One day a truck pulled up in front of our house and a crew got out with a tree and began to dig a hole. Mom looked out the window, saw what they were doing, and immediately went out and told them to stop. The foreman came up to her and stated they were from the city and they were planting trees in the neighborhood. His statement suggested this was to happen without question, and with authority he returned to the hole and continued digging. Mom came up to him and demanded that he stop. She stated that she had not been informed of this action and she did not want a tree planted at the edge of her yard. As Jan recalled the scenario, Mom's voice was clear and firm and the look on her face showed she meant business. The foreman stopped, replaced the grass he had moved, retrieved the tree and told the crew they were leaving. The city never did plant a tree in our yard next to the sidewalk. Jan remembers this scenario as key to her understanding of the power a female possesses in taking a stand, assuming authority, and making a difference.

My second initial childhood scenario depicting my memory of riding in the car with my mother was somewhat productive as a catalyst for additional scenarios, providing a key exemplar depicting expectations and assumptions. This scenario involved an incident with a poor driver who nearly caused an accident. After skillfully explicating our car from the near disaster, my mother commented that she was not surprised it was a man who was driving. This scenario was analyzed in two ways, examining the biased assumption of male performance and examining the roles and skills of females. In our discussion, additional scenarios on female skills emerged. In one scenario known as the pot-holder incident, Pam recalled a verbal encounter Mom had with Pam's Girl Scout troop leader. Pam, along with all the other girls in her troop, was expected to knit a pot-holder for a badge. Pam described her engagement in this activity as clueless and disinterested. At the mother-daughter gathering held to award badges, the troop leader publicly chastised Pam and another girl for not completing the knitting activity (suggesting that every girl should learn the skill of knitting). Pam recalls two aspects of Mom's response to the troop leader that strongly resonated with the idea of individual skills and interests: 1) the many accomplishments which Pam had completed that earned badges, and 2) the quandary over why the troop leader would focus only on the one badge effort that was obviously something in which Pam was not interested. Pam recalled how powerful this was as an example of supporting individual skills and interests over gender-specific expectations.

The third initial scenario recounted a moment from my first year as an assistant professor involving a research presentation. In this scenario I described my response to a gender study where teachers were seen as spending more time with boys than with girls in the classroom. The researcher suggested that such teacher actions reflected a preference for male students. I questioned the assumption of the results of the study, suggesting that perhaps more time with the boys reflected an expectation of less potential and thus a need for more help. (For the complete scenario, see Appendix B.) It was interesting to me, 22 years later, to reflect back on this particular scenario and still feel that same conundrum of assumptions: when male students are afforded more instruction and attention it signals favoritism. Research around the time of this presentation supported the notion that when teachers paid more attention to boys it represented a preference toward males (American Association of University Women, 1992; Sadker & Sadker, 1994). As I discussed with my critical friends, I still would argue that a very different explanation is quite plausible for that earlier research data. I would suggest (and did) that the additional time spent with male students may signal an acknowledgement of need rather than of favoritism, arguing that an assumption of greater potential is directed toward the female students who require less support for their learning. This particular scenario raised questions from my critical friends regarding my thinking about practice and about how the world worked. Why did my thinking seem to differ so much from others' thinking? What are the influences in my life that have impacted how I view the world and how I make sense of what I see? We saw an influence on my thinking emerging from our analysis of my lived experiences within my family culture.

MAKING CONNECTIONS

We used my three initial scenarios as the basis for discussing and analyzing family protocols and engagements. As these initial scenes spurred additional childhood scenarios, I used a type of mapping to document the connections of the content discussed and to show the direction of the discussions as they occurred. Figure 1 provides a visual representation of one example of mapping, reflecting our discussion of the holiday scenario where multiple connections evolved. Eventually, the momentum of the emerging scenarios subsided, resulting in a substantial collection of protocols and engagements, which we used as the narrative data representative of our matriarchal upbringing. Across our discussions and examination of the various scenarios, four major themes emerged as values we learned through our life experiences: the value of being female, the value of individuality, the value of following one's own interests, and the value of being independent. These four over-arching themes emerged from the process of collapsing smaller themes into larger conceptual understandings of the data. These larger themes often interconnected across scenarios. Figure 1. Diagram of additional scenarios that emerged from discussion of the Holiday Meal Scenario.

The value of being female was a dominant theme in the holiday meal scenario, especially depicted in the manner in which the senior female and other female family members were paid deference by the senior (and only) male in the family. This

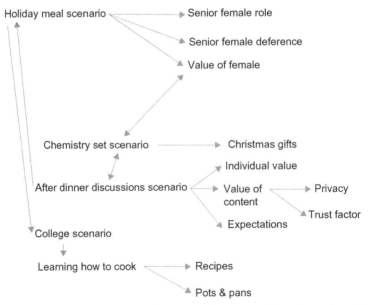

Figure 1. Diagram of additional scenarios that emerged from discussion of the Holiday Meal Scenario

sense of female value was an undercurrent in many of the scenarios we discussed, sometimes more blatant and other times less so. But the pervasive messages we heard as we examined the scenarios we discussed were that it is good to be female, it is important to be female, it is desirable (preferred) to be female. In the driving scenario, Mom's implication of males as less effective drivers also suggested that females had better skills for driving (such as making judgment calls for distance and in problem solving). Mom's pervasive bias in favor of female problem solving abilities, female performance, and female productivity became apparent in many of the scenarios that emerged. These biases, while framed as opinions, were often supported in our discussion of examples recalled from social encounters where male actions provided confirmation for her biases.

Values of individuality and of following one's own interests were overlapping themes seen in many of the scenarios that emerged in our discussions. This notion of individuality reflected the value my family placed on the individual outside of gender-specific expectations as seen through respecting and encouraging an individual's interests, an individual's actions, and an individual's experiences. We found this an interesting paradox in our discussions. The lack of focus on gender in our family's expectations was in and of itself a gender expectation that females can and do succeed across a wide range of contexts. When we initially began discussing the holiday meal scenario, our focus was on the senior female's role and her subsequent lead in the family dinner protocol. We saw the deference shown to her as reflecting the value we held for the senior female, but it was also deference to her skills as an individual. Rather than seeing cooking as the role of the female, we saw these skills as an individual's specific talent to organize, to orchestrate the support from others in preparing the various courses for the meal, to multi-task as she created a culinary feast. We recognized in our analysis of this discussion of cooking that it could, indeed, be interpreted as a traditional female role. But within the context of our family view of her talents, we did not perceive her individual skills as a female stereotype. Perhaps part of the influence on this was the family history of hearing stories of our mother's mother being a salad chef in hotels in the South as her professional career. Our discussions often came back to this view of seeing the individual for the actions and abilities revealed rather than for the gender connected to the individual. This discussion on the value placed on the individual was reflected in the additional scenario describing the post-dinner discussions, where each individual's story was seen as valued and important.

Our discussion of storytelling also reflected the larger theme of individual interests. During these evening stories, Mom would ask us about our current interests and about what we thought of current events and politics. These kinds of conversations happened outside of the after-dinner discussions as well. The interests that we shared often would be reflected in the kinds of gifts we received. Pam recalled a scenario where she received a chemistry set as a Christmas gift, following her sharing of an interest in chemistry and chemistry sets. We realized how critical it was to our understanding of who we were as individuals that our interests were honored. In fact, the variety in gifts that we were given, from Tonka® trucks to Barbie® dolls to train sets to cooking books, always reflected whatever we found to be interesting. There were no limits set for what our interests could be, nor were expectations given for what types of interest young girls should have. In the analysis of these scenarios it became clear that the individual and her interests were prized over gender-specific expectations. The idea of the importance of individual interests over gender expectations was seen also in how we were supported publicly. We saw in the pot-holder scenario a concern from our Mom not so much about disavowing the issue of gender-based tasks but more about acknowledging the interests of the individual – rejecting the requirement that all be the same, that all perform the same tasks with alacrity and skill.

Across our discussions and analyses, we discovered a paucity of gender-specific expectations and an abundance of opportunities to express our individual selves and to value our lives as females. Many of the scenarios we discussed focused on the intelligence, skills, and expectations of females with an overarching theme of being independent. Jan provided an example of independence in the practical presents scenario. During high school, Mom and Dad began giving us presents for Christmas and for birthdays that were earmarked for our first apartment, such as pots and pans - not as a trousseau, but as a part of our planning for being independent and living on our own when we went to college. Jan recalled other scenarios where Mom provided financial guidance on being independent, such as teaching us how to balance a checkbook and how to budget our money. Pam and I recalled Mom modeling for us how to cook along with sharing her recipes – not as a female skill but as a competency for being independent and caring for oneself. It was made very clear that developing cooking skills was important for us and our own well-being, not for serving others. Jan recalled how Mom taught us social graces not so much as a female skill but as a skill of an accomplished individual, enabling us to carry on a conversation with any adult. Part of the argument for learning to converse was to feel competent and independent when talking with a group of people, whether males or females. Jan recalled very clearly that Mom's focus was not on learning how to be coy and woo boys, but rather on how to engage in meaningful conversation. For me, the ultimate scenario on fostering independence was what I called the marriage scenario. Mom would consistently remind us "anybody can get married." This statement came across to me and to both my sisters as suggesting marriage was a low priority. We recognize now that for females growing up in the 1950s and 1960s, this was an unusual comment for a mother to make. But for us at the time it did not seem unusual, it just seemed normal. Pam recalled going to college and coming into contact with young women who were there to find a husband. This was such a contradiction to what we knew that Pam found this focus on marriage rather than education unfathomable, reflecting an overly dependent and needy approach to life. An interesting footnote here is that all three of us did eventually marry, but not until we were older, had finished college, and were working and living independently.

Our matriarchal family structure, as analyzed through scenarios of our experiences, appears to foster independence, to place high value on being female, to value individuality and to support individual interests. We saw in our experiences growing up in a matriarchy an environment where women have high prestige. This matriarchy was not a result of being raised in a single mother household, a matriarchal dynamic described in some of the research. Our family culture was defined by both of our parents, not just our mother. Our father instigated and substantiated the engagement, actions and dynamics that revealed the value of being female. It was a collaborative effort between both our parents that created our family environment.

What intrigued all three of us in this research was how much we learned through scenario analysis, from broader relational understandings to the intricacies of engagement. I have come to understand through this self-study the strong influence my family culture has played in my thinking, resonating particularly in the high value I place on being female. We see this matriarchal upbringing as an influential legacy which promotes power in being female and which emboldens high expectations for who we are as individuals.

MAKING SENSE OF THE IMPACT OF A MATRIARCHY ON MY VIEWS AS AN EDUCATOR

It became clear in our discussions and interpretations of actions and interactions within the scenarios that matriarchy influences perception. It can be argued that our life experiences constantly reinforced the value of being female, the value of the individual and individual interests, and the value of being independent, which became the lens through which we view the world. The story I shared in the scenario as a new professor discussing a plausible different explanation on research illustrates the influence of my family culture on my professional thinking. As we discussed the reasoning embedded in this alternative view on research, we saw the possibility of male need over male potential and the possibility of female competence over obscurity which informed my interpretation of teacher actions. More specifically, as a classroom teacher I realize that while my approach to teaching boys and girls was more or less the same, it was my thinking on that teaching and my expectations that were different.

In reflecting back to my early professional years as a classroom teacher, I recognize the impact of those values lived in a matriarchy on my work with children. I had taught mostly in the intermediate grades with fifth and sixth grade students ranging in age from 10 to 12-year-olds. As an elementary classroom teacher with a degree in physical science, much of my teaching was in the sciences, as well as in reading and mathematics. Since my elementary school teaching was early in my educational career, after so many years in higher education these iconic recollections of my earlier teaching focus more on general patterns of engagement that hold fast in my memory rather than the day to day interactions of my teaching. In a sense, these iconic scenarios represent archetypes of my teaching. For example, within a general dynamic in the classroom where a student did not understand a class assignment, I recall a boy's lack of understanding as not unexpected. It was important to address his misunderstanding by explaining the assignment in different ways, attempting to provide him with ample opportunities to understand and to approach the task successfully. This use of multiple approaches to instruct about specific content is considered good practice, to provide diverse ways of thinking about and approaching a concept or task in order to facilitate different ways of knowing. I recall this effort to provide a wide range of approaches to learning as intentional on my part, as my professional development within the district and my ongoing graduate coursework had made me very aware of the importance of such diversity. Interestingly, I do not recall as clearly that girls had difficulty understanding lessons. It seems my recollection of my teaching reflects several of the childhood scenarios we analyzed (and in particular the riding in the car scenario), where there is an implication that males may lack the skills needed to perform as well as females.

My instructional time with girls is remembered more as extending and expanding the lesson, and engaging in conversations about their work. When I compare my memories about those conversations with girls to my mother's modeling of interactions in the after-dinner scenario, I can see how my remembered engagement with my female students reflected some of those same types of interactions I experienced with my mother – asking questions about the content, asking about their interests, and connecting what they were doing to my own experiences. I do remember engaging with boys in similar ways, but what I find interesting is that when I generalize about those practices (of providing remediation for a skill versus providing expansion of a skill), females are remembered as receiving more complex instruction. Whether those extensions and expansions of lessons occurred in equal measure between boys and girls may or may not be the case, but what reflects the value of the female in my matriarchal history is that I remember my more sophisticated engagement and interactions with my female students with greater clarity than I do similar engagements with my male students.

In discussing these variances in my teaching with my critical friends, what emerged were my biases toward the expectation of success of female students and toward the expectation of need for instructional support for male students. While my professional zeitgeist would suggest an appreciation of diverse ways of knowing within the individual, my iconic memories suggest a pervasive bias within my expectations of boys and of girls. The tension in this divergence within my expectations creates an interesting contradiction: the importance of valuing the individual as represented in our scenario analyses versus ignoring the individual as represented in my generalization of performance for a particular gender group. Moreover, these biases reflect a reversal of archetypal biases in favor of male students found in the literature (Sadker & Sadker, 1994; Sadker & Zittleman, 2009). Much of the research on teacher engagement with students suggests boys are given an advantage over girls in the classroom. "A large body of research indicates that teachers give more classroom attention and more esteem building encouragement to boys" (American Association of University Women Educational Foundation, 1992, p. 2). What I find particularly enlightening from this self-study is my understanding of the potential for bias embedded within my professional thinking.

For my teaching life, I need to reconcile the potential biases emerging from my matriarchal experiences that could impact my practice. I can see the connection between these potential biases and the larger themes that emerged from the various scenario data. The first theme of placing value on being female can influence my thinking about the expectations I have for female and male students. As a professor of literacy education for elementary and secondary preservice and in-service teachers, a majority of my students are female. In my university teaching, my belief in the value of being female is realized through my daily expectations of my female students, where I see their contributions as thoughtful problem solving and skillful meaning making. Such expectations can be argued to be a very positive environment for female students, providing a learning dynamic that challenges and honors the female learner. In this context I see placing high value on being female as a very good thing, and a very natural thing. However, this self-study reveals the potential for gender biases that can emerge from such a focus. The struggle within my teaching can be seen when the value I place on being female creates dynamics within the classroom that play out as a reverse bias for my male students. I see this bias as creating tensions, and impacting my ability to develop an equitable effective environment for both male and female students. What I would prefer to see happen within my classroom is the creation of an environment that helps to eliminate bias (Zimmerman, McQueen, & Guy, 2007).

Recognizing the value of individuality and the value of pursuing students' interests can provide opportunities for students to use their own ways of thinking and to connect their own interests in making sense of course content. Such an environment has great potential for providing accessibility to learning and for meeting the needs of each student. This may help both me (as the instructor) and the students to reduce oppressive structures that may undermine their learning and agency (Langan & Davidson, 2005). I see these values of individuality and of personal interests working hand in hand in the classroom with the value of independence. I have often argued that independence is a hallmark of university instruction, both for the professor and for the student. By addressing this value in my teaching I would suggest that such an environment would foster independent thinking and problem solving, and would nurture the pursuit of interests and strengths independent of generalized expectations. But as I discussed my thinking about practice with my critical friends, I came to realize how my culture (both macro and micro) has influenced the value I place on being independent and on students' independent endeavors. I can see where placing too much value on the individual working independently conflicts with values placed on relational knowledge (Barnes-Holmes, Barnes-Holmes, & Cullinan, 2001; Hayes, Fox, Gifford, Wilson, Barnes-Holmes, & Healy, 2001) and on collaboration (Swenson & Strough, 2008). By venerating independence, I recognize the potential for tensions within my teaching. Such a focus on independent learning can infringe upon collaborative and collegial engagement, ultimately contradicting efforts to create accessible learning environments that foster diverse ways of knowing.

Examining my life scenarios has impacted my thinking about my practice and about the potential tensions within my teaching. I see many strengths and positive aspects of growing up within a matriarchy, especially the development of a sense of self and the value I feel in being female. By examining these scenarios that reflect my family culture and my teaching experiences, I have been pushed to consider the potential for bias within my practice that impacts my thinking about my teaching and my engagement with students (both positive and negative). This awareness of bias becomes especially important in my efforts to create an instructional environment of caring and bias-free engagement (Zimmerman, McQueen, & Guy, 2007). The understandings I take from this self-study inform my thinking about my teaching practice in several ways. I recognize the potential for the values uncovered within our matriarchal family culture, and realize these values may create tensions within my practice, but may also be used to inform and improve my practice. By using my world values as the lenses through which I craft my teaching, and by acknowledging and examining potential tensions within my teaching, I see a greater opportunity for me to create a more thoughtful, engaging and equitable learning environment. In addition, I would suggest that this process of analyzing scenarios would be helpful for researchers who are interested in examining how their own cultural views of the world inform their thinking, engagement, and actions around issues of gender.

REFERENCES

American Association of University Women. (1992). *How schools shortchange girls.* Washington, DC: AAUW & National Education Association.

Banks, J. A. (2001). *Cultural diversity and education.* Needham Heights, MA: Allyn & Bacon.

Bardsley, A. (2006).Girlfight the power: Teaching contemporary feminism and pop culture. *Feminist Teacher, 16*(3), 189–204.

Barnes-Holmes, Y., Barnes-Holmes, D., & Cullinan, V. (2001). Education. In S. C. Hayes, D. Barnes Holmes, & B. Roche (Eds.), *Relational frame theory: A post Skinnerian account of human language and cognition* (pp. 181–196). New York, NY: Kluwer.

Bauer, D. M. (2009). Authority. In R. D. Crabtree, D. A. Sapp, & A. C. Licona (Eds.), *Feminist pedagogy: Looking back to move forward* (pp. 23–26). Baltimore, MD: John Hopkins University Press.

Buchman, C., Diprete, T., & McDaniel, A. (2007). *Gender inequalities in education: ISERP working paper 07-15.* New York, NY: Columbia University in the City of New York—Institute for Social an Economic Research and Policy.

Bullough, R. V. (1994). Personal history and teaching metaphors: A self-study of teaching as conversation. *Teacher Education Quarterly, 21*(1), 107–120.

Clandinin, D. J., & Connelly, F. M. (2000). *Narrative inquiry: Experience and story in qualitative research.* San Francisco, CA: Jossey-Bass.

Dee, T. S. (2007, Summer). Teachers and the gender gap in student achievement. *Journal of Human Resources 42*(3), 528–554.

Ember, C. R. (1974). An evaluation of alternative theories of matrilocal versus patrilocal residence. *Cross-Cultural Research, 9*(2), 135–149.

Engels, F. ([1884] 1972). *The origins of family, private property, and the state.* New York, NY: Pathfinder.

Frazier, E. F. (1968). *The Negro family in the United States.* New York, NY: Macmillan.

Gatson S. N. (2007). Matriarchy. In W. A. Darity, E. Bonilla-Silva, P. Costanzo, P. L. Mason, P. McClain, D. & Scott, T. Singleton (Eds.), *International encyclopedia of the social sciences* (2nd ed., pp. 28–31). Farmington Hills: Macmillan/Thomson Gale.

Goettner-Abendroth, H. (2004). Matriarchal society: Definition and theory. In G. Vaughan (Ed.), *The gift: A feminist analysis.* Retrieved from http://www.gift-economy.com/athanor/anthanor_005.html

Goettner-Abendroth, H. (2005). *Modern matriarchal studies: Definition, scope and topicality.* Paper presented at the 2nd World Congress on Matriarchal Studies, Austin, TX, September 29–October 1.

Gough, K. (1961) The modern disintegration of matrilineal descent groups. In D. M. Schneider & K. Gough (Eds.), *Matrilineal kinship* (pp. 631–654). Berkeley, CA: University of California Press.

Hayes, S. C., Fox, E., Gifford, E. V., Wilson, K. G., Barnes-Holmes, D., & Healy, O. (2001). Derived relational responding as learned behavior. In S. C. Hayes, D. Barnes-Holmes, & B. Roche (Eds.), *Relational frame theory: A post-Skinnerian account of human language and cognition* (pp. 21–50). New York, NY: Kluwer.

Heath, C., Hindmarsh, J., & Luff, P. (2010). *Video in qualitative research: Analyzing social interaction in everyday life.* Thousand Oaks, CA: Sage.

Hoskins, J. (2005) Matriarchy. *New dictionary of the history of ideas.* Retrieved August 20, 2013, from http://www.encyclopedia.com/doc/1G2-3424300460.html

Kitchen, J. (2009). Passages: Improving teacher education through narrative self-study. In D. L. Tidwell, M. L. Heston, & L. M. Fitzgerald (Eds.), *Research methods for the self-study of practice* (pp. 35–53). Berlin: Springer.

Kluckhohn, C. (1949). *Mirror for man.* New York, NY: McGraw-Hill.

Kroeber, A. (1952). *The nature of culture.* Chicago, IL: University of Chicago Press.

LaBoskey, V. K., & Cline, S. (2000). Behind the mirror: Inquiry-based storying in teacher education. *Reflective Practice, 1*(3), 359–375.

LaBoskey, V. K., & Hamilton, M. L. (2010). "Doing as I do": The role of teacher educator self-study in educating for reflective inquiry. In N. Lyons (Ed.), *Handbook of reflection and reflective inquiry* (pp. 333–350). New York, NY: Springer.

Langan, D., & Davidson, D. (2005). Critical pedagogy and personal struggles: Feminist scholarship outside women's studies. *Feminist Teacher, 15*(2), 132–145.

Lapadat, J. C., Black, N. E., Clark, P. G., Gremm, R. M., Karanja, L. W., Mieke, M., & Quinlan, L. (2010). Life challenge memory work: Using collaborative autobiography to understand ourselves. *International Journal of Qualitative Methods, 9*(1), 77–104.

Laquer, T. (1992). The facts of fatherhood. In B. Thorne & M. Yalom (Eds.), *Rethinking the family: Some feminist questions* (pp. 155–175). Boston, MA: Northeastern University Press.

Lynch, K., & Feeley, M. (2009). *Gender and education (and employment): Lessons from research for policy makers.* Brussels: European Commission.

Moynihan, D. P. (1965). *The Negro family: The case for national action.* Washington, DC: Office of Policy Planning and Research, U.S. Department of Labor. Retrieved from http://www.dol.gov/oasam/programs/history/webid-meynihan.htm

Sadker, M., & Sadker, D. (1994). *Failing at fairness: How America's schools cheat girls.* New York, NY: Maxwell Macmillan

Sadker, M., & Zittelman, K. (2009). *Still failing at fairness: How gender bias cheats girls and boys in school and what we can do about it.* New York, NY: Scribner.

Schneider, D. (1961). The distinctive features of matrilineal descent groups. In D. Schneider & K. Gough (Eds.), *Matrilineal kinship* (pp. 1–29). Berkeley, CA: University of California Press.

Swenson, L. M., & Strough, J. (2008). Adolescents' collaboration in the classroom: Do peer relationships or gender matter? *Psychology in the Schools, 45*(8), 715–728.

U.S. Department of Labor. (2011). *Women's employment during the recovery.* Washington, DC: US Department of Labor.

Zimmerman, L. W. McQueen, L., & Guy, G. (2007). Connections, interconnections, and disconnections: The impact of race, class and gender in the university classroom. *Journal of Theory Construction & Testing, 11*(1), 16–21.

APPENDIX

Three Initial Scenarios

Holiday Meal

It is the Christmas holiday season. The house is decorated with a large Christmas tree in the living room, and the dining room table is set for five with our best china and glassware. All five of us, Mom, Dad, my older sister, my younger sister, and I, are helping in the kitchen, either getting out the serving dishes for the food, helping with the preparation of the food, or finishing up the table settings. Once all the food has been placed on the table, we all come into the dining room and stand behind our chairs, waiting for Mom to come to her seat and sit down. As she approaches her chair, my Dad moves the chair out to help seat her. Once she is seated, the rest of us take our seats. My Dad waits until all the girls are seated before he sits down. To me, what I saw in this moment, replayed over again and again at holiday meals, was the deference given to the senior female of the family and the overall deference given to female members in general.

Scenario Addendum after discussion: Platters of food are passed around the table and each of us fills our plates with food. Once all the platters are passed, we wait for Mom to take the first bite. After she has, we all then begin to eat.

Riding in the Car Scenario

It is late in the afternoon, and my mom and I are sitting in the front seat of our family car, a 1963 maroon Ford four-door station wagon with rounded tail lights protruding from round-shaped panels that flowed on each side from the back door to the tail light. This car was my favorite from my childhood. It had lots of room in the back seat when my two sisters and I sat together, it had a pleasing rounded oblong shape, and its taillights always reminded me of red glowing owl's eyes. Though we called it the family car, Mom probably drove this car the most, especially around town and taking us to and from different events. On this particular day, Mom and I were returning home from shopping at the local grocery store.

We were driving down the main thoroughfare that was four lanes wide. As we came to the intersection a car waiting to our right at the cross section pulled out suddenly in front of us, causing Mom to quickly hit the brakes to avoid hitting the driver. As usual in an emergency, Mom was very calm and slowed the car down to give us distance between ourselves and the other driver as she commented under her breath "idiot!" Once the other car had accelerated enough to move at least two car distances in front of us, Mom accelerated as well and turned on the left blinker to move into the other lane to pass. Mom glanced over at the driver as we passed the car and said with absolute conviction, "I knew it. It was a man." This was a common scenario for me as a child. It seemed that whenever some odd driving maneuver happened in traffic or someone drove recklessly or demonstrated lack of good driving skills, the culprit was consistently a man. How I understood this was to generalize that poor drivers were typically male, and that as a female it was critical to watch out for such drivers and to give them wide berth.

Research Presentation Scenario

It is my first year as a university professor. I attend a special presentation by a guest researcher who is presenting her research on high school students in an urban high school in England. Her research focuses on the conduct of males and females in a history class, where males take up most of the room and females sit in tight groups avoiding the encroachment of males into their space. Much of her presentation is on this particular class that she observed over several months. She closes with a summary of some key issues in education that reflect the dominance of males in education and the predilection of teachers to focus their energies on the male students over the female students. She shares her data on the observations of teacher engagement in the class she observed to support the dominance of males on teacher attention, arguing that the teacher (as do most teachers) does not provide the support to encourage females in the way that they do male students. I find her data intriguing, but I also am listening to her description of what the teacher in her study was doing with the male students. The engagement of the teacher with the male students focused on providing support to the male students who had not completed an assignment or who had not attempted an assignment. When asked about how the teacher had addressed the female students who had not completed or attempted assignments, the researcher admits that most of the female students actually attempted the work and some completed the assignments, though the quality varied greatly.

As I listen to her description of what was happening in that classroom, I cannot help but see a possible different explanation for the scenario, that the female teacher provided more help to the male students because they needed the support while the female students were more able/capable to attempt the assignment without that additional support. Could it be possible, I ask her, that the teacher was seeing a need in the male students that she didn't see in the female students. Was her expectation of males different (less) than that of females, resulting in additional support provided to the male students in order for them to be able to complete the assignment. Could it be that the male students, over time, receiving less expectation from the teacher resulted in their living down to that lesser expectation? The researcher responds to my queries with a generalization that most researchers would not agree with my take on the scenario and that my particular suggestion is not commonly held as viable. But I keep thinking beyond the *what* in the teacher's actions, to the *why*. My life experiences and my worldview no doubt influenced the lens through which I saw some other possibilities for the explanation of the teacher's engagement with her students.

D. L. TIDWELL, P. T. SCHWARTZ & J. T. DUNN

AFFILIATIONS

Deborah L. Tidwell
Professor & Coordinator - Literacy Education,
Department of Curriculum and Instruction,
University of Northern Iowa,
Cedar Falls, Iowa

NATHAN D. BRUBAKER

GENDERED DISCOURSE IN THE EVANGELICAL SOUTH: FASHIONING A CONSERVATIVELY CRITICAL PEDAGOGY OF TEACHER EDUCATION

For five years I taught diversity courses to undergraduate and graduate elementary teacher education students in the middle of the Bible Belt (the hub of socially conservative evangelical Protestantism in the Southeastern United States). As the most churched region in the country—widely perceived as a *place* while the rest of the U.S. (north, east, and west) are simply *directions* (Reynolds & Webber, 2009)—the South proved quite different culturally from areas I had previously inhabited northeast of the Mason-Dixon (the line separating northern and southern states in the U.S. Civil War era). Religion, for one, occupied a more central position in everyday life than I had previously perceived in other communities. The practice of Weekday Religious Education in area schools, for example, was widely embraced, and was reinforced by passages of Scripture regularly cited in local news outlets. Combined with recurring emotionally-charged conflicts in the community and in class concerning diverse perspectives on the history of slavery and segregation, I quickly realized my regional assumptions were at odds with the cultural landscape of my new environment. There would be no shortage of opportunities to heighten my awareness of the subtleties of my own and others' outlooks on the world concerning our multiple layers of social identity. The complex intersection of religion, race, and sexuality provided a particularly powerful context for discerning more deeply the social construction of gender as a significant component of self within the community.

It did not take long for such contrasting cultural viewpoints about the intersection of gender and other social identities to be manifested in my teaching. Consistent with U.S. teaching demographics (Cochran-Smith & Zeichner, 2005; Schulte, 2009), my students were overwhelmingly female, white, and Christian. Many emerged from houses of worship to encounter ideas about critically questioning core aspects of their identities as prospective teachers. Many more invariably returned to such spaces to help dispel any doubts produced from examining their deeply rooted assumptions about themselves and others in their studies. Over twenty-five times teaching the course, *Diversity in Elementary Education*, no topic energized our classroom discussions about diversity as much as gender. Embedded in the evangelical outlook of our community were convictions about morality (Berliner, 1997) that triggered occasionally explosive classroom encounters. Sexual orientation was a predictable

M. Taylor and L. Coia (Eds.), Gender, Feminism, and Queer Theory in the Self-Study of Teacher Education Practices, 111–125.

provocateur. My interactions with students concerning family diversity over five years ranged from hostile to harmonious. Discussions about religious values frequently paralyzed our progress. Cultivating spaces in which diverse identities were both affirmed and challenged—with gender an interpretive category for making sense of our social practices as well as a social relation that influenced other activities (Lazar, 2007)—put my pedagogy to the test.

The purpose of this chapter is to examine how my interactions with evangelically-minded students helped shape my pedagogy of teacher education concerning gendered discourses in teacher education. Specifically, I deconstruct a class discussion about Christian privilege (Schlosser, 2010) in which my students' assumptions about gendered discourses were collectively perturbed and my own explicitly confronted. In analyzing the authority relationships embedded in our interactions (Johnson-Bailey & Lee, 2005), I illuminate the complexities of dialogical pedagogies that simultaneously construct and are constructed by gendered identities and privileges (Johnson, 2006; McIntosh, 1988). While my experiences in the South both confronted and confirmed my pedagogical assumptions, I conclude that such experiences ultimately challenged me to develop my practices in ways that were more congruent with my commitments to diversity and democracy. Such growth as a teacher educator has helped me respond more effectively to a fuller breadth of diversity in my practice. In particular, I have come to show a greater sensitivity to the complex intersections of identity in my own and others' experiences in ways that have made more prominent the position of gender in my practice as a teacher educator.

STANCE

As one component of larger webs of identity (Harro, 2000) that help define our social standing, I consider gender a socially constructed conception of self that situates us relationally (Weiler, 2001). It is one aspect of broader pedagogies of positionality (Maher, 1999) that are continually foregrounded in our teacher education practices. As such, it is an essential aspect of diversity to which prospective teachers must be consciously sensitized to effectively meet the needs of diverse learners and help construct a more just society. Within our contemporary cultural and historical context, I share the view that it is not a matter of whether sexism is a part of who we are, but how broadly and deeply it is ingrained in us (Johnson, 1997). Making a difference in undermining the widespread prevalence of gender oppression must begin by recognizing that we have a collective responsibility to end the corrosive effects of oppression in all its manifestations (Blumenfeld, 1992).

Like hooks (1984), I consider feminism the struggle to end sexist oppression instead of a movement to make women the social equals of men. Such a conception necessarily directs our attention to systems of domination and the interrelatedness of race, class, religion, and other forms of social oppression concerning gendered identities. A broad ethic of criticality is necessary for confronting the culture of male domination to which we are collectively accustomed and for discerning diverse perspectives about gender in contemporary schooling (Hofman, 2008; Sax, 2005). The combination of such responsibilities presents a broad imperative for teacher educators to develop practices congruent with democratic ideals and the quest for social justice. Through research, we can more clearly illuminate gender as a social and discursive practice (Pullen & Simpson, 2009) which is done, undone, and constructed in specific contexts (Nentwich & Kelan, 2013).

METHODOLOGY

The discussions described in this chapter took place in the graduate course, *Teaching for Critical Thinking*, at a comprehensive public university in the Southeastern U.S. I had previously taught a similar course with undergraduates at another university in the Northeastern U.S. and offered it as an elective at Southeast State University (a pseudonym to protect the confidentiality of my research participants) in the summer 2010 term due to student request. Ten students enrolled in the course, each of whom I had previously taught in the course, *Diversity in Elementary Education*, across different sections over three semesters. All students enrolled in the course identified as female, of whom one was of African-American ancestry and all others of European-American descent. Students ranged in age from 21-23 and were in the first term of their graduate year as part of a five-year M.A.T. program for teaching children in grades PK-6. Nine of the ten students provided their consent to participate in the research as it was approved by the university's institutional ethics process. I identified as of European-American ancestry and in my mid-thirties, and was one of only two full-time male faculty members (amongst eighteen females) in elementary education—the largest department in the College of Education and home to one of the largest majors on campus. More than sixty percent of all students across campus, and ninety percent of students enrolled in elementary education, were identified in university enrollment figures as female.

While the teacher education program in which I conducted the study was well regarded for its commitments to constructivist practice, differentiated learning, and teacher inquiry, the curricular attention to critical thinking and diversity was confined to just a handful of courses. In the course, *Diversity in Elementary Education*, I used a critically-reflective and discussion-based approach to help introduce students to diversity concepts (e.g., race and ethnicity, language and culture, exceptionalities, social class, religion, gender, sexual orientation, and pedagogical diversity) by helping them question common assumptions and perspectives, reflect on personal experiences, and develop strategies and resources for applying diversity content to their future elementary teaching. In the course described in this study, *Teaching for Critical Thinking*, I extended students' previous study of diversity by situating it within the broader methodological framework of the classroom community of inquiry (Brubaker, 2012b; Lipman, 2003; Sharp, 1993). As what I considered to be the best currently-available means of teaching for critical thinking across disciplines using a dialogical and non-indoctrinating approach, the classroom community of inquiry accompanies the internationally-recognized Philosophy for Children program (Lipman, 1988; Lipman, Sharp, & Oscanyan, 1980). I used novels and discussion plans from the Philosophy for Children curriculum (e.g., Lipman, 1982; Lipman, Sharp, & Oscanyan, 1984) to promote the pedagogical focus of the course while integrating theoretical and practical texts from the organization, *Rethinking Schools,* as well as from other sources, to highlight diversity themes.

As a self-study of my own teaching, I hoped to grapple with the challenges, frustrations, and dilemmas that emerged from my classroom context while reinterpreting and reframing my experiences in ways that extended beyond myself (Pinnegar & Hamilton, 2009; Samaras & Freese, 2006). LaBoskey's (2004) five characteristics of self-study research provided the basis for the study. As part of a larger research project, I audio recorded and selectively transcribed all activities associated with the course throughout the term while also maintaining a personal journal and using students' written assignments as data. For this particular study, I used the concept of critical moments (Tripp, 1993) to help unpack the problematic aspects of my practice and illuminate unconscious biases, beliefs, and "interactional misfires" (Macgillivray, 1997) embedded in my teaching.

A single discussion comprised the central focus of the study, which occurred in the final week of the course and consisted of one hour and fifty-three minutes of classroom talk (68 typed pages). I selected this particular discussion due to its unique emotional intensity, its relevance to gendered discourse in the Evangelical South, and because the pedagogical process I used to facilitate our discussion was representative of my broader efforts to cultivate a classroom community of inquiry.

I analyzed the discussion transcript using the constant-comparative method (Glaser & Strauss, 1999), for which I used the computer software program, QSR Nvivo 8.0, to facilitate the process of constant comparison. I also drew from traditions of feminist critical discourse analysis (Lazar, 2007) to help show the complex, subtle, and sometimes not-so-subtle ways in which frequently taken-for-granted gendered assumptions were discursively produced, negotiated, and challenged in our discussion. As a male examining my own practice in the predominantly female occupation of elementary education, I hoped to produce scholarship of relevance to men's participation in feminism, more broadly, and feminist teaching more particularly (Breeze, 2007).

CONTEXT OF THE CRITICAL MOMENT

The critical moment that comprised my focus for the study arose from my efforts to involve students in a process of open inquiry about the topic of religion. While I had not previously attempted to have students openly inquire into religion to such an extent, my efforts to address religion in this context more broadly throughout my first three years at the university had presented me with several challenges. In my first semester, for example, I had a particularly unique combination of students.

Some identified as personal friends with Jerry Falwell, a conservative televangelist who founded the Thomas Road Baptist Church and Liberty University, and co-founded the Moral Majority political lobby group for evangelical Christians— all known for their commitments to ultra-conservative causes. Others adamantly refused to entertain the topic of sexual orientation in the classroom on the basis that one should love the sinner but hate the sin, and because of their perception that the country was founded as a Christian nation. Others, from their written assignments and contributions to class, clearly considered feminism a slippery slope toward the "homosexual" agenda (Reynolds & Webber, 2009).

In the initial weeks of the course, preceding the critical moment, we had explored such topics as civil rights, child labor, and critical literacy with passion, focus, and commitment. Our group discussions were highly participatory, engaging, and co-facilitated. The relationships within the class were strong, with an increasing sense of community throughout the term. I purposefully scheduled the topic of religion for the final week of the course to ensure we had sufficient time to develop our group dynamics. While I anticipated the topic could be challenging for the group, from having already touched on it in previous semesters, I figured our skills in collaborative inquiry would have been sufficiently developed by then to tackle most any topic. My purpose for the session was to model the community of inquiry process (Lipman, 2003) using a chapter from *Harry Stottlemeier's Discovery* (Lipman, 1982) as the stimulus text, featuring fictional children engaged in classroom dialogue concerning the Pledge of Allegiance, idolatry, and religion. Upon reading the text as a class in round robin fashion, I invited students to identify something that was "interesting, confusing, puzzling," and to put their interest "in the form of a question." I reminded them that their questions did not "have to come from" the text, but could be derived from "something that it made [them] think about" or something that they had "already been thinking." We generated a list of eleven questions, of which we collectively decided to focus on two—as written in students' words—to begin our discussion:

1. Are the ideas discussed in the articles something that is religious-based or society-created?
2. Why are the people in the Christian religion made to feel guilty?

Both questions were implicitly connected to the texts concerning religion I assigned in the course syllabus for students to have read before class. The first, on Christian privilege (Schlosser, 2010), listed eighteen advantages concerning religious holidays, history, and traditions of relevance to Christians (e.g., "I can assume that I will not have to work or go to school on my significant religious holidays," p. 246). The second, on the unacknowledged norm of Christian beliefs in U.S. public schools (Joshi, 2010), focused on the impact of such norms on non-Christians (e.g., feelings of exclusion, becoming targets for discrimination, receiving unequal educational experiences), with suggestions for remedying such impact in school classrooms (e.g., by becoming more informed about diverse religious traditions).

Our discussion of the first question, about whether the ideas in the assigned readings were religious-based or society-created, proceeded smoothly and uneventfully. Bridget (all names used in this study are pseudonyms, with the exception of my own) considered the authors' perspectives "unfair," since Christianity was originally brought to the country for purposes of "religious freedom." Those who are "angry" about Christianity "being the main religion" in the USA have their "own country" in which to celebrate their "own religion." Kendra asked, "[D]oes that mean...we don't need to be sensitive to other religions?" Bridget replied: "[I]t's important to teach about other religions," but Christians should not be considered "bad people" because they're privileged. Teagan added, "[I]t depends on your own personal views and your religion," because "everyone deserves an equal and fair chance," but it "depends on the situation." Leanna added: the list of privileges could be "rewritten if you went [to other] places." In Palestine, for example, one could likely write a list of "Muslim privileges." Colette concluded that the ideas in the articles were "society-based" because "it's not like...Christians all came together one day and said...we're going to come up with all these things." Since no one had any "different thoughts," we shifted our focus to the second question, about why Christians were made to feel guilty. From there, our critical moment emerged.

CRITICAL MOMENT OVERVIEW

Exploring the reasons why Christians were "made to feel guilty" by the ideas in the readings prompted a sudden shift in our class dynamics. Within moments, the tenor of the room turned from thoughtful to tense. The change began when I asked Teagan: "[I]s the feeling of guilt...triggered by...the fact that these ideas make people question? Like is the questioning cause for feeling guilty?" Teagan stated that she was "confused" by my question. Bronwyn interjected: "[D]o you feel guilty because some of these [privileges] have like some meaning?" I clarified: "[D]o these [privileges] make you question your standing in society so therefore make you guilty because...now [you] might be more privileged than [you] realized?" I explained that my question was not "just for [Teagan]" but was a "broad[er] question." Teagan responded: "I'm very aware that I'm privileged. I mean, I'm a white Christian. Obviously." She elaborated: making others feel guilty, as she perceived the authors to have "aimed," is not "fair" because "I would never want someone of another religion to feel guilty or embarrassed or singled out." She concluded: "It's not what I believe in. That's not what I feel like my religion is about." I responded: "So it calls into question your view of your faith or your view of your participation in it. Or do you just think that the author was like an evil intended...."

Before I could finish my question, the mood palpably shifted. Colette, who had been uncharacteristically quiet for much of the discussion, swiftly and decisively stepped to Teagan's defense. In dramatic fashion, with raised voice, she demanded: "How could you phrase a question like that to her?" She elaborated: "That's such a condescending way to ask that question." She asked the group: "[A]m I the only one that feels like that was like a really ridiculous question to throw out there?" Kendra shared her view that it came across as "very polarizing." Teagan added: "[I] t's not fair...to ask me if I'm questioning my faith because that's something personal that...I would go through personally." I clarified that my question was not "intended to be nasty" and suggest that anyone was a "bad person," but to see if we could "distinguish between what the author was intending and what the impact [was]"—to discern whether the author had "evil" or "malicious intentions" and was *trying* to make people feel guilty or was just making them feel guilty by virtue of the substance of what he had written. Our discussion proceeded for another hour beyond that point, but our exploration of the topic at hand effectively came to a screeching halt. The dramatic encounter shifted our focus from Christian guilt to what had caused the atmosphere of our discussion to change so suddenly.

Our ensuing dialogue—about the readings, the practical implications of our views, and the relevance of our discussion process—provided the basis for the findings of the study. Central to our deliberations were questions, implicitly, concerning such gendered issues as control, voice, and context (Kaufman & Kimmel, 2011). From such considerations emerged three themes pertaining to how gender was constructed in our classroom discourse: shaping the agenda, distributing participation, and bridging differences. Below, I elaborate on each of these themes.

SHAPING THE AGENDA

Shaping the agenda represented a dimension of our gendered discourse that commanded considerable attention throughout the discussion. Immediately following the critical moment, two students objected to how my text selections were ultimately detrimental to the discussion since they had helped frame the session in a biased manner. According to Colette, both articles "painted a negative picture for those...[of] Christian faith" without "anything" that was "a positive promotion of the majority of religion." From her perspective, a more positive view was necessary to "balance out" the discussion and counter the "one side of the argument" that was not a "fair" or "accurate position of the other side"—the "Christian side." Bridget felt that the article on Christian privilege in particular made it seem as though "Christians are intolerant people who are ruling the United States unjustly," which she considered "overkill." When I asked where such views would be "coming from"—whether we could "trace [them] to one particular part" of the readings— Colette lamented that there were "no examples" of teachers who were "inclusive" or "understanding." From such a perspective, I had unfairly shaped the class agenda to promote a distorted view of the topic.

In further reflecting on our discussion, I shared my perspective that at least the discussion process we had followed enabled us to explore our own ideas rather than be required to accept someone else's. I expressed: "I'd like to think that the process of what we were doing was allowing...religion to be inquired into and to be examined and...reasoned about, but that no one set of religious beliefs was being propagated."

Leanna immediately countered: "I think it was more the reverse." Colette agreed: the readings were more "like negating" and were "against" Christianity, which "led to a discussion that was more in the defensive or like in the negative aspect of Christianity. It...wasn't like promoting it but it certainly wasn't like a non-biased discussion...because of the articles." From her view, "the articles that we read [throughout the course]...set the tone for our conversations every day," and the two on religion "set the tone for like a more defensive, attacking perspective on Christianity." While I reminded students of how we had spent nearly forty minutes collaboratively constructing a shared agenda for the day's discussion—reading aloud a short text, constructing questions with partners, methodically deciding as a group which of our questions to discuss from those we had publicly identified—students nevertheless assumed the readings would comprise the central agenda regardless of their contributions.

Questioning social norms can be expected to evoke resistance due to fear, guilt, cognitive dissonance, and strong religious beliefs (Goodman, 2011). Discussing privilege in particular can evoke defensiveness from students of all political persuasions due to the tendency to credit one's successes to personal merit over structured advantage (Mueller & O'Connor, 2007). My selection of readings for this particular discussion nevertheless blurred the boundaries between broadly exposing students to diverse perspectives of others and privileging particular views to help them focus on challenging their own. To this extent, my selections implicitly exercised control over the discussion agenda and constituted an act of privileging certain voices while silencing others. While males commonly seek to be in control, make decisions, and provide for others (Kaufman & Kimmel, 2011), I considered myself to have been actively countering such conventional constructions of masculinity. I had, after all, explicitly involved students in determining what we would discuss by cultivating consensus around students' questions and positioning my own as possibilities and proposals for further deliberation without imposing them. Some students nevertheless had difficulty seeing beyond the perspectives I provided in the readings to realize the reality I was attempting to create—complicating my efforts to actualize such a reality.

DISTRIBUTING PARTICIPATION

Distributing participation, as an important component of enacting equity in our interactions, represented a second component of gendered discourse that was prominent throughout the class. As Remlinger (2005) has documented, males commonly use talk to control and silence ideas that do not fit those of the dominant ideology and to limit the participation of others in constructing a shared culture. Using interruption to hold the floor and to silence others' voices is one way of using talk as a form of control. Another approach is to employ the concept of extended development to restate and recycle old topics, maintain the conversational flow, and dominate floor space. Such actions ultimately privilege certain turns and ideas while silencing others (Remlinger, 2005).

The use of talk in this setting, however, was equitable and focused on students' concerns. Sixty-nine percent of all words uttered in our discussion, for example, were by students. Twenty-one percent—more than one out of five—of students' contributions were an average of 137 words in length, with seven contributions exceeding 200 words. In contrast, my longest contributions were an average of 97 words in length. My contributions were mainly procedural, concerned with seeking clarification (e.g., "What do you mean by [that]?"), requesting elaboration (e.g., "Why?"), and inviting additional participation (e.g., "Any other thoughts?"). Consequently, students' contributions were overwhelmingly concerned with offering their own perspectives and providing reasons and examples to support their views.

In this way, we used talk across our session to counter conventional norms of masculine discourse. From my perspective, social change towards more democratic classroom spaces was a primary goal of feminist pedagogy. It was necessary for moving beyond schools as training grounds for obedience to authority (Crabtree & Sapp, 2003) and for helping students form a community of support essential for breaking patterns of domination and subordination in learning to be teachers. In authentic democratic teaching and learning, those in silenced, marginalized, oppressed, subordinate positions must be enabled to speak and build solidarity so they no longer occupy such status. In doing so, they will no longer need to turn to male authority for validation as they instead will learn to trust their own judgments and ideas (Brantlinger, Morton, & Washburn, 1999). Through using teacher authority to activate multiple perspectives and emphasize community interaction, we distributed participation in a manner that contributed to feminist aims (Sikes Scering, 1997).

BRIDGING DIFFERENCES

Bridging differences represented a third dimension of our gendered discourse. From students' comments, it was evident that a combination of pedagogical, cultural, and personal differences complicated our discussion. Pedagogically, when I asked, for example, if students would consider using, with children, the philosophical novel—*Harry Stottlemeier's Discovery* (Lipman, 1982)—from which we had collectively read a couple of chapters in class, students expressed views that were largely disapproving. Bridget expressed concern that doing so could prompt children to actually question. She said: "[I]f you start to question something like the Pledge of Allegiance...it could just be like a downturn." She elaborated:

> [I] would rather avoid having...students be like, 'well, if we don't have to say the Pledge then why do we have to line up? And why do we have to raise our hands? And why do we have to do this?'...[I]f they're questioning something as simple in the classroom as the Pledge, then it could just be chaos.

Leanna agreed that such questioning could result in "all-out rebellion." Regarding the topic of religion specifically, Colette said she would never bring it up with children "for the safety of your job, and the politics involved."

Culturally, students expressed concerns that religion was too sensitive of a topic to discuss within the particular context of the area. To Leanna, it would be "a really slippery slope when it comes to parents" in elementary schools because in her practicum school, "six kids…had to leave the room" for a televised speech by President Obama "encouraging education" because their parents "sent in notes" and "held very strong onto the fact that like they didn't support [him]." Colette explained how teachers in her practicum school were "not even allowed to read *Harry Potter*… for religious reasons" so if "you can't even read like a world-renowned children's book, like yeah right, like you could ever talk about religion." For Leanna, attempting to "grow diversity" in such a context would be "really risky"—particularly since, as Bronwyn asserted, "they can think that you're like preaching at their children."

Personally, students expressed concerns about discussing religion due to the fact that, for some of them, it was very central to their own identity. As Leanna expressed, religion was "personally grounded" which, Kendra observed, promoted a sense of "defend[ing] our thinking instead of challenging it." For Teagan, the topic of religion was "sensitive material" which involved "a lot of emotion" and "personal ties" and it was therefore "more draining" to discuss because it promoted "more disagreement than normal." For Colette, "religion is like the heart of many people" and is "where they find their identity." Consequently, in such discussions, you're "inevitably…defending yourself," which "completely changes…the questions that are…acceptable." As Teagan explained:

> [R]eligion is difficult [to discuss] because [unlike one's race or other aspects of identity], a lot of people come to find it on their own or they choose it for themselves. So, it's like, you made that, you believe in it. You can't necessarily prove it to someone else, so…you tend to feel more intense [about it] because [it's] yours.

Kendra added: "I think that it requires self-disclosure too. I'm obviously white, I'm obviously female, but I'm not obviously Christian. So in order to have meaningful conversations, it requires self disclosure…[w]hich can be uncomfortable." For Colette, such sentiment was particularly salient since she had been "attacked for being a Christian" and had received "threatening voice mails" on her phone because she was "a Christian," and had her "tires slashed" because she "stood up for [her] faith" even though she was "in the majority." Such comments suggest that the broader context was more complicated than simply considering religion an interesting source of intellectual inquiry, as I essentially had.

Approaching religion in class as something students could consider discussing in future classrooms highlighted differences in our experiences. In implicitly imagining others to have inhabited a similar position in the gender hierarchy as myself, I overlooked the extent to which students' socialization was likely quite different from my own. As women, they had likely learned to see themselves in terms of appearance and beauty instead of intellect and attitude—to realize that in teaching it is men who occupy most positions of power and exercise control over women's opportunities for professional independence and judgment (Griffin, 1997). In pushing students to question their personal assumptions, I implicitly embodied the extent to which I had constructed my masculinity in the predominantly female field of elementary education around traditionally male characteristics of willingness to take risks, experience discomfort, and accumulate new experiences (Perra & Ruspini, 2013). As Pullen and Simpson (2009) identified, token or marginal men manage difference by doing masculinity and appropriating femininity so that masculinity is partially subverted and partly maintained. By activating projects of femininity, they reconstruct their job so as to minimize non-masculine associations. In leading difficult conversations, I rejected traditional masculinity, and in so doing acknowledged and reinforced its dominant status.

DISCUSSION

In this study, I have attempted to demonstrate how gender was constructed in a graduate level teacher education course. Through shaping the agenda, distributing participation, and bridging differences, gender was constructed in the class in a manner that was contradictory and conflicting—simultaneously upholding and undermining conventional authority relations. While I occupied a privileged status as a male within the larger power structure of a male-dominated society, I also exhibited actions which actively disrupted conventional gender hierarchies. Of what value, then, was my experience in the Evangelical South? As discerned from the findings of this study, how did my interactions with evangelically-minded students help shape my pedagogy of teacher education concerning gendered discourses in teacher education?

Personally, my interactions with evangelically-minded students helped me reflect more deeply on the extent to which I have long been conscious of my status as a male doing what's commonly considered women's work. The stigma of such a non-traditional role is widely associated with assumptions of homosexuality, sexual perversion, and being a sexual predator (Pullen & Simpson, 2009; Simpson, 2005). While my female colleagues may have few qualms about having students to their homes, holding private conversations behind closed doors, and nurturing students through sensitive relationship matters, as a single man, the same standards do not apply. The societal perceptions of sexual deviance (Smith, 2004) make the stakes of imperfection high. As a man in elementary education, I must be more distant emotionally and recognize that my motivations are automatically suspect because I'm male. This is partly justified by patriarchal domination, yet a culture of femininity, I believe, is no more the answer. I must heed such occupational realities or else face considerable risk.

Professionally, my experiences in the Evangelical South ensured I developed a deeper understanding of the complexity of male positionality in predominantly female environments. How gender was constructed across the programmatic, university, and professional contexts in which I was immersed, I learned, was more complicated and nuanced than I had initially realized. While I frequently interpreted the gender relations I experienced in these environments as symptoms and manifestations of male hegemonic power and privilege, I became increasingly mindful throughout my experience of the jointly constructed nature of gender oppression. As Brantlinger et al. (1999) assert, women may not command the same attention and respect as men, and may not be heard in the same way for saying the same things. Such inequity, however, is not always attributable to dominant and domineering males.

> Women may collude in undermining their own authority as they construct feminine or maternal roles and images for themselves within persuasive and pervasive sexist ideologies. Women may be encouraging and helpful but wary that by asserting a strong message or imposing an unbending moral stance, they may be perceived as unfeminine. (p. 499)

So long as sexist attitudes, practices, and structural inequalities continue to allow men more power and opportunity than women, in ways that are jointly constructed, re-enacted, and perpetuated by all involved, gender divisions will persist and the success of education reform will remain inextricably tied to gender (Hubbard & Datnow, 2000).

Pedagogically, my interactions with evangelically-minded students helped me fashion a conservatively critical pedagogy of teacher education (Loughran, 2006). To me, this meant developing a deeper acceptance of "critical acquiescence" (Carbado, 2005)—criticizing and rejecting those aspects of teaching practice directly linked to gender privilege, while recognizing that my practices as a teacher educator were still helping to reproduce such discourses in my own and others' teaching. As this study suggests, I could neither position my practice completely outside of such discourses nor within them, but rather needed to simultaneously question and comply with prevailing gender hierarchies—working against while working within the multifaceted realities of sexism. While I embodied male hegemonic oppression, I also helped students contribute to our discussions in ways that supported their questioning of the gender status quo—both actively disrupting conventional gender hierarchies and supporting students in finding their voice against oppressive norms.

While I aspired to teach in a manner that was increasingly democratic, equitable, and just, I have learned that effectively meeting students' needs sometimes means moving in a direction opposite of one's intuition and desire. Effectively meeting students where they are, for me, means approaching students more carefully, conventionally, and conservatively to involve them gradually in processes of democratic learning (Brubaker, 2012a). It means being more careful, guarded, and inclined to err on the side of caution—being sure not to wear my political beliefs on my sleeve—neither promoting nor prohibiting religious beliefs, while ensuring all perspectives are considered in the course of discussing sensitive topics (Frederick,

1995). It also means being satisfied with less as a means of accomplishing more—while maintaining a commitment to even stronger and more robust feminist action.

CONCLUSION

Fashioning a conservatively critical pedagogy of teacher education may not go far enough. It nevertheless presents a politically useful and manageable starting place for developing a liberatory consciousness necessary for living with awareness and intentionality (Love, 2010). In this respect, my time in the South provided a metaphor of sorts for broader social possibilities concerning gendered identities. Like Lincoln and Mandela, who sought to make partners out of adversaries and bridge regional divides in their own historical eras, I perceived a similar responsibility. Without efforts to actively work together and reconcile our differences, how can we be assured our future teachers will use their teaching to honor the right of oppressed people to decide for themselves how to win their liberation (Gorski, 2008)? How can we be assured they will use the classroom community of inquiry as an essential tool and beginning point for women's liberation (Daniel, 1994)—as a site of feminist and critical resistance (Kawai & Taylor, 2011)? How can we be assured they will take advantage of teachable moments to make knowledge contestable and engage young children in spontaneous explorations of gender (Lyman, 2011)? To me, the act of speaking "with" was the ideal discourse position as a male feminist teacher, providing the only hope of getting beyond typical positions of male authority to join women in solidarity (Breeze, 2007). Forming pedagogical partnerships in the face of fundamentalism is a long road to feminism, though I'd be inclined to do it again.

REFERENCES

Berliner, D. C. (1997). Educational psychology meets the Christian right: Differing views of children, schooling, teaching, and learning. *Teachers College Record, 98*(3), 381–416.

Blumenfeld, W. J. (1992). *Homophobia: How we all pay the price*. Boston, MA: Beacon Press.

Brantlinger, E., Morton, M. L., & Washburn, S. (1999). Teachers' moral authority in classrooms: (Re) Structuring social interactions and gendered power. *The Elementary School Journal, 99*(5), 491–504.

Breeze, W. (2007). Constructing a male feminist pedagogy: Authority, practice, and authenticity in the composition classroom. *Feminist Teacher, 18*(1), 59–73.

Brubaker, N. D. (2012a). Multiple layers of self in an evolving pedagogy of teacher education: Conflict and compromise in a quest for classroom democracy. *Studying Teacher Education, 8*, 3–18.

Brubaker, N. D. (2012b). Negotiating authority through cultivating a classroom community of inquiry. *Teaching & Teacher Education, 28*, 240–250.

Carbado, D. W. (2005). Privilege. In E. P. Johnson & M. G. Henderson (Eds.), *Black queer studies: A critical anthology* (pp. 190–206). Durham, NC: Duke University Press.

Cochran-Smith, M., & Zeichner, K. M. (Eds.). (2005). *Studying teacher education: The report of the AERA panel on research and teacher education*. Mahwah, NJ: Lawrence Erlbaum Associates.

Crabtree, R. D., & Sapp, D. A. (2003). Theoretical, political, and pedagogical challenges in the feminist classroom: Our struggles to walk the walk. *College Teaching, 51*(4), 131–140.

Daniel, M. F. (1994). Women, philosophical community of inquiry and the liberation of self. *Thinking: The journal of philosophy for children, 11*(3 & 4), 63–71.

Frederick, P. (1995). Walking on eggs: Mastering the dreaded diversity discussion. *College Teaching, 43*(3), 83–92.

Glaser, B. G., & Strauss, A. L. (1999). *The discovery of grounded theory: Strategies for qualitative research*. New York, NY: Aldine de Gruyter.

Goodman, D. J. (2011). *Promoting diversity and social justice: Educating people from privileged groups* (2nd ed.). New York, NY: Routledge.

Gorski, P. C. (2008). *The evolution of a pro-feminist*. Retrieved from http://www.edchange.org/publications/pro feminist.pdf

Griffin, G. (1997). Teaching as a gendered experience. *Journal of Teacher Education, 48*(1), 7–18.

Harro, B. (2000). The cycle of socialization. In M. Adams, W. J. Blumenfeld, H. Casaneda, H. Hackman, M. L. Peters & X. Zuniga (Eds.), *Readings for diversity and social justice: An anthology on racism, anti-Semitism, sexism, heterosexism, ableism, and classism* (pp. 15–21). New York, NY: Routledge.

Hofman, S. (2008). Miles of aisles of sexism: Helping students investigate toy stores. In A. Pelo (Ed.), *Rethinking early childhood education* (pp. 29–33). Milwaukee, WI: Rethinking Schools.

Hooks, B. (1984). *Feminist theory: From margin to center*. Cambridge, MA: South End Press.

Hubbard, L., & Datnow, A. (2000). A gendered look at educational reform. *Gender and Education, 12*(1), 115–129.

Johnson-Bailey, J., & Lee, M. Y. (2005). Women of color in the academy: Where's our authority in the classroom? *Feminist Teacher, 15*(2), 111–122.

Johnson, A. G. (1997). *The gender knot: Unraveling our patriarchal legacy*. Philadelphia, PA: Temple University Press.

Johnson, A. G. (2006). *Privilege, power, and difference* (2nd ed.). New York, NY: McGraw-Hill.

Joshi, K. Y. (2010). "Because I had a Turban". In N. P. Gallavan (Ed.), *Multicultural education: Annual editions* (15th ed., pp. 29–31). New York, NY: McGraw-Hill.

Kaufman, M., & Kimmel, M. (2011). *The guy's guide to feminism*. Berkeley, CA: Seal Press.

Kawai, H., & Taylor, E. R. (2011). The work children do: Unpacking gendered conflict in an elementary classroom. *Harvard Educational Review, 81*(4), 646–666.

LaBoskey, V. K. (2004). The methodology of self-study and its theoretical underpinnings. In J. Loughran, M. L. Hamilton, V. K. LaBoskey & T. Russell (Eds.), *International handbook of self study of teacher education practices* (pp. 817–869). Dordrecht, The Netherlands: Kluwer Academic Publishers.

Lazar, M. M. (2007). Feminist critical discourse analysis: Articulating a feminist discourse praxis. *Critical Discourse Studies, 4*(2), 141–164.

Lipman, M. (1982). *Harry Stottlemeier's Discovery*. Upper Montclair, NJ: Institute for the Advancement of Philosophy for Children.

Lipman, M. (1988). *Philosophy goes to school*. Philadelphia, PA: Temple University Press.

Lipman, M. (2003). *Thinking in education* (2nd ed.). New York, NY: Cambridge University Press.

Lipman, M., Sharp, A. M., & Oscanyan, F. S. (1980). *Philosophy in the classroom* (2nd ed.). Philadelphia, PA: Temple University Press.

Lipman, M., Sharp, A. M., & Oscanyan, F. S. (1984). *Philosophical inquiry: An instructional manual to accompany Harry Stottlemeier's Discovery*. Lanham, MD: University Press of America.

Loughran, J. (2006). *Developing a pedagogy of teacher education: Understanding teaching and learning about teaching*. New York, NY: Routledge.

Love, B. J. (2010). Developing a liberatory consciousness. In M. Adams, W. J. Blumenfeld, C. Castaneda, H. W. Hackman, M. L. Peters & X. Zuniga (Eds.), *Readings for diversity and social justice* (2nd ed., pp. 599–603). New York, NY: Routledge.

Lyman, K. (2011). Girls, worms, and body image. In E. Marshall & O. Sensoy (Eds.), *Rethinking popular culture and media* (pp. 138–146). Milwaukee, WI: Rethinking Schools.

Macgillivray, L. (1997). Do what I say, not what I do: An instructor rethinks her own teaching and research. *Curriculum Inquiry, 27*(4), 470–488.

Maher, F. (1999). Progressive education and feminist pedagogies: Issues in gender, power, and authority. *Teachers College Record, 101*(1), 35–59.

McIntosh, P. (1988). *White privilege and male privilege: A personl account of coming to see correspondences through work in women's studies*. Retrieved from http://www.lamission.edu/sociology/mekelburg/SOC2%5CWhite_Privilege_handout.pdf

Mueller, J., & O'Connor, C. (2007). Telling and retelling about self and "others": How pre-service teachers (re)interpret privilege and disadvantage in one college classroom. *Teaching and Teacher Education, 23*, 840–856.

Nentwich, J. C., & Kelan, E. K. (2013). Towards a topology of 'doing gender': An analysis of empirical research and its challenges. *Gender, Work and Organization, 21*(2), 121–134.

Perra, M. S., & Ruspini, E. (2013). Men who work in 'non-traditional' occupations. *International Review of Sociology: Revue Internationale de Sociologie, 23*(2), 265–270.

Pinnegar, S., & Hamilton, M. L. (2009). *Self-study of practice as a genre of qualitative research: Theory, methodology, and practice.* Dordrecht, Netherlands: Springer.

Pullen, A., & Simpson, R. (2009). Managing difference in feminized work: Men, otherness and social practice. *Human Relations, 62*(4), 561–587.

Remlinger, K. A. (2005). Negotiating the classroom floor: Negotiating ideologies of gender and sexuality. In M. M. Lazar (Ed.), *Feminist critical discourse analysis: Gender, power and ideology in discourse* (pp. 114–138). New York, NY: Palgrave Macmillan.

Reynolds, W., & Webber, J. A. (2009). *The civic gospel: A political cartography of Christianity.* Rotterdam: Sense.

Samaras, A. P., & Freese, A. R. (2006). *Self-study of teaching practices: Primer.* New York, NY: Peter Lang.

Sax, L. (2005). *Why gender matters: What parents and teachers need to know about the emerging science of sex differences.* New York, NY: Doubleday.

Schlosser, L. Z. (2010). Christian privilege: Breaking a sacred taboo. In M. Adams, W. J. Blumenfeld, C. Castaneda, H. W. Hackman, M. L. Peters & X. Zuniga (Eds.), *Readings for diversity and social justice* (2nd ed., pp. 246–247). New York, NY: Routledge.

Schulte, A. K. (2009). *Seeking integrity in teacher education: Transforming student teachers, transforming my self.* Dordrecht, The Netherlands: Springer.

Sharp, A. M. (1993). The community of inquiry: Education for democracy. In M. Lipman (Ed.), *Thinking children and education* (pp. 337–345). Dubuque, IA: Kendall Hunt.

Sikes Scering, G. E. (1997). Themes of a critical/feminist pedagogy: Teacher education for democracy. *Journal of Teacher Education, 48*(1), 62–68.

Simpson, R. (2005). Men in non-traditional occupations: Career entry, career orientation and experience of role strain. *Gender, Work and Organization, 12*(4), 363–380.

Smith, J. (2004). *Male primary teachers: Disadvantaged or advantaged?* Paper presented at the Australian Association for Research in Education, Melbourne.

Tripp, D. (1993). *Critical incidents in teaching: Developing professional judgement.* New York, NY: Routledge.

Weiler, K. (Ed.). (2001). *Feminist engagements: Reading, resisting, and revisioning male theorists in education and cultural studies.* New York, NY: Routlendge.

AFFILIATIONS

Nathan D. Brubaker
Lecturer,
Faculty of Education,
Monash University,
Melbourne, Australia

JULIAN KITCHEN

INQUEERIES INTO SELF-STUDY:
QUEERING THE GAZE ON TEACHER EDUCATOR
IDENTITY AND PRACTICE

Teacher educators engaged in the self-study of teacher education practices are reflective about many aspects of practice. At the same time, most have probably given little thought to heterosexual privilege or the experiences of those who identify as lesbian, gay, bisexual, or transgender (LGBT). In "Queering the Gaze," Doll (1998) used the pun on gays/gaze as an artful way of thinking about identity, gays/queers, and perception. In the hope that "we can re-cognize what the 'normal' mind views as 'natural'" (p. 287), I offer queer theory as a useful lens for viewing identity, experience and practice as straight and queer teacher educators.

A small conference I attended several years ago began with an icebreaker activity. Sue, the event organizer, passed along a ball of string and invited participants to break off a length. We were then invited to tell about ourselves as we wound the string around a finger. Sue began by telling about her family and her work. Others followed in the same vein. I felt uncomfortable as I listened to others and waited my turn as the second last speaker. Other than my colleague, Matt, I did not know anyone in the room. While openly gay, I did not feel ready to share my personal life with a group of strangers. I snapped off most of my string. Deborah, who was not married, did the same. When my turn came, I spoke only of my professional work. Later, Matt told me that he felt uncomfortable wondering about my predicament. Over the course of the two-day event, I casually spoke of my personal life and my relationship with my husband.

This commonplace experience is presented as a critical incident (Tripp, 1993) indicative of underlying patterns of heteronormativity in society. I hope that you feel mildly uncomfortable as you reflect on the incident from the perspectives of the four characters in the story. You may empathize with my discomfort as I quickly tried to assess whether this was a safe place for disclosure. Viewing the story from Deborah's perspective, you may feel awkward about the degree to which marriage and children are regularly privileged in conversation. Putting yourself in Sue's shoes may be more disquieting. Her intentions were good yet, by not pausing to consider the sexual and gender politics, she inadvertently made participants uncomfortable. You may recall similar incidents in your past. As a gay man, I can tell you that it happens all the time.

M. Taylor and L. Coia (Eds.), Gender, Feminism, and Queer Theory in the Self-Study of Teacher Education Practices, 127–141.

Let's end our critical examination of the incident on a more positive note. Through empathy, Matt rose above his heterosexual male positioning to notice how this incident might make sexual minorities feel. This incident proved critical for me because it revealed how a straight teacher educator might apply a queer gaze (Doll, 1998) to teacher identity and practice. It also caused me to reflect on how I as a queer teacher educator can help teacher candidates and teacher educators to understand heteronormativity and consider the experiences of LGBT people.

As a teacher educator, my primary unit for understanding the world is experience, rather than practice or theory. Clandinin and Connelly (2000) write:

Following Dewey, the study of education is the study of life—for example, the study of epiphanies, rituals, routines, metaphors, and everyday actions. We learn about education by thinking about life, and we learn about life by thinking about education. (p. xxiv)

A grounding in narrative inquiry and the self-study of teacher education practices has made me suspicious of theory that runs counter to experience. At the same time, as I can habitually slip into the comfortable groove of rituals and routines, I need to regularly challenge myself and the culture in which I work. I have found that theoretical knowledge, used judiciously, removes blinkers, sharpens thinking, and helps one to experience the world with new eyes. Enacted in the context of experience, theory deepens understanding, uncovers unexamined elements of practice, and enhances one's pedagogy of teacher education (Pinnegar & Hamilton, 2009).

The world is a complex place. We can better understand ourselves, others, and the world around us when we deliberately apply multiple lenses in order to interpret experience. The lenses of critical theories, by offering alternative renderings of the world in which we live, challenge the orthodoxies of the dominant groups in our society. Feminism (Olesen, 2000) helps me grapple with the male privilege and the challenges this poses for women. Critical Race Theory (Ladson-Billings, 1998) aids me in appreciating the unexamined racial and cultural assumptions endemic to society and engrained in traditional views of education. In my work in Aboriginal teacher education (e.g., Kitchen, Hodson & Cherubini, 2011), Tribal Crit (Brayboy, 2005) has helped me critique mainstream approaches to Aboriginal education and appreciate the importance of culturally responsive schooling for Indigenous people.

Queer theory offers a *bent*, rather than *straight*, perspective on people, texts and contexts. "Queer theory offers educators a lens through which they can transform praxis so as to explore and celebrate the tensions and new understandings created by teaching new ways of seeing the world," according to Meyer (2012, p. 10). While experience guides us in understanding ourselves and our practices, we do not see what we don't look for. Sometimes things hide in plain sight, overlooked until our attention is drawn to them by circumstances, the observations of others or something we have read.

I begin this in*queery* into self-study with an outline of queer theory, in which I focus on three orientations that may be useful in queering the gaze. Queer theory is then applied to my own practice through a critique of a self-study paper I wrote. As

128

queer theory can be useful in examining our identities as educators, the next section considers the intersection of queer theory and autobiography. I examine my educational story through the dual lens of queer theory and autobiography. My goal is to prompt questioning by disrupting normalized assumptions in a manner that focuses on tensions rather than alternative certainties. And in a way that is playful and generous.[1]

A GUIDE TO QUEER THEORY

Queer theory is a critical discourse that offers deep insights into personal identity, social relationships, and social hierarchies. Unfortunately, many gay and straight people are reluctant to wade through the theoretical musings, dense prose and impractical solutions (Adams & Holman Jones, 2011) found in many queer theory articles and chapters. In this section, I attempt to make queer theory more accessible by identifying three main orientations. First, queer theory is a critical theory that seeks to understand gendered identity and critique orthodox conceptions of gender and sexual orientation that privilege heterosexuality (Alexander, 2008). Second, it challenges the binaries of sexual orientation and gender identity. Third, queer theory sometimes adopts a subversive and transgressive tone through artistry, inventiveness and humour (Adams & Holman Jones, 2008) to challenge orthodoxy and highlight tensions regarding understandings of sex and gender.

On the Contrary

First and foremost, "queer theory seeks to disrupt and to assert voice and power" (Tierney & Dilley, 1998, p. 59). With roots in feminism, gay and lesbian studies, identity politics and post-colonial theory, it "offers methods of critiques" (Britzman, 1995, p. 154) against white, male discourse that normalize identity and shield power and privilege. This begins with challenges to heteronormativity—the assumption that heterosexuality and traditional gender roles are normal, while other orientations and representations of gender identity are abnormal and threatening (Quinn & Meiners, 2011). The most passionate theorists, who view sexual minorities "as exhibiting revolutionary potential" (Pinar, 1998, p. 6), offer radical critiques in the hope that these will "transform past experiences with abjection, isolation and rejection into legibility, community and love" (Halberstam, 1998, p. 221).

These critiques of heterosexual privilege and heteronormativity have led queer theorists to remap "the terrain of gender, identity, and cultural studies" (Alexander, 2008, p. 108). School and other institutions are critiqued as instruments of masculine agency and straightness, as involving the uncritical acceptance of gender roles and identities (Pinar, 2007). The norms of schooling are viewed as promoting "curricular and instructional changes that aim towards more inclusive learning environments" (Luhmann, 1998, p. 147). This critique extends to confronting the homophobic and transphobic harassment and bullying that permeates schools as agencies of social reproduction (Meyer, 2012; Quinn & Meiners, 2011).

This critical lens is also turned towards the LGBT identities and communities (Alexander, 2008, p. 108). Efforts to protect the privacy of gays and lesbians are seen not as a move towards freedom, but as "a kind of confinement" while "simultaneously restricting access to the public sphere" (Quinn & Meiners, 2011, p. 138). The conceptualization of lesbian and gay as a single community is challenged for simplifying "complex internal differences and complex sexualities" (Gamson, 1998, p. 597). Some queer theorists dismiss gay pride as an assimilationist effort to appear normal (Halberstam, 1998). Objective categories are dismissed as instruments of homogenization and erasure in favour of sexual and gender identity as complex and fluid (Anzaldua, 1987).

A queer gaze, by challenging heteronormativity and gay response to it, helps one understand sexual orientation and gender identity within a wider social context. By challenging our assumptions about what is normal, it creates space for asking questions about schools as places that privilege heterosexuality and for considering how to incorporate LGBT lives into pedagogy and curriculum. By aligning with feminist and other critical perspectives, queer theory helps in "remapping the terrain of gender, identity, and cultural studies" (Alexander, 2008, p. 108).

In Tension

While queer theory values political commitment and is aligned with critical pedagogy, much of its richness as a discourse stems from its challenge to fixed identities, particularly in relation to gender identity and sexual orientation (Adams & Holman Jones, 2008). As Sedgwick (1993) observes, "when constituent elements of anyone's gender, of anyone's sexuality aren't made to signify monolithically" one can observe "the open mesh of possibilities, gaps, overlaps, dissonances and resonances, lapses and excesses of meaning" (p. 8). A queer gaze, by looking beyond surface appearances, provides us with the awareness to tell "a story about being half in and half out of identities, subject positions, and discourses and having the courage to be fluid in a world relentlessly searching for stability and certainty" (Adams & Holman Jones, 2011, p. 114). Queer theory, by reminding us that "[g]ender codes constrain all individuals" (Meyer, 2011, p. 11), encourages all educators to question the gay-straight binary, while challenging the uncritical acceptance and perpetuation of heteronormativity in the classroom and curriculum.

The tensions inherent in remapping the terrain of identity sometimes make queer theory seem like a "minefield... strewn with fragrant flowers as well as shattering mortars" (Chinn, 1994, p. 244). By tearing away the veil of heteronormative convention, they expose us to the richness and complexity of identity.

At Play

While much queer theory focuses on challenging the status quo and identifying tensions in heteronormative paradigms, queerness can also be artistic, humorous and playful (Morris, 1998). *Camp* humour, for example, employs a secret, satiric language to deflate pretension, dismantle hierarchy (Halperin, 2012) and question normality (Bronski, 2011). It works from "a position of disempowerment to recode social codes whose cultural power and prestige prevent them from simply being dismantled and ignored" (Halperin, 2012, p. 217). Through a camp sensibility, films such as *Rocky Horror Picture Show* or *Priscilla, Queen of the Desert* can be seen as possessing a double nature through which the normative and the transgressive are engaged in a dynamic relationship that simultaneously honours and subverts cultural norms. As Russo (1981) writes, *Rocky Horror Picture Show* is a "truly subversive and anarchistic film on the subjects of sexuality, movies, sex roles and the homosexual as monster" (p. 52) that makes deviance visible and tangible. While queer theory is serious business, it is worthwhile maintaining a sense of irony and humour. Indeed, in my experience, a playful approach often breaches defences that are impervious to sermons and instruction.

QUEER THEORY IN ACTION: CRITIQUING MY PRACTICE

In order to consider how queer theory might be applied in the self-study of teacher education practices, I examine "Making It Better for Lesbian, Gay, Bisexual and Transgender Students through Teacher Education: A Collaborative Self-study" (Kitchen & Bellini, 2012). In this article, Christine Bellini and I studied a series of teacher education workshops we conducted titled "Sexual Diversity in Secondary Schools." Below, I highlight how queer theory informed our study, and then critique our work using the three orientations of queer theory.

On the Contrary

The first section of the paper identified the need to address LGBT issues in teacher education. We began by proposing that the need for such workshops was great given the high levels of homophobia and homophobic bullying in schools, according to Canadian and American data. In doing so, we confronted the degree to which harassment permeates the school system and challenged ourselves to make this explicit to teacher candidates through our pedagogy and curriculum. We framed our work in relation to the heteronormative tendency to pathologize LGBT teens and minimize attention to their needs. We drew on queer theory, paying particular attention to the marginalization of sexual minorities and activism in response to homophobia. At the same time, we were careful to create a safe environment in which all teacher candidates would feel respected and cared for (Lee, 2011). Although we identified ourselves as committed to equity, diversity and social justice, "we were reluctant to take a strongly ideological stance" (Kitchen & Bellini, 2012, p. 211) and "avoided engaging overtly in ideological debate" (p. 215) so as to help teacher candidates feel safe during the workshop.

While queer theory has become relatively common in some discourse communities, it has seldom been examined in the self-study literature. Our article was the first in *Studying Teacher Education* to feature queer subject matter, and my review of the self-study literature for queer content located only one article (Conley & Colabucci, 2009) and one chapter (Manke, 2005).

Although our paper critiqued the dominant discourse and attempted to remap the terrain of gender and sexual orientation in schools, we could also be critiqued for being insufficiently critical and disruptive in our approach. Rather than truly confront the pervasiveness of systemic discrimination, we could be viewed as settling for incremental change. Our concern with the safety of the predominantly heterosexual teacher candidates could be viewed as a reluctance to challenge the unexamined heteronormativity that is the basis of homophobia. Indeed, we acknowledged that our political commitment is tempered by other factors. We justified this in terms of a pedagogical commitment to "developing a relatively safe space for teacher candidates to examine and challenge their professional identities" (Kitchen & Bellini, 2012, p. 223), but this could just as easily be viewed as cowardly, apolitical, and assimilationist by some queer theorists.

In Tension

One of my goals in this work was to problematize heteronormativity for teacher candidates and teacher educators. While I had not employed queer theory in my own research, extensive reading in this area had made me aware of the issues. Also, through my application of critical theories and critical pedagogy in my research on Aboriginal education (e.g., Kitchen, Cherubini, Trudeau & Hodson, 2009; Kitchen, Hodson & Cherubini, 2011), I had a heightened awareness of power and privilege. Christine also drew on queer theory for her research on gay straight alliances in schools (Bellini, 2012). My particular interest is in queer theory as a challenge to fixed identities regarding gender identity and sexual orientation. As gender codes constrain everyone, I prefer to embrace ambiguity and tension rather than critique individuals, including predominately heterosexual teacher candidates, based on identity. In our *Studying Teacher Education* article, Christine and I "pragmatically focussed on creating a discursive space in which teacher candidates could safely struggle with alternative conceptualizations of sexual identity and the duties of teachers" (Kitchen & Bellini, 2012, p. 211). The first activity, involving the matching of terms and definitions, opened the floor for discussion of pejorative, clinical and preferred terms for gender identity and sexual orientation. The group work on case studies also provided space for the discussion of both personal values and professional strategies. Embracing ambiguity and rendering the invisible visible is liberating both to teacher candidates who are challenged to see beyond their heteronormative worldviews and to us as teacher educators.

One of the commonalities between queer theory and the self-study of teacher education practices is their shared embrace of ambiguity and tension. Reflective teacher educators have long been aware of the "indeterminate swampy zones" (Schön, 1987, p. 3) where practice occurs. Berry (2007) introduced the notion of *tensions* "as a way of representing and better understanding the ambivalence and contradictions so intrinsic in the nature of pedagogy" (p. 139). We explored four of these tensions "as a means of framing our experiences conducting [the] workshop" (Kitchen & Bellini, 2012, p. 213). By examining tensions, both with a self-study and a queer gaze, we were able to interpret the ways in which we navigated the central tensions underlying our practice as teacher educators. For example, one of the tensions was between telling and growing (Berry, 2007). As queer theorists and advocates, we were motivated to transmit as much of our knowledge and understanding as possible within a two-hour timeframe. On the other hand, as educators, "we worried that our commitment to the topic might blind us to the learning needs of teacher candidates" (Kitchen & Bellini, 2012, p. 213). Therefore, "[w]hile there was much telling about the need to respect sexual diversity and gender identity, we made a determined effort to select content that would prompt reflection" (p. 215). In this regard, we were mindful of Dewey (1938), who wrote, "teachers discriminate between experiences that are worthwhile educationally and those that are not" (p. 33). At the same time, based on the feedback received from teacher candidates, we have noted considerable growth in acceptance over the years we have conducted LGBT workshops at the university. Therefore, in planning workshops for the next year, we modified content and delivery to recalibrate the tension between safety and challenge. While I am generally satisfied with the balance we have struck, I recognize that some queer theorists and activists might criticize us for not focussing more on the unsettling effects of heteronormativity and homophobia.

At Play

Queerness can also be viewed as an aesthetic reading and interpretation of texts. While our workshop and subsequent article were not particularly artistic in sensibility, we did carefully construct personal stories to share with participants. Like actors, "we sought to understand how our personal identities and experiences motivated our involvement with LGBT issues in schools and contributed to our efforts to make our interactions with teacher candidates educative" (Kitchen & Bellini, 2012, p. 214). The employment of personal stories, according to participants, made us as presenters "more credible" and "made the class a safe, comfortable learning environment" (p. 219). Another found that it put "a *human* perspective on academic material" (p. 220). My performative self—a gentle, non-judgemental manner—helped dispel stereotypes and increased safety. Also, the stories told were selected to gently unsettle. For example, I recalled my opposite-sex dating experiences in high school and recounted the story of a masculine male friend who has subsequently identified as trans. While the content was serious, teacher candidates indicated appreciation for a lightness of tone that conveyed an ironic acceptance of complexities of identity and an acceptance that heterosexual privilege is not about to disappear. Playfulness in tone seems important as we—queer theorists and teacher educators—seek to simultaneously honour and subvert cultural norms that privilege heterosexuals, males, whites, and the wealthy.

A camp sensibility can also help us to see ourselves ironically as teacher educators and change agents. Why do I mention that I dated girls in high school? Why do I dress conservatively? Why do I avoid *gay* mannerisms or *camp* behaviour? To what extent am I straight-*acting*? Are there signs of internalized homophobia in my self-identity and performative self? Why do straights *act* straight? What is *normal?* These fair questions, which might otherwise seem judgemental, are more palatable when asked with a sense of playfulness and inquiry.

QUEERING THE SELF: QUEER THEORY AND AUTOBIOGRAPHY

Queer theory can be employed by self-study practitioners as means of critically and playfully examining tensions related to sexuality, gender and heteronormativity in their professional practice. As queer theory challenges normative assumptions, many queer theorists share self-study's interest in the self, the practice, the context in which practice takes place, and the interplay of these elements. Autobiographical writing informed by queer theory can help educators understand the lived experiences of LGBT people as nested in the folds of a complex heteronormative culture.

"The value of autobiography in researching our own practice lies in our ability to understand how the past impacts our present," write Coia and Taylor (2009). While the experiences are personal, we must employ cultural lenses to recognize that the "dilemmas and questions come from the specific and inescapable cultural context within which we live and breathe" (p. 5). Connelly and Clandinin (2000) stress that teacher knowledge is always knowledge in context. While all autobiographical writing has the potential to "transform our relationships to ourselves, to our students and to the curriculum" (Samaras, Hicks, & Garvey Berger, 2004, p. 909), the potential for insight "is more likely to be realized when practitioners engage in exercises that stimulate rigorous reflection and thinking" (Kitchen, 2009, p. 39). These exercises could be reflective, such as the use of personal experience methods used to uncover, recount and examine one's stories (e.g., Connelly & Clandinin, 1988). Or, they could be critical approaches to exploring self, practice and context. Queer theory, by challenging heteronormativity, offers a lens through which one can gain new insights into previously unexamined elements of the self and how they are manifested in the context of practice.

One of the limitations of autobiography is that "educators use autobiography in ways that reinforce classroom representations of a knowable, always accessible conscious self who progresses, with the help of autobiographical inquiry, from ignorance, to knowledge of self, other, and 'best' pedagogical and curricular practices" (Miller, 1998, p. 367). While Miller may be harsh in her critique of autobiographies that are not informed by critical theory, there is merit to her concern that "[s]uch normalized versions of autobiography serve to limit and close down rather than to create possibilities for constructing permanently open and resignifiable selves" (p. 367). Combining autobiography with queer theory offers an alternative lens through which to hold ways of knowing in tension in order to re-examine normative assumptions about oneself, one's practice and one's context. At their best, both autobiography and queer theory acknowledge ambiguity and view life as an open text. As Adams and Holman Jones (2011) observe, "We write to leave room for interpretation, for misunderstandings, for not knowing. We write to leave things unfinished and unanswered" (p. 108).

Queering the gaze, in short, is both a way of highlighting otherwise unexamined issues and a way of accepting and embracing the tensions of experience rather than attempting to contain and regularize experience in pre-formed boxes. It is of potential use to both queer educators, who have clashed with normativity, and straight educators, who may not have examined issues of gender identity or sexual orientation reflectively or critically.

In order to consider how queer theory and autobiography might be applied in the self-study of teacher education practices, I examine and re-examine an unpublished manuscript I wrote for a course on language, identity and culture many years ago. In "Lost between the Lines: A Personal Search for Cultural Identity" (Kitchen, 1995), written before I was aware of queer theory, I drew on cultural theory and stories of cultural identity to reflect on my identity as an immigrant from Great Britain and as a gay man. First, I present excerpts from the paper that illustrate how a critical queer gaze can expose unexamined assumptions about identity and culture. In this construction of my narrative of experience, "there is a reflexive relationship between living a life story, telling a life story, retelling a life story, and reliving a life story" (Clandinin & Connelly, 2000, p. 71).

Lost between the Lines: A Personal Search for Identity

A course on cultural identity, with an emphasis on experience, caused me to reflect on "my sense of not having an identity" and "appearing like an insider while feeling like an outsider" (Kitchen, 1995). I embarked on "a journey towards a deeper understanding of my life between the lines, or in the borderlands." The paper became "an annotated text in which I reconstruct and deconstruct my experiences in order to recover the hidden meanings and expose the individual behind the masks."

I felt "lost between the lines," "invisible," and a "chameleon" due to the invisible stigma of being gay and my invisible identity as an immigrant of English and Spanish heritage.

> Everyone else had an identity, but I had none. Or, perhaps too many identities. Some were valid while others were false identities I assumed or had imposed on me. Others were real yet denied or suppressed. Overall, I was caught between identities, uncertain which, if any, were truly me...

135

Heteronormativity was prominent in my earliest recollections of traditional families and "shameful stereotypes of pathetic, effeminate outcasts." This led me to mimic "straight mating habits as I entered in romantic liaisons with girls to whom I was not attracted" and profess "disdain for the *jocks* whose prowess I secretly admired." In puzzling over my experiences, I reflected:

> It is hard to become whole—to unite the *private* and *public*—when society denies your sexuality—part of the core of your private identity. This means that in order to function one is expected to hide this secret and act as if part of the majority. The consequence, as Paul Monette (1992) laments, is "the gutting of all our passion till we are a bunch of eunuchs, our zones of pleasure in enemy hands" (pp. 1-2). Worse than external stigmas is the self-delusion and self-hate this engenders in the victim.

While *coming out* to myself, family and friends proved a liberating experience, I did not want to be entirely defined by this facet of my identity: "Labels are true as identifiers but are often used falsely to reduce rather than understand a person... we lose tone and shade when we reduce ourselves to caricatures and stereotypes." When I became a teacher, I initially hid my sexual orientation. As I attempted to make sense of my experiences, I wrote, "All these experiences have influenced me as a teacher. My sense of alienation has diminished me as a teacher, but my sympathy for outsiders and love of diversity have enhanced my teaching." I indicated that I felt "stronger and wiser" after better understanding my identities and expressed optimism about my ability to "cope with change and thrive on chaos." In the next two decades, I have been open about my queer identity while reluctant to be defined by it. In re-visiting my narrative 19 years later, I work at the intersection of autobiography and queer theory.

On the Contrary

Autobiography and queer theory can deepen understanding of self and contribute to a richer discourse in education. As Proust (1913; 1981) observes, the voyages of discovery involve learning to see with new eyes. One way of seeing with new eyes is to view the landscape with different lenses. Applying critical theory to my experiences prompted me to ask questions that yielded new discoveries about myself. Initially, I felt I was neither part of the mainstream nor a member of another culture. By questioning my identity, I was able to make the themes and theories in the course meaningful to me. As Miller (1998) notes, autobiography "provided an incentive and a reason...to tell how my life and my love exceeded the academic discourses, frameworks, and contexts that tried to contain them" (p. 367). At the same time, the critical lens enabled me to "queer both the subject and forms" (Miller, p. 367) in order to disrupt approaches to sanitize and normalize identity.

Stories of my 30 year relationship with my same-sex partner, for example, expose marriage as both a personal act of love and a political act nested in a public institution.

When combined with queer theory, such stories of experience can provide both authors and readers with richer contextual and critical understandings of themselves and their world. They can prompt both queer and straight educators to make explicit the ways in which the personal and political are intertwined.

The authenticity of personal experience is one of the strengths of autobiography. While theorists may expose social forces such as heteronormativity and homophobia, narrative accounts convey how these phenomena affect real people in the contexts in which they live. My awareness of heterosexual norms reflects the reality that most youth, queer or straight, equate marriage to an opposite sex mate with acceptance and respectability (Evans, 2002). Schools need to question such implicit codes rather than passively allow them to be taken for granted by students constructing their own identities and coming to understand other people. The reality that "queer-as-deviant can be invoked at any moment" to undercut acceptance, respect and self-respect (Evans, 2002, p. 116) illustrates how homophobia is interwoven into heteronormativity. This is reflected in my references to "my shameful secret" and "shameful stereotypes." It is also evident in the self-denial that led me to deny my same-sex attraction in order to date girls.

My reluctance to be stereotyped could be interpreted as an acceptance that sexuality and gender are not static categories, and that identity is fluid and multi-faceted (Adams & Holman Jones, 2008). On the other hand, as Monette (1992) observes, there remains "lingering self-hatred" and "closets in closets" (p. 173) that make it difficult to fully love and accept oneself. This can result in being more concerned with "acceptance from the mainstream" and more inclined to "use terms that are palatable to the mainstream" (p. 116). Either way, or allowing both possibilities to exist simultaneously, it is important that heterosexual privilege and the *othering* of non-conforming identities be challenged and critiqued (Kumashiro, 2002). Understanding our gender identities and sexual orientations has the potential to make us more responsive as educators to a wide range of diversities in our students and communities.

In Tension

"The story of a single life is always entangled in the complex folds of culture," according to Leibowitz (1989, p. xvii). Narratives serve as means of making meaning from experience by refiguring "the past to create purpose in the future" (Connelly & Clandinin, 1988, p. 24). Understanding the tensions in our own narratives serves as a basis for understanding the lives of our students and the complex social dynamics that inform their understandings of themselves. By telling and retelling my story, I better understood how experiences of heteronormativity shaped my identity. By employing a critical lens, I questioned taken-for-granted assumptions about sexual orientation and gender identity.

Queer theory provides me with the tools to understand the oppressive forces of masculinity and heterosexuality. Writing about the tensions I experienced as a gay male helps me appreciate the complexities and tensions of marginalization. As a gay man, I am both a beneficiary and a victim of a society that privileges maleness. In developing my teen identity while hiding my self-loathing, I was quick to divide my world into *us* and *them* (Monette, 1992) in order to feel more confident. This made me no better than the athletic students I disdained. Looking back with a critical lens, I am reminded of the importance of avoiding labels that privilege one group at the expense of others; community can only be built on the basis of respect for all individual and group identities (Milner, 2004) and minority groups are not well served by engaging in stereotyping or labelling the majority.

At Play

A life history, according to Tierney (2000), serves as a portal through which readers can "understand a culture different than their own" (p. 545), as well as a process for understanding "the semiotic means by which someone else makes sense of the world (p. 545). By artfully constructing a narrative of experience, I both heighten my own awareness of self and offer a text to help others understand from within what it is like to grapple with sexual and gender identity in a heteronormative world. The particulars of personal experience, such as my grappling with multiple identities and layers of privilege, add depth and texture to the rendering of a challenging topic. The combination of autobiography and queer theory can both help straight educators better understand themselves and better serve the queer people in their midst. As gender and sexuality are often constituted through the reiteration of norms, most people give little thought to how they are historically and socially inscribed through language and cultural practices (Butler, 1990). Reading about the experiences of sexual minorities can help one understand how heteronormativity pervades our world and, in particular, how it creates discomfort for those it excludes. Also, as Evans (2002) observes, educators have an obligation to make queer students and teachers feel welcome and safe in their midst.

Inquiring into one's own experiences with a queer lens has the potential to render visible tacitly held assumptions that guide how one lives life and practices as an educator.

CONCLUSION

"Experience is limited by all the causes which interfere with perception of the relations between undergoing and doing," according to John Dewey (1934/2005, p. 46). Good theory, by dispelling interference, helps us better understand experience. Queer theorists highlight the distorting effects of homophobia, heterosexual privilege and heteronormativity. Although the esoteric and exclusive nature of some queer theory interferes with perception, this should not diminish the many insights one can gain by applying a queer theory lens to the fields of education and teacher education.

While writing this chapter, I was also coding and analyzing survey and interview data for a research project on gay straight alliances in schools (Kitchen & Bellini, 2013). The teacher-participants in the study often drew attention to the ways in which school cultures privilege heterosexuality and, as a result, create a school climate that can be less welcoming to sexual minority students. Queer theorists, particularly those who have applied theory to bullying and school climate, helped me to understand the sexual and gender dynamics at play in schools (Meyer, 2012; Short, 2013). Applying the lens of queer theory reminds me again and again of the pervasiveness of heteronormativity both in the schools studied and in my own context as a professor.

In this chapter, I have drawn on my experiences as an educator and teacher educator to demonstrate that queering the gaze can help teacher educators think in new ways about their identities and practices. Queer theory offers a forceful critique of heteronormativity, heterosexual privilege, and homophobia. It highlights the fluidity of gender identity and sexual orientation, while offering a subversive and transgressive slant on what is perceived as normal. While queer theory is only one lens through which to view education, it does illuminate areas of self and practice that are often overlooked as we go about our daily lives. As the opening story illustrates and subsequent examples reinforced, reflection on and analysis of heteronormativity and heterosexual privilege can sharpen our perceptions of ourselves and our contexts as educators. Enhanced perception can lead to more educative experiences for our students and contribute to the development of social justice for all.

NOTE

[1] Similarly, I acknowledge the tensions prompted by the contested language of gender and sexual identity. I generally use *gay* to describe my life and *queer* to convey my intellectual positioning and sense of belonging to a larger LGBT community. I sometimes add 'Q' and/or other letters to LGBT to acknowledge additional layers of complexity, but have opted for the simpler formulation here. Although I occasionally use 'sexual minorities' as a synonym, I recognize that it has its own nuances and limitations.

REFERENCES

Adams, T. E., & Holman-Jones, S. (2008). Autobiography is queer. In N. K. Denzin, Y. S. Lincoln, & L. T. Smith (Eds.), *Handbook of critical and indigenous methodologies* (pp. 373–390). Thousand Oaks, CA: Sage.

Adams, T. E., & Holman-Jones, S. (2011). Telling stories: Reflexivity, queer theory and autoethnography. *Cultural Studies Critical Methodologies, 11*(2), 108–116.

Alexander, B. K. (2008). Queer(y)ing the postcolonial through the west(ern). In N. K. Denzin, Y. S. Lincoln, & L. T. Smith (Eds.), *Handbook of critical and indigenous methodologies* (pp. 101–134). Thousand Oaks, CA: Sage.

Anzaldua, G. (1987). *Borderlands/la frontera: The new mestiza.* San Francisco, CA: Spinsters/Aunt Lute.

Bellini, C. (2012). The pink lesson plan: Addressing the emotional needs of gay and lesbian students in teacher education. *Journal of LGBT Youth, 9*(4).

Berry, A. (2007). *Tensions in teaching about teaching: Understanding practice as a teacher educator.* Dordrecht, The Netherlands: Springer.

Brayboy, B. M. J. (2005). Toward a tribal critical race theory in education. *The Urban Review, 37*(5), 425–446.

Britzman, D. (1995). Is there a queer pedagogy: Or stop reading straight. *Educational Theory, 45*(2), 151–165.

Bronski, M. (2011). *A queer history of the United States.* Boston, MA: Beacon.

Butler (1990). *Gender trouble: Feminism and the subversion of identity.* New York, NY: Routledge.

Chinn, S. (1994). Queering the profession, or just professionalizing queers? In L. Garber (Ed.), *Tilting the tower: Lesbians teaching queer subjects* (pp. 243–250). New York, NY: Routledge.

Clandinin, D. J., & Connelly, F. M. (2000). *Narrative inquiry: Experience and story in qualitative research.* San Francisco, CA: Jossey-Bass.

Coia, L., & Taylor, M. (2009). Co/autoethnography: Exploring our teaching selves collaboratively. In D. L. Tidwell, M. L. Heston, & L. M. Fitzgerald (Eds.), *Research methods for the self-study of practice* (pp. 3–16). Dordrecht, The Netherlands: Springer.

Conley, M. D., & Colabucci, L. (2009). Researchers who surf: Riding the waves of analysis in self-study research. *Mid-Western Educational Researcher, 22*(4), 26–35.

Connelly, F. M., & Clandinin, D. J. (1988). *Teachers as curriculum planners: Narratives of experience.* New York, NY: Teachers College Press.

Connelly, F. M., & Clandinin, D. J. (2000). Teacher education—A question of teacher knowledge. In A. Scott & J. Freeman-Moir (Eds.), *Tomorrow's teachers: International and critical perspectives on teacher education* (pp. 89–105). Christ Church, New Zealand: Canterbury Press.

Dewey, J. (1938). *Experience and education.* New York, NY: Collier Books.

Dewey, J. (1934/2005). Art as experience. New York, NY: Perigree.

Doll, M. A. (1998). *Queering the gaze.* In W. F. Pinar (Ed.), *Queer theory in education* (pp. 287–299). Mahwah, NJ: Lawrence Erlbaum.

Evans, K. (2002). *Negotiating the self: Identity, sexuality, and emotion in learning to teach.* New York, NY: RoutledgeFalmer.

Gamson, J. (1998). Must identity movements self-destruct? A queer dilemma. In P. M. Nardi & B. E. Schneider (Eds.), *Social perspective in lesbian and gay studies* (pp. 589–604). New York, NY: Routledge.

Halberstam, J. (2005). Shame and white gay masculinity. *Social Text, 23*(3–4), 219–233.

Halperin, D. (2012). *How to be gay.* Cambridge, MA: Belknap Press.

Kitchen, J. (1995). *Lost between the lines: A personal search for identity.* (Unpublished graduate course paper). University of Toronto, Toronto, Canada.

Kitchen, J. (2009). Passages: Improving teacher education through narrative self-study. In D. L. Tidwell, M. L. Heston, & L. M. Fitzgerald, (Eds.), *Research methods for the self-study of practice* (pp. 35–51). Dordrecht, The Netherlands: Springer.

Kitchen, J., & Bellini, C. (2012). Making it better for lesbian, gay, bisexual and transgender students through teacher education: A collaborative self-study. *Studying Teacher Education, 8*(3), 209–225.

Kitchen, J., & Bellini, C. (2013). Making schools safe and inclusive: Gay-straight alliances and school climate in Ontario. *Canadian Journal of Educational Administration and Policy, 19*(146).

Kitchen, J., Cherubini, L., Trudeau, L., & Hodson, J. M. (2009). Aboriginal education as cultural brokerage: New aboriginal teachers reflect on language and culture in the classroom. *McGill Journal of Education, 44*(3), 355–375. Retrieved from http://mje.mcgill.ca

Kitchen, J., Hodson, J., & Cherubini, L. (2011). Developing capacity in Indigenous education: Attending to the voices of Aboriginal teachers. *Action in Teacher Education, 33*, 615–627.

Kumashiro, K. (2002). *Troubling education: Queer activism and antioppressive pedagogy.* New York, NY: Routledge.

Ladson-Billings, G. (1998). Just what is critical race theory and what's it doing in a nice field like education? *International Journal of Qualitative Studies in Education, 11*(1), 7–24.

Lee, Y. A. (2011). Self-study of cross-cultural supervision of teacher candidates for social justice. *Studying Teacher Education, 7*(1), 3–19.

Leibowitz, H. (1989). *Fabricating lives: Explorations in American autobiography.* New York, NY: Alfred

A. Knopf.

Luhmann, S. (1998). Queering/querying pedagogy? Or, pedagogy is a pretty queer thing. In W. F. Pinar (Ed.), *Queer theory in education* (pp. 141–156). Mahwah, NJ: Lawrence Erlbaum.

Manke, M. (2005). A queer path across straight furrows: A series of reflections. In C. Mitchell, S. Weber and K. O'Reilly-Scanlon (Eds.), *Just who do you think you are? Methodologies for autobiography and self-study in teaching* (pp. 193–205). London, UK: RoutledgeFalmer.

Meyer, E. J. (2012). From here to queer: Mapping sexualities in education. In E. R. Meiners & T. Quinn (Eds.), *Sexualities in Education: A Reader* (pp. 9–17). New York, NY: Peter Lang.

Miller, J. L. (1998). Autobiography as a queer curriculum practice. In W. F. Pinar (Ed.), *Queer theory in education* (pp. 365–374). Mahwah, NJ: Lawrence Erlbaum.

Milner, M. Jr. (2004). *Freaks, geeks and cool kids: American teenagers, schools and the culture of consumption.* New York, NY: Routledge.

Monette, P. (1992). *Becoming a man: Half a life story.* San Francisco, CA: Harper.

Morris, M. (1998). Unresting the curriculum: Queer projects, queer imaginings. In W. F. Pinar (Ed.), *Queer theory in education* (pp. 275–286). Mahwah, NJ: Lawrence Erlbaum.

Olesen, V. L. (2000). Feminism and qualitative research at and into the millennium. In N. K. Denzin & Y. S. Lincoln (Eds.), *Handbook of qualitative research* (2nd ed., pp. 215–255). Thousand Oaks, CA: Sage.

Pinar, W. F. (1998). Introduction. In W. F. Pinar (Ed.), *Queer theory in education* (pp. 1–48). Mahwah, NJ: Lawrence Erlbaum.

Pinar, W. F. (2007). A queer conversation, toward sustainability. In N. M. Rodriguez & W. F. Pinar, *Queering straight teachers: Discourse and identity in education* (p. 12). New York, NY: Peter Lang.

Pinnegar, S., & Hamilton, M. L. (2009). *Self-study of practice as a genre of qualitative research: Theory, methodology and practice.* Dordrecht, The Netherland: Springer.

Proust, M. ([1913]1981). *In search of lost time.* London, UK: Chatto and Windus.

Quinn, T., & Meiners, E. R. (2011). Teacher education, struggles for social justice, and the historic erasure of lesbian, gay, bisexual, transgender and queer lives. In A. F. Ball & C. A. Tyson (Eds.), *Studying diversity in teacher education* (pp. 135–151). Lanham, MD: Rowman & Littlefield.

Russo, V. (1981). *The celluloid closet: Homosexuality in the movies.* New York, NY: Harper and Row.

Samaris, A. P., Hicks, M. A., & Garvey Berger, J. (2004). Self-study through personal history. In J. Loughran, M. L. Hamilton, V. LaBoskey, & T. Russell (Eds.), *International handbook of self-study of teaching and teacher education practices* (pp. 905–942). Dodrecht: Kluwer.

Schön, D. A. (1987). *Educating the reflective practitioner.* San Francisco, CA: Jossey-Bass.

Sedgwick, E. K. (1993). *Tendencies.* Durham, NC: Duke University Press.

Short, D. (2013). *That's so gay! Queers, bullying and making schools safe.* Vancouver, Canada: University of British Columbia Press.

Tierney, W. G. (2000). Undaunted courage: Life history and the postmodern challenge. In N. K. Denzin & Y. S. Lincoln (Eds.), *Handbook of qualitative research* (2nd ed., pp. 537–554). Thousand Oaks, CA: Sage.

Tierney, W. G. & Dilley, P. (1998). Constructing knowledge: Educational research and gay and lesbian studies. In W. F. Pinar (Ed.), *Queer theory in education* (pp. 49–72). Mahwah, NJ: Lawrence Erlbaum.

Tripp, D. (1993). *Critical incidents in teaching: Developing professional judgement.* London, UK: RoutledgeFalmer.

AFFILIATIONS

Julian Kitchen

Faculty of Education,

Brock University,

Hamilton, Ontario, Canada

ADRIAN D. MARTIN

FROM ADAM AND EVE TO DICK AND JANE: A LITERARY NOMADIC INQUIRY ON GENDER AND SEXUALITY IN TEACHING AND TEACHER EDUCATION

As institutions reflective of the larger social discourse, schools are prime sites for the reinforcement and perpetuation of the status quo with regard to gender and sexuality. It is incumbent upon teachers and teacher educators to consider how their beliefs about gender and sexuality influence pedagogy and construct limits for the education of students. In response, they need opportunities to develop counter practices for their schools and classrooms. Do we allow our male students the opportunity to express emotion? Do we hold the same expectations for girls in our classrooms as we do for boys? Are men encouraged to become early childhood educators? Are women encouraged to become educational leaders? Do we assume all of our students are heterosexual?

In this chapter I aim to hold a microscope to my own understanding and knowledge of self as a teacher and to gender and sexuality in public education. More specifically, I aim to deconstruct a mythological narrative in relation to narratives of my practice to examine consequences for conforming or not conforming to gender norms. As an educator I am responsible for the academic development and learning experiences of my students irrespective of race, class, or gender. However, while issues pertaining to social class and racial difference have become the focus in many teacher preparation programs (Cochran-Smith et al., 2009; Villegas & Lucas, 2002) and part of some public schools' curriculum (Johnson, 2003), scant attention is paid to gender (Galman & Mallozzi, 2012). It should therefore come as no surprise that although my own academic background and professional development have focused on culturally and linguistically responsive teaching, examinations of gender and sexuality have been noticeably absent.

Straut and Sapon-Shevin (2002) suggest that lack of attention to gender and sexuality in education is undergirded by four assumptions. First is the fallacy that all students identify as either men or women and as heterosexual. Second is the hegemonic norm privileging heterosexuality and its pervasive, tacit influence. Third are the potential political, social and professional sanctions from engaging in teaching practices or enacting a curriculum that counters this norm. Fourth is the lack of space in K-12 schools or preservice teacher education to incorporate attention to curricular activities that focus on these issues. Although there are some recent

M. Taylor and L. Coia (Eds.), Gender, Feminism, and Queer Theory in the Self-Study of Teacher Education Practices, 143–156.

initiatives to support the inclusion of all students in the school community (e.g., the Gay, Lesbian, & Straight Educator's Network 2011 policy statement on transgender and gender nonconforming students), gay, lesbian, queer and gender nonconforming youth continue to experience marginalization in institutions of education (Lambda Legal Defense, 2011; Robinson & Espelage, 2012; Society for Public Health, 2012). It is apparent that educators are in dire need of opportunities for reflection on the assumptions identified by Straut and Sapon-Shevin (2002). Such reflection could potentially serve as a first step towards moving such students from the margins towards the construction of an inclusive school climate.

In contrast, non-inclusive school climates support the traditional gender binary and its corollary assumption of heteronormativity (heterosexuality as the natural and privileged form of sexual expression) (Sullivan, 2003), constraining the human capacity for a subjectivity beyond the sex, gender, and sexual orientation triad. These constructs place limits on the expression of masculinity and femininity. Therefore, the denotative and connotative definition of male and female become fixed and mutually exclusive. Like pieces on a chessboard, each gender can only "be" and "exist" within particular boundaries. Hence, identities, experiences, feelings, and expressions embodied by men and women are not self-selected or decided, but ascribed to them through social discourse, culture, and religion (Sarup, 1993).

Self-study provides an opportunity for teachers and teacher educators to examine and reflect upon their teaching and interactions with students in relation to gender and sexuality as well as to enhance knowledge of their praxis (Loughran, 2004; Taylor & Coia, 2009). While I turned the analytic lens inward to examine myself, I also opted to extend beyond reflections on my own professional history towards the realm of the literary. In doing so I aim to link the normative views and discourses on gender and sexuality across mythological foundations and reflections on my own narratives. This method assisted me in linking critical incidents from my own teaching with theory and myth to problematize gender and sexuality in education.

To explore these themes through self-study, I have chosen to experiment with a methodology I have termed literary nomadic inquiry. The nomad represents movements from striated space to smooth space (Deleuze & Guattari, 1987). Deleuze and Guattari suggest that striated spaces are identities, conditions, or settings where motions or movements are subject to pre-existing patterns of migration. They write, "…it can be said that space is susceptible to two kinds of breaks: one is defined by a standard, whereas the other is irregular and undetermined, and can be made wherever one wishes to place it" (Deleuze & Guattari, 1987, p. 477). This "other", open-ended field of operationalization potent with unregulated potentialities (all that is capable of being but not yet in existence) is the smooth space. Therefore, smooth space, whether physical, emotional, psychological, or social, is receptive to the unexpected, the atypical, the unusual, and all that deviates from the norm. Conceptually, gender non-conformity and non-heteronormative sexualities are smooth spaces that counter the status quo male-female gender binary and heterosexual paradigm.

144

My construction of literary nomadic inquiry, an extension of St. Pierre's (2000) conceptualization of nomadic inquiry, provided a smooth space to work rhizomatically, connecting literary, academic, and personal accounts in contrast to the binary division between personal and professional. Such a research endeavor, "…is not motivated by the desire to produce knowledge for knowledge's sake…" (p. 259). Rather, a literary nomadic inquiry is a non-linear, a-temporal bouquet of texts, anecdotes, research, and observations that melds theory with experience and literature. This approach was particularly useful towards making connections between my own experiences (the micro) with the myth and theoretical constructs employed (the macro).

Working with the methodology of literary nomadic inquiry, I contemplated how gender issues related to my teaching practice. Specifically, I wanted to explore how gender conformity or deviance surfaced in the classroom and the school environment. I journaled throughout one academic semester. These entries were not only accounts of daily experiences with students and colleagues, but also dipped into the well of my memory of past teaching experiences. I journaled about being the only male member of a teaching staff. I wrote about learning to teach students whose behavior in class was not conducive towards learning, and how gender differences influenced my views of such students and hence my teaching approach. I wrote about being a gay man teaching elementary school, and how such a revelation was interpreted by parents, colleagues, and school administrators. Ultimately, these reflections focused on understanding myself in the classroom, my positionality in relation to my students, and my teaching.

Throughout the journaling I consciously sought to connect my teaching experiences with theory. Each time I returned to the text I wore different theoretical spectacles, but found that my preferred reading glasses were post-structural and informed by queer theory. The former permits me to see the construction of what is currently considered normal and natural, while the latter applies such critiques to gender and sexuality. Therefore, post-structuralism served as the theoretical starting point when examining the entries. Employing this lens I recognized how particular practices or experiences are framed by larger social norms (e.g., the gendering of student learning centers, such as the housekeeping center for girls or the block area for boys). I then moved towards queer theory to specifically identify emergent themes in my practice in relation to gender and implications for teachers and teacher education.

Queer theory reflects the Deleuzo-Guattarian concept of smooth space. Its critical deconstruction of gender and sexuality serve as an analytic tool that can highlight the extent to which heteronormativity saturates human thought and experience. By shedding light on the performative construction of gender and sexuality, queer theory deconstructs prior definitions of masculinity and femininity, gay and straight, and seeks an understanding of self beyond essentialist identity labels (Sullivan, 2003). Using both post-structuralism and queer theory was conceptually liberating as I was able to branch beyond the confines of one theory towards the other.

Looking through these frames, I assumed the role of the nomad, the Deleuzo-Guattarian metaphorical figure that encapsulates resistance to norms and assumptions that prohibits questioning and investigation.

At the end of the academic semester, I (the nomad) read over the journal entries. I examined the texts to determine which entries or narratives reflected or commented on the assumptions previously suggested by Straut and Sapon-Shevin (2002). In considering which would be best suited for further analysis and investigation, I selected two that reflect heteronormative/sexist norms within the classroom and within the school community. To amplify these norms I used the theoretical concept of the Body without Organs from post-structuralists Deleuze and Guattari, and queer theorist Butler's notion of gender as performative. I elected to include the story of the fall of "man" from the book of Genesis. I selected this story due to the privileged status of Christianity in Western society. The Adam and Eve myth, or symbolic story "…describing how the universe and its inhabitants came to be" (Womack, 2005, p. 81), highlights how pervasive and deeply rooted heteronormative/sexist views are, a potential manifestation of the collective unconscious (Jung, 1990). Lastly, I engaged reflectively with these narratives and texts to discern an understanding of myself and possible implications for my teaching.

The narratives, theories and analytic reflections in this chapter are interwoven (differentiated by a roman or italic font). Engaging in this work, *you become* the nomad, reading this intellectual expedition that veers away from the rigidity of traditional qualitative research (striated space) into/through an atypically constructed (smooth space) chapter. My intent is that you reflect on the construction of gender and sexuality in education and possible implications for educators.

As researchers and teacher educators, we can choose to march within striated space, or dance unabashedly upon smooth space, embracing the nomad. To continue to march can be likened to supporting traditional fixed notions of male and female, enamored with the gender fallacy, a product of discursive progressions (Butler, 1990; Halberstam, 2012). This march represents a sole reliance on research practices considered standardized or valid without consideration for experimental or emergent approaches, thereby furthering the discourse on what counts as legitimate and relegating all other investigations that do not conform to such a paradigm as problematic.

Consequently, it is not enough for methodology to mirror the research question. Methodology must be expansive enough to include the unexpected and the irreconcilable. As teachers and teacher educators, I invite you to embrace a paradigm outside of binaries. Self-study is one approach. I offer you these spectacles to place upon your face, and gaze not only outward, but inward as well. Queer as they might be, the lenses may help you to understand your students, your praxis, and yourself through a spectrum of colors.

PANTS, PENMANSHIP AND PARTY DRESSES

In *Gender Trouble* (1990), a foundational text in queer studies, Butler proposes that the social construction of gender is performative. Namely, the enactment of gender does not solely define the individual, but the collective enactment of gender (specifically the gender binary) affects social discourse. The result is the gradual construction, production and reproduction of embodied norms for men and women. This binary excludes non-gender conforming and intersex individuals (Wilchins, 2004).

When I think about first year teachers, I usually think of them as working in "survival mode." They arrive at their schools each morning and commence another day learning the "professional ropes": how to attend to students, work with parents, plan instruction, and cover the curriculum. These most likely form the core of their chief concerns. I know they were for me. I began my teaching career with a bilingual first grade class in an urban school district. My classroom was housed in a 100 year old building. The aging room was filled with wooden desks, blackboards covered the walls, and towering glass windows let light in while chalk dust clung to the air. I had about 30 students of various Latin American nationalities who spoke English with different degrees of proficiency. With the impassioned convictions of a beginning teacher, I felt it my duty to teach them, guide them, instill a sense of pride in who they are, and have them achieve academic success. At this novice phase in my career, issues of gender and sexuality in education were not at the forefront of my mind. Yet, at a certain point within that first year, a small experience would serve as a catalyst for what would later become an area of academic exploration.

I do not recall the exact date. The child may very well have transferred to the school and entered my classroom a few months into the school year. Among the students, this child was distinguished by a profound silence and quiet stillness unusual for a first grader. Genesis always wore jeans, had hair cut short and wrote with an impeccable penmanship. Today, years later, I remember that Genesis had difficulty with her speech. This may have been the source for such a quiet demeanor.

Now whether it was the first week of school or whether it was one of Genesis' first days in my classroom does not matter much. The students stood in the hallway waiting to use the bathrooms. There were two lines of boys and girls intermixed. I stood before them, watching students as they entered and exited the bathrooms, walking from the front of the lines and eventually rejoining at the back. Soon, Genesis was at the front.

"OK, you can go," I said.
Genesis began to walk towards the girl's room.
Without a moment to think, I stated, "Um, no. That's not where you..."

I stopped my sentence midway. The child looked at me. She looked up at me. While what was said is not clear to me now, I do recall the look on the child's face as she stared into my eyes. In that instance devoid of words there was an explicit understanding between a seven year old girl and her twenty three year old male teacher that an error in assumption had been made.

"I'm sorry, go ahead."
She continued her walk to the bathroom.

Butler argues that the performative nature of gender is intimately tied to biological sex. The pronouncement at birth, "It's a boy" or "It's a girl" each carries with it a series of assumptions, beliefs and expectations for the new born. The gendering process begins immediately, starting with the name. The child is repeatedly identified by gender throughout the toddler years.

"What a good girl you are!"
"My! You are such a big boy!"

Genesis was a girl. By all appearances one would have guessed that she was a boy. I felt embarrassed at my mistake. But my embarrassment was overshadowed by my concern as to how my assumption that she was a boy could possibly influence/affect her. At her seven years of age Genesis unlikely recognized the gender deviance that she displayed. Certainly a parent or older sibling dressed her for school. Perhaps she had older brothers who provided hand me downs. As a child from a family of immigrants who lived in the poorest section of town she likely lived at the poverty line. Maybe wearing jeans and having short hair were of secondary importance if her family was struggling for food and rent money.

Clothing serves to aid in the gendering process, as well as the assumed identification with a parent or role model of the same gender who will serve as a "gender representative" for the child to gender assimilate. As children grow older, the boundary between male and female widens, and by adolescence it is assumed (and heteronormatively desired) that the child has embraced his or her respective gender and will continue a lifelong enactment of that role in society.

Heterosexuality becomes an assumed added layer, the next progression in this link between biological sex and gender. Butler suggests that this discursive regime is cyclical. However, the "trouble" begins in the mismatch, when one's sex does not match one's gender or sexual preference.

It was my mistaken assumption (a product of a lifetime of heteronormative gender ideology), not my students. I have no recollections of any child picking on her, laughing at her or saying, "Genesis is a boy!" The only one in that classroom at that time with a "fixed" sense of what boys and girls looked like was me. Reflecting on subsequent academic years, I recall other students who had also been in such "trouble." I recall the differential treatment some experienced from their peers. As a teacher, I struggled seeing students who were marginalized in the classroom community for their differences. As a gay man, I grappled with recollections of my own schooling experiences and moments of having felt "othered," different, or an outsider. Additionally I recall the absence, the void of thought or consideration in school and in professional organizations to advocate for them (or for me). Collectively, it seems we would prefer to believe that these expressions are a "stage" and turn a blind eye.

Later that year, the school community held a celebration for Cinco de Mayo. Genesis attended and wore a party dress. She had shiny white shoes, her dress was covered in laces and frills, her short hair combed back with a large red, green, and white bow and she held a tiny purse with satin ribbons in her hand. She smiled when she entered the classroom that day. I remember hearing her laugh. Genesis seemed to be thoroughly enjoying her attire and feeling good about how she looked. But what did it mean to perceive someone as one sex when in fact he or she is the other... or neither...or both?

THE BEGINNING, THE BODY WITHOUT ORGANS, AND EDUCATION

Written over 2000 years ago, the book of Genesis offers the contemporary reader a mythological account of the foundations of universal existence. The first book of the Bible commences with God's construction of the entire universe and details the creation of the first man and woman. According to the text, the progenitors of the human species, Adam and Eve, lived in divine, ignorant bliss in the paradise known as Eden.

Deleuze and Guattari present the concept of the Body without Organs (BwO) in *A Thousand Plateaus* (1987). The BwO exists in and beyond the field of the present or the physical, enveloped in an a-temporal reality situated between our sensory perceptions and fantasy. It is not a thing but a set of practices, a field we find space in, open up toward, and can lean into. As they write, "It is nonstratified, unformed, intense matter, the matrix of intensity, intensity = 0; but there is nothing negative about that zero, there are no negative or opposite intensities" (Deleuze & Guattari, 1987, p. 153).

For Adam and Eve, the bounty of the earth was theirs to enjoy and the only condition for this eternal elixir of delights was abstinence from the Forbidden Fruit of the Tree of Knowledge. God said to Adam, "Of every tree of the garden thou mayest freely eat: But of the tree of the knowledge of good and evil, thou shalt not eat of it: for in the day that thou eatest thereof thou shalt surely die" (Genesis 2: 16-17, King James Version).

Eve (to whom God had not given this directive), described as vain and narcissistic with an insatiable desire to know (Walker, 1988), encountered a serpent in Eden. As Genesis maintains, the serpent (whom traditional Christian interpretations associate with the Devil, in binary opposition to God) used his cunning to convince Eve that the Forbidden Fruit prohibition denied her God-like status, and urged her to eat of the fruit so that her eyes "...shall be opened, and ye shall be as gods, knowing good and evil" (Genesis 3:5). Eve did take it. Having plucked the apple off the branch, she held it before her lips and inhaled the sweetly intoxicating scent and felt the blazingly red taut skin tear between her teeth. She ate, consumed the bittersweet flesh and felt the electric spark of power and knowledge course through her body, mind, and spirit. She shared this ecstasy with her husband. As Genesis continues, the first couple realized their nudity and covered themselves with fig leaves and vines, hiding those parts of their anatomy that had now become both sources of pleasure and shame.

Beyond our sex and desires, we are the BwO. We are this unfurled mass of intensity situated beyond our subjectivities (the organs) that serve to define our purpose, or place, and our function. The human body is composed of various systems, organs working with one another to produce "life." Meaning and function are ascribed to the heart, the liver, and the brain. We construct explanations for the workings of the body and believe that we "know" or "understand" the inherent nature of all of our parts.

Socially, such stratifications are extended in relation to gender and sexuality. Gender is defined through the perceived binary of the sexes. At this starting and terminal point, the BwO is evaded and a constructed self (a human) is produced. The parts covered by Adam and Eve became infused with sexual meaning and the construction of humanity locked the BwO in Pandora's box, holding all potentialities, epistemologies, and ontologies outside of humanity as sinful. Across (and within) time, the discourse on gender arises, systems of patriarchy spiral outward, and an inherent nature is imposed upon the penis and the vagina. Their meaning extends beyond what lay beneath the fig leaves of Adam and Eve, towards fixed, stable, and coherent notions of masculinity and femininity culminating in the socially sanctioned heterosexual paradigm of today (Bravmann, 1996).

Now God, believed to see and know all, arrived at the garden and found his creations clothed and with "their eyes open." They attempted to hide from him, and when Adam was interrogated by the divine architect, he readily pointed the finger at his spouse, and blamed Eve, the woman, for transgressing God's divine law. Adam said, "The woman whom thou gavest to be with me, she gave me of the tree, and I did eat" (Genesis 3:12). In turn, Eve admitted to eating due to the enchantment of the serpent.

While Adam was punished to till and toil upon the earth (yet remain its master), Eve's sentence was that her husband, "...shall rule over" her (Genesis 3:16).

This Biblical story in Genesis suggests that the tacit, essentialist identities ascribed by God were realized by Adam and Eve upon eating the apple. The Garden of Eden (the BwO) was dismantled, and in its place perceptions of male and female arose along with the confining walls of language that hinder thought and prevent an outlet to the BwO. In my own teaching, the loss of the BwO has been felt through my own assumptions about my students as boys and girls, including how they look and who they might be as adults. I assumed boys would have short hair and girls long hair. I assumed that the girls would prefer dolls and the boys would prefer trucks. I assumed that the girls would likely become mothers whereas the boys would likely become breadwinners for their families.

Focusing on such considerations suggests that public education perpetuates the masking of the BwO. Teachers continue to call on "boys and girls." Administrators are still largely male with the predominantly female teaching force. Research suggests attention to gender in education has waned since the mid 1990s (Galman & Mallozzi, 2012). Sexuality continues to be a taboo issue in K-12 classrooms and teacher education. The striated spaces of the classroom, the principal's office and gymnasium turn a blind eye to the sexualities and genders that exist outside of male-female heterosexuality. Heteronormativity deems the queer teacher a perverse fiction, while the legend of the ever giving, forever forgiving, asexual, culturally devoid virgin/mother at the head of the classroom is heralded as the preferred natural, moral "truth" that students "need" (Weems, 1999). As an early childhood educator, this discourse has rendered me as the invisible, the unspeakable: a gay man who teaches children.

Heteronormativity/sexism is not a jinn that emerges into social discourse in the realm of adulthood. It is actively cultivated throughout our lives across time and space. It extends past our collective consciousness into the depths of the pre-historical, the mythical, towards the present day. In Western culture it begins with that first differentiation among newborns in the ways they are dressed and spoken to, wrapped in pink or blue, initiating a trajectory of lifetime events that the now-sexed infant will be assumed to experience. With such an understanding that the influence of heteronormativity begins from the moment of birth, is there not an ethical and moral responsibility to actively purge our world, our kindergartens of it?

Reflecting on my experiences with Genesis my student, and Genesis the text, it became evident to me that all educators need to be aware of the tacit and explicit forms of marginalization of individuals outside of the heteronormative matrix. As teacher educators, it is urgent that we explicitly and openly examine how such oppression has influenced the lives of our students and the potential manifestations of differential treatment along gender lines and the privileging of heterosexuality in our schools. The BwO is a theoretical tool, an outlook that we can apply and with which we can work. As theoretical spectacles, it invites us to see our teaching as contributing towards this massive social illusion, bringing forth the underpinning gender/sexual assumptions in our work. Although at the time I recognized my error regarding Genesis' gender, it was not until recently (by engaging with theory in this self-study) that I realized the larger societal constructions with which my mistake aligned and of which was a product. As a teacher, the BwO propels me to see my students as individuals with multiple subjectivities and not solely as gendered beings. This suggests that students can learn in a classroom environment where they are not defined or pinned down by a particular identity or gender. Students (and teachers) can bask in smooth space wherein they approach learning as an inquiry into the unknown rather than a journey towards the predetermined end point of womanhood for girls and manhood for boys.

ACCUSING EVE IN THE 21ST CENTURY

What does it mean to teach "boys and girls" instead of students? Why not look upon those who enter our classrooms as individuals rather than imposing gendered expectations? Would there be a difference/change in learning outcomes? If I affirm the sexed identities of my students, am I denying the falsity of gender in favor of an essential self? In this final narrative I retell an incident that occurred among staff members. The commentary from this meeting reflects the aforementioned spiralling discourse on gender, and how as teachers, we unknowingly re-inscribe the social gender norms.

Our grade level meetings usually take place at the end of the school day. On this particular occasion, the meeting was held in a kindergarten classroom. The students had been dismissed and the halls in the building were devoid of the usual chatter and movement of children and teachers. Each week we gathered to discuss curriculum, co-plan our lessons, and talk about our students and our work. I walked into the room with my teacher editions and sat at one of the tiny tables with tiny chairs. The classroom teacher, Ms. Reynolds, was cutting gingerbread men out of construction paper for a bulletin board. Ms. Holmes was grading spelling tests, and Ms. Hernandez was glancing through the pages of Rethinking Schools. On Ms. Reynolds' desk was a bright red apple, a token of affection from one of her students.

"Pablo gave that to me," Ms. Reynolds said. "He said he wasn't familiar with this custom till a friend told him. He said that teachers don't get apples in Mexico."

"No, they don't get apples in Mexico. They get respect," Ms. Hernandez replied.

We chuckled at the honest humor.

"It's not like this over there," Ms. Hernandez continued. "I'm telling you, the whole approach that people have towards teachers is totally different. Families respect what they do for their children. It's not like here." "Yeah, here we're the blame for everything," Ms. Holmes replied. "The market goes down, people can't find jobs, the economy starts going bad and it's all on our shoulders."

"I don't think it's all about families though," I said. "I think that it's more than just the families we work with. I think the whole media and so much of public rhetoric finds us to be the easy target to blame for everything wrong with the country." Ms. Reynolds replied, "Yes now, but some of these parents just don't know what they're doing with their children. Honestly, students these days are worse than they were when I started teaching. What are the parents doing? I had one child who said she stays up till one in the morning watching television. No wonder she's constantly falling asleep at school! I told the mother and she just looked at me disgruntled. She was angry at ME for mentioning that her daughter needs a full night's rest. I just don't get it."

"There you go, you said it. The mother. If she's not doing what she should with her children, then there is no way that what we do with them will work," Ms. Holmes said. "Truthfully, we know it all starts in the home."

As humans living in an era of neoliberalism, we continue to position ourselves as free agents with an innate, rational, human identity that seeks expression along "normalized" lines. Believing that one can exclude the "sexed" identity of another is to fall prey to such humanistic myths that we can exist outside the influence of social discourse. The myths of social discourse (from Adam and Eve to present day gender roles) can be unwound, exposed and deconstructed to recognize their social origins. Assuming such a stance, I can begin to acknowledge the performativity of gender in my classroom. However, poststructuralists might respond that to believe one can "escape" a particular discourse is to fall into another.

Although I was intrigued with the conversation, I saw Ms. Reynolds' jar of homemade chocolate chip cookies and couldn't help myself from getting out of my seat to get one. Thoughts of curriculum planning and the current state of public education were temporarily placed on the back burner as I opened the jar and bit into moist, sweet cookie dough with dark chocolate chips. I quickly had another.

"Careful there," said Ms. Holmes as she gathered her gingerbread men. "You know Sherri uses way too much sugar and butter in those."

"Well if you think they're so unhealthy, don't eat them!" said Ms. Reynolds with a chuckle. Ms. Holmes and Ms. Reynolds had been teaching together for over twenty years. Their warm camaraderie was reflected in their friendly jostling. But I really didn't care about Ms. Holmes' warning, and even though I knew the calories in the cookie would do me no favors, I couldn't help myself from removing the lid of the jar once more and having another taste of sinful indulgence.

"I think it's more than just what starts at home. It's way more than that. It has a lot to do with parenting," said Ms. Reynolds as she returned to the topic at hand. "Well we all know that," said Ms. Holmes.

Ms. Reynolds continued, "Yes, but there was a story on the news the other night. There was a study on middle age men, and the reporter discussed how many of these middle age men were facing the same types of issues in their lives, both medical and familial. The point of the segment was that researchers found that the men's problems all stemmed from prenatal issues. Issues during pregnancy and the mother's health were all related to what these men were experiencing and having trouble with, from divorce to illness to addiction issues. They used to think that everything wasn't predetermined, but this segment suggested that how the mother cares for her children is the overriding influence on everything."

"It all comes back to the egg," said Ms. Reynolds.

Peering through post-structural and queer spectacles, I have reflected on this dialogue among colleagues and the underlying suggested implication. The conversation demonstrates the reinforced narrative that women are to blame for the ills of society, emphasizing how this discourse stemming back from the Garden of Eden continues to permeate and infect our schools and society at large. A queer gaze further magnifies such a consideration. By applying Butler's theorization of performativity, this dialogue reveals the reproductive nature of such social discourse on gender. While this is made most explicitly clear when Ms. Reynolds suggests that the quality of prenatal care a woman provides for her unborn child is the deciding factor for a lifetime of failure or success (with the egg bearing sole responsibility), the finger Adam pointed at Eve continues to be pointed at her in the 21st century.

Yet, throughout this dialogue I remained virtually silent. What did it mean that I, as a teacher among my colleagues (and the only male), failed to disrupt this flow of ideas, or attempt to present a counter view? I can suggest that I was very young, had no knowledge of Deleuzo-Guattarian concepts such as the BwO or queer or post-structural insights. Yet, does ignorance of academic theorizations absolve me from countering a deficit view that I felt to be wrong?

While the analysis of this scenario through self-study caused me to reconsider this dialogue through my adopted theoretical spectacles and amplifies particular notions, I do not believe that such insight is required to recognize sexism. Although the veil of heteronormativity is slowly being recognized (and lifted) in our current time, the struggle for social equity between the sexes, the women's liberation movement, and the persistent battle for women's reproductive rights continue to be urgent and real issues. Therefore, even as one voice among many, I could have suggested that perhaps the egg is not solely responsible for social conditions. Adam too ate of the apple.

FROM ADAM AND EVE TO DICK AND JANE

This research experience has served as a means to examine and analyze my teaching and my being a member of the teaching community. It has helped to highlight how gender and sexual discourses permeate school as a hidden curriculum disseminated through both teaching practices and teacher talk. Employing theory as an analytic tool, I began to recognize the illusions of heteronormativity within the classroom and recognized its performative effects. I cannot deny the lived consequences of heteronormativity. My own assumption about Genesis and my silence in the second narrative serve as examples. But, I can begin to unravel dominant social constructions on gender through queer theory.

Reflecting on these themes has aided in my recognition that heteronormativity is an attempt to perpetuate essentialist identities based on the body parts the primordial couple covered in fig leaves and vines. The original binary of Adam and Eve, God and the devil (a myth!) are actualized in the reality of patriarchy, misogyny, homophobia and heteronormativity that pervade not only human existence, but the human interpretation of the world itself. While some bask in the rainbow of possibilities found in smooth spaces, unencumbered by rigid gender notions and expectations, others continue to believe that girls will be mothers and wives, and boys fathers and husbands. When they do not, such individuals ask, "What went wrong?"

Perhaps a post-structural queer lens would suggest that educators acknowledge the gendered social construction of their students while simultaneously attuning to the Body without Organs (BwO). Rather than a deconstructive approach (replacing a heteronormative outlook with an inclusive ontology), this lens articulates the fabricated boy/girl, man/woman divide and recognizes the open space, the affective realm wherein we connect, understand and know irrespective of Adam and Eve or Dick and Jane. The BwO means seeing all and seeing one. I must see my students and self as we believe ourselves to be, as society has constructed us, and as more than either of these. I must see the space beyond what has been socially ascribed as normal. I must tune into the emotional denial that my male students are expected to maintain. I must consciously enact a praxis that dismantles different assumptions for girls. I must work towards enacting a pedagogy that draws from the well of our collective experiences and surrenders the assumption that all within the classroom will be heterosexual and gender conforming.

This self-study has helped me make connections between my work, theory, and myth. Contemplating as a nomad, wearing these theoretical spectacles, I suggest that dialogue on gender and sexuality in education becomes an integral part of all teacher education programs. We can no longer assume or believe that all of our students conform to one of the two binary options when it comes to their gender/sex/sexual orientation. Although social discourse on men and women has continued from the past, the potential for change lies within reach in the present. Charged with professionally orienting individuals entering the teaching profession, teacher educators must prepare candidates who are critically conscious not only on issues of race and class, but of gender and sexuality as well.

As I move forward professionally and prepare for an upcoming school year, I find that this self-study has aided in my recognizing how vitally important it is to discuss gender and sexuality not only with students, but with educators as well. This self-study has highlighted how we as teachers perpetuate gender norms. As a result of this investigation, I feel that I must adopt teaching practices that are attentive to the representation of gender norms in curriculum and learning materials. In addition, I must take steps to actively promote dialogue that seeks to counter discursive gender assumptions and include a myriad of representational possibilities for all members of the school community. Working with young children, this might be reflected by attending to gender assumptions held by the students and facilitating a classroom conversation to examine what lies behind the assumptions. With members of the school community (including preservice teachers) it includes promotion of reflective practice on our own assumptions about gender, sexuality, our students, and ourselves. I urge us, as teachers and teacher educators, to realize that not all boys will grow up to be Adam, and not all girls will grow up to be Eve. Perhaps such a realization will aid us in moving further away from the current gender norms towards queer possibilities, inclusive and affirmative of all.

REFERENCES

Bravmann, S. (1996). Postmodernism and queer identities. In S. Seidman (Ed.), *Queer theory/sociology* (pp. 333–361). Cambridge, MA: Blackwell.

Butler, J. (1990). *Gender trouble: Feminism and the subversion of identity.* New York, NY: Routledge.

Cochran-Smith, M., Shakman, K., Jong, C., Terrell, D., Barnatt, J., & McQuillan, P. (2009). Good and just teaching: The case for social justice in teacher education. *American Journal of Education, 115*(3), 347–377.

Deleuze, G., & Guattari, F. (1987). *A thousand plateaus: Capitalism and schizophrenia.* Minneapolis, MN: University of Minnesota Press.

Galman, S. C., & Mallozzi, C. A. (2012). She's not there: Women and gender as disappearing foci in U.S research on the elementary school teacher, 1995-present. *Review of Educational Research, 82*(3), 243–295.

Gay, Lesbian and Straight Educator Network. (2011). Model district policy on transgender and gender nonconforming students: Model language, commentary, and resources. *GLSEN*. Retrieved August 28, 2013, from http://glsen.org/modeltranspolicy

Halberstam, J. J. (2012). *Gaga feminism*. Boston, MA: Beacon Press.

Holy Bible: King James Version. (2002). Grand Rapids, MI: Zondervan.

Johnson, L. (2003). Multicultural policy as social activism: Redefining who "counts" in multicultural education. *Race Ethnicity and Education, 6*(2), 107–121.

Jung, C. G. (1990). *The archetypes and the collective unconscious,* R. F. C. Hull (Trans.). London, UK: Routledge.

Lambda Legal. (2012). *Facts: Gay and lesbian youth in schools. Lambda Legal*. Retrieved August 28, 2013, from http://data.lambdalegal.org/pdf/158.pdf

Loughran, J. J. (2004). A history and context of self-study of teaching and teacher education practices. In J. J. Loughran, M. L. Hamilton, V. K. LaBoskey, & T. L. Russell (Eds.), *International handbook of self-study of teaching and teacher education practices* (pp. 7–39). Dordrecht, The Netherlands: Kluwer Academic.

Robinson, J. P., & Espelage, D. L. (2012). Bullying explains only part of LGBTQ- heterosexual risk disparities: Implications for policy and practice. *Educational Researcher, 40*(8), 309–319.

Sarup, M. (1993). *An introductory guide to post-structuralism and postmodernism* (2nd ed.). Athens, GA: University of Georgia Press.

Society for Public Health Education. (2012). Lesbian, gay, bisexual and transgender youth: Embracing diversity and promoting Inclusion. *Sophe*. Retrieved August 28, 2013, from http://www.sophe.org/Sophe/PDF/LGBT_Youth.pdf

St. Pierre, E. A. (2000). Nomadic inquiry in the smooth spaces of the field: A preface. In E. A. St. Pierre & W. S. Pillow (Eds.), *Working the ruins: Feminist poststructural theory and methods in education* (pp. 258–283). New York, NY: Routledge.

Straut, D., & Sapon-Shevin, M. (2002). "But no one in the class is gay": Countering invisibility and creating allies in teacher education programs. In R. M. Kissen (Ed.), *Getting ready for Benjamin: Preparing teachers for sexual diversity in the classroom* (pp. 19–31). Lanham, MD: Rowman & Littlefield.

Sullivan, N. (2003). *A critical introduction to queer theory*. New York, NY: New York University Press.

Taylor, M., & Coia, L. (2009). Co/autoethnography: Investigating teachers in relation. In C. A. Lassonde, S. C. Galman, & C. M. Kosnik (Eds.), *Self-study research methodologies for teacher educators* (pp. 169–186). Rotterdam, The Netherlands: Sense.

Villegas, A. M., & Lucas, T. (2002). *Educating culturally responsive teachers: A coherent approach*. Albany, NY: State University of New York Press.

Walker, J. M. (1988). *Milton and the idea of woman*. Urbana, IL: University of Illinois Press.

Weems, L. (1999). Pestalozzi, perversity, and the pedagogy of love. In W. J. Letts & J. T. Sears (Eds.), *Queering elementary education: Advancing the dialogue about sexualities and schooling* (pp. 27–48). Lanham, MD: Rowman & Littlefield.

Wilchins, R. A. (2004). *Queer theory, gender theory: An instant primer*. Los Angeles, CA: Alyson Books.

Womack, M. (2005). *Symbols and meaning: A concise introduction*. Lanham, MD: AltaMira.

AFFILIATIONS

Adrian Martin

Teacher Education and Teacher Development,

Montclair State University,

Montclair, New Jersey

LESLEY COIA & MONICA TAYLOR

A CO/AUTOETHNOGRAPHY OF FEMINIST TEACHING: NOMADIC JAMMING INTO THE UNPREDICTABLE

"LISTENING FOR THE SECRET, SEARCHING FOR THE SOUND…"
(PETERSON & LESH, 1974)

Lesley: I have all the data now, Monica. The course is over, the videos complete, my notes and journals all done. But I am just so disappointed. When I look at it all, and when I look back it seems clear the course was all about power and authority.

Monica: Of course we knew that. We could have predicted that before we started.

Lesley: Then what did we learn? Why did I bother collecting all that data if we already knew what we'd find? How can we learn if we already know?
(Skype conversation, Dec. 12, 2012).

We approach self-study as the people we are: We take from our self-studies what we can. We are reminded of Deleuze (1990/1995) writing about the students who took his courses: "nobody took in everything, but everyone took what they needed or wanted, what they could use" (as quoted by St. Pierre, 2004, p. 139). As we grapple with what we have learned from our self-study, we are tempted to present our findings as clear and delineated, an orientation we are all too familiar with in teacher education with our reliance on standards, criteria, and rubrics. Yet, as many self-studies demonstrate, what we learn is not always concrete, able to be stated definitively, or replicable in other teaching contexts. As we show through this self-study, our learning as teachers is complex and not always articulable as propositional knowledge.

We come to our research with interests and a personal history. Although questions appear to emerge organically, those that surfaced during this self-study were ones that have preoccupied us throughout our teaching lives: negotiating power and authority (Coia & Taylor, 2009; Taylor & Coia, 2006, 2009). We know there are issues we don't see in our data or in our subsequent analysis. Someone who observed the class with a very different orientation, maybe with the question "Could this course be taught on-line?" would come up with different themes and concerns. But this is a

M. Taylor and L. Coia (Eds.), Gender, Feminism, and Queer Theory in the Self-Study of Teacher Education Practices, 157–169.
© 2014 Sense Publishers. All rights reserved.

self-study. We are interested in improving *our* practice (LaBoskey, 2004; Loughran, 2004). Who we are is important (Hamilton & Pinnegar, 1998; Korthagen & Russell, 1995; LaBoskey, 2004). Who we are includes our social identities (Deaux, 2001), what we identify with and care about (Frankfurt, 1987), and importantly our past experience. As LaBoskey (2004) writes, "[w]e teach who we are" (p. 829). In this study we primarily self-identify as feminist teachers analyzing a class about gender and education. Whether we explicitly acknowledged it or not, we were looking for feminist themes and issues. And we found them.

Do we in the end continue to write the same paper because it is about us? Do we have to confront the shibboleth of self-study: solipsism. As Banks (2004) says in his novel, *The Algebraist,* "Any theory which causes solipsism to seem just as likely an explanation for the phenomena it seeks to describe ought to be held in the utmost suspicion" (p. 368). Fortunately, solipsism is not something we need to consider because the post-structural feminist approach we use in co/autoethnography, our self-study methodology, precludes it. We start with the idea that our identities are not fixed: they are discursively produced. At root, our identities are constructed and while they may seem unique and private, this is itself a construction. Another way of putting this is to say that it would be a mistake to think that when we start a self-study we are somehow at the beginning. On the contrary, as Moore (2010) writes "we enter the various worlds in our lives in media res, in the middle of a story already being constructed both for us and through us" (p. 63). Thus when we begin a self-study, as opposed to those Hollywood moments that suggest as Glinda, the Good Witch of North says "It's always best to start at the beginning" (Wizard of Oz, 1939), self-studies always start somewhere in the middle.

Although the story we tell is in relevant respects familiar, continued study of our practice from a feminist perspective yields important insights. In this study, close attention to the details of the everyday events of the class, of which we have chosen to address two in this chapter, revealed the importance of the unpredictable in feminist teaching.

"BLAME IT ON A SIMPLE TWIST OF FATE…"
(DYLAN, 1974)

In this co/autoethnographic self-study, we examine the teaching of an upper level course on gender and education. As is often the case in our research, we hoped to examine how content, pedagogy, and biography intersect in our feminist teaching. The course provided the opportunity, impetus, and focus, but as a co/autoethnography (Coia & Taylor, 2009; Taylor & Coia, 2009) it draws on other teaching and life experiences.

The course on gender and education at the center of the study was taught at a small liberal arts college for women in the southeastern United States. We planned to study this course almost from the moment Lesley began to develop it. From the beginning, we shared and discussed possible readings, topics, and assignments. The course was taught for the first time in the fall of 2012, the period of the self-study. The students were invited to be part of the study and all requisite permissions were obtained for the class to be taped and data to be collected. Throughout that semester and the one following we used our regular meeting time to discuss the course and what we were learning. This resulted in the present self-study.

This is not the first self-study we have undertaken. We have spent the past fifteen years collaboratively writing into each others' lives as we engage in self-studies that explore our past, present, and future as women and educators. Early on in our work together, we moved apart to work at relatively distinct institutions: Lesley teaches at a small liberal arts college in the south and Monica teaches at a large state university in the northeast. Determined to continue our collaboration and friendship, we found alternative means to carry on with our self-study work during that time developing a methodology called co/autoethnography. Conducting self-studies has nurtured both our professional and personal relationships: each Skype session, sometimes every day and at other times every week, reflects the congruence of our personal and professional lives. We share the same commitments to feminism, social justice, and ultimately teacher education as a way of realizing these values.

For this particular self-study we constructed the co/autoethnography using a combination of Lesley's narrative reflections from her teaching, video from her class sessions, emailed dialogue between us, personal narratives from the past and present about our lives as women, quotes, articles, and videos that inspire us, and collaborative writing. We present two narrative episodes that creatively draw on these texts.

In the self-study we incorporate our feminist past, particularly our experience with feminist pedagogy. The fundamental purpose of co/autoethnography is the co-construction of meaning and self through writing about the self in its social, historical, and cultural context. As such, it draws heavily on poststructural feminism (Ellsworth, 1989; Lather, 2001; St. Pierre, 2000). As Randall (2010) reminds us, this points to the discursive and contingent nature of identities, including gender. Co/autoethnography, as we have elaborated in an earlier work (Coia & Taylor, 2009), "acknowledges the personal while recognizing the social construction of our identity and practices" (p. 15). Central to the process is recognition of the importance of relationships in the creation of meaning that is facilitated through collaborative analysis. Through writing our teaching lives we bring together and create aspects of ourselves. Via this perspective we analyze our practice to see if we can say something meaningful about what we learn through our teaching; how it is learned, and ultimately how we, as teachers, learn at all.

"THERE IS A ROAD NO SIMPLE HIGHWAY BETWEEN
THE DAWN AND THE DARK OF NIGHT…"
(HUNTER & GARCIA, 1970)

In order to capture our process of coming to understand our teaching experience in a situation where we are teaching about a particular pedagogy whilst enacting that pedagogy, we borrow the metaphor of the "nomad" (Deleuze & Guattari, 1987) to describe our writing approach. A nomadic inquiry helps to illustrate how our co/autoethnography is focused on the small moments of our teaching practices. Although the term nomad often elicits the idea of a placeless, itinerant person, in this context Deleuze and Guattari (1987) categorize a nomad as living in "the intermezzo" (p. 380).

Semetsky and Lovat (2008) envision nomads as always being in "between here and there, between now and then" (p. 174). From this perspective, nomads are not considered aimlessly wandering. They are aware of the various points on their path (to get water, rest, or assemble supplies), but they focus on the journey. We illustrate our co-autoethnography nomadically because we see a connection between where the lens is focused both for a nomad and for ourselves in self-study. We are interested in examining the planned unpredictable moments in the classroom where crucial elements of our feminist pedagogy emerge. Writing nomadically reminds us that the usual checkpoints in our teaching: to planning, to reflecting, to evaluating our students, and then to planning again; are not necessarily where we should focus. Those points are predictable moments. Our interest is in the unpredictable, spontaneous, small moments that are out of our control, as we suspect it is in these moments that learning occurs.

How do we compose a chapter nomadically? Some write that nomadic groups are like improv jazz groups, explaining that the coherence of either group stems inherently from the "activity of improvising itself" (Holland, 2005, p. 188). In many ways, engaging in and writing co/autoethnography involves a sort of shared improvisation and a willingness to cross boundaries: in this case the boundaries of context, pedagogy, and biography. For us, we see nomadic writing as similar to the improvised jamming of a band like the Grateful Dead. To a great extent, their improvisational style at live shows became their trademark. Like the nomad who has stops along her path, every Grateful Dead show had a predictable structure and format that could be anticipated. The band started on time, there were always two sets with an intermission in between, and often songs were grouped in pairs or triplets. In the second set, there was always a set of drums and space when the musicians experimented with sounds. But also like the nomad who focuses on " the intermezzo," there was an improvised set list each night and improvised jams during songs. This made them different from other bands that rehearsed a standard set and then played it each night of the tour. As Jerry Garcia stated in a 1966 interview, "We don't make up our sets beforehand. We'd rather work off the tops of our heads than off a piece of paper" (Gans & Simon, 1985, p. 17). Besides making improvised selections from a list of over a hundred songs, the Grateful Dead also incorporated a jam in each song. A jam is defined as an "extended musical improvisation over rhythmic grooves and chord patterns, and long sets of music that cross genre boundaries...drawing from a range of traditions including blues, bluegrass, funk, jazz, rock, psychedelia and even techno" (jambands.com, 2007). The jam is the planned unpredictable moment of the song, and is only possible because of the shared commitment of the Dead musicians.

There is also a sort of unspoken communication that involves deep listening to each other that allows a jam to come into its own. In this chapter, the narratives of two teaching episodes from Lesley's course are our version of what we are calling nomadic jamming.

Nomadic jamming borrows from the structure and format of a Grateful Dead Show and also from our understanding of nomadic inquiry. This means that as the reader you will have opportunities to both be comforted by the academic conventions in place at the front and the end of the chapter but you will also have the nomadic jam experiences in the middle of the chapter where we explore the teaching episodes. These jams function as times when, and places from which to think about our practice in Lesley's course. Analogous to musical jam sessions, in this co/autoethnography we write about our teaching lives together and in so doing develop a communal practice that yields new interpretations of our work. Thus, we plan to come together but what is produced is unpredictable. It is always new and, if it works, it creates new knowledge.

"NOTHING'S FOR CERTAIN, IT COULD ALWAYS GO WRONG. . ."
(HUNTER & GARCIA, 1970)

"I would like to tell the class what happened to me this weekend. Is that ok?"
(Email correspondence August 30, 2012, first day of class).

I don't recognize the name. I haven't met this student. Class starts in twenty minutes. I am going to say yes. After all, this is what this course is truly about: I want this course to be shared, for the course to be about the students, meshing experience and different ways of knowing. It is for them. It is about them. This is an opportunity.

The beginning of the semester, the first class. Those moments before we meet the students when we are ready and unready at the same time. We have thought through the class. We have the order of events planned. We even know, or think we know, how things will go: Where the sticking places will be, where the students will start to come together. While always flexible of course, we have planned and we feel confident that we know where we are going. We are in control. It is our course.

It is fifteen minutes into the course and Julie, the author of the email, is telling a difficult story. She is talking about how the police stopped her and her boyfriend this weekend; how she spent the night in jail; how the police shouted at her, accused her, and beat up her boyfriend. She is outraged, shocked, and scared. It is a terrifying story. Although she was calm when she started talking, now she is shaking with emotion and using language that some students might find offensive.

This is a classroom but it doesn't feel like one. Someone once said to me, "Education isn't therapy." Can a classroom handle this level of emotion? What do we, as teachers, do here? It feels like it is spiralling away. Where is this class going?

I hope I appear calm and supportive. I fear I am using my coffee mug as a shield against what is happening, as I sip and sip and peer over the rim. I am horrified by what Julie has suffered. I am appalled at the indignity, injustice, and humiliation. I am also very aware that it is now half an hour into the course and I have ceded control to Julie. I don't know how long she will talk. The managerial side of teaching is on my mind, eclipsing the ethical. All eyes appropriately are on Julie, but I don't know those eyes. This is a new class. Am I reading them, their body language, correctly? What are they thinking? What do I know?

Control. Control. Are we in control? The ideal would be to let go.

I let go. I stop being worried. I stop worrying about being a teacher. I trust the students and the pedagogy. For now that means being here with my role as teacher being transformed by the interaction. I am going to let the situation play out. I am in an in between space. I am not totally part of the group, but I am of the group.

Being in between. This is a space we think about. We talk about this all the time. What does it mean here? How can we make sense of who we are, our responsibilities here? Is this the time to be thinking about control?

Julie finishes. She is worn and torn and angry. There is a pause and then Siobhan speaks directly to Julie and tells her about an alumna, a lawyer, who can help. Another student, Tiffany, tells Julie about a student group that can give immediate support. I marvel at the seriousness and concern shown by the class for Julie. There is recognition, outrage, but no surprise. Phone numbers and names are given to Julie. It is a supportive but calm moment. There is a slow easy transition to further discussion of the course.

The moment is over. It naturally evolved and resolved, at least for now. What really happened? Was this teaching? How do we know? And the students. What were their perceptions?

Later that day, I have lunch with Lucy, a student from the course who I know well. It is a pre-arranged appointment to talk about a long term project on which she is working. I ask for her views on what happened in class. She says that what it did for Julie, the feeling of community and real support from her new academic "home" is worth any annoyance or irritation other students may have felt. In short, the positive for Julie means it was worthwhile.

First day of class and already a real sense of community and support. Discomfort by students possible but maybe it is this shared dissonance that brings a community together.

Another student, Amanda, says something similar later that day when she comes to my office to talk about another matter, pointing out that any discomfort other students may have felt would be fleeting – they would forget it in a week or two – but the empathy expressed for Julie's experience may have had a lasting effect on her. It was worth it.

This is an uncertain story. Does it end here? Was it planned? Does it matter? Will the unexpected stick?

Now that it is evening I take time to reflect in my journal on Julie, the class, and some of my subsequent conversations. Of course I could have done things differently. Amanda seemed amused to learn that I had not found out what Julie wanted to talk about. Interestingly, she said that when Julie started talking she thought Julie and

I had planned this as the beginning of the course to make a point about feminist pedagogy.

Was it planned? In some ways it was. It was a planned unplanned moment: less deliberate and more abstract but stemming from our orientation, from our understanding of what feminist pedagogy is.

Somehow I was, those first minutes of class, living the principle that the course should not be "mine" from the outset. It was important to me that I didn't know what was going to happen or at least knew as little as the other members of the class. The students were in as much control of the class during that first half hour as it was possible to be. Although it was Julie who spoke, and it was me that gave her the authority to do so, it involved us all.

A planned unpredictable moment. And how many ways can it be interpreted? Endlessly, maybe. "Nothing's for certain. . ."

Planning this first class, the illusion of control was masked in my understanding of teaching and my experience. But in the teaching moment, I called on my wits, my feelings, and my ethics. And it was in that moment that I was reminded that control is measured.

Each time we teach we plan for the unpredictable. To allow for the possibility of jamming, of connecting with our students.

"WAKE UP TO FIND OUT THAT YOU ARE THE EYES OF THE WORLD. . ." (HUNTER & GARCIA, 1973)

I stand at the front of the class with Sameeda, a student from Pakistan visiting the class to talk about gender and education in international contexts. I introduce her and sit so I can listen along with the other students. She talks with eloquence and passion of her experience as a woman studying in Pakistan, life in her family, and her informal literacy and consciousness raising work with young girls in her extended community.

Sometimes you just have to open your eyes, be quiet, and listen.

As she talks I feel a stiffness, that I hadn't realized was in the class, melting. At the time I feel us as a community, listening and participating in Sameeda's story and in so doing, changing.

Listening can sometimes change you. It seems this is something we know and yet cannot always do: listen to our students rather than search for what we want to hear. No matter how many times we remind each other, it is a hard practice when you are "the teacher" with things to manage and stuff to teach. Playing the same melody with a new arrangement can open our eyes.

Some things in the class had, before this moment, felt known and predictable: I "knew" Anna's position on the impossibility of negotiating authority; I could finish Martha's sentence on the notion of privilege, or Brittany's on cultural relativism. We had, midway through the semester, settled into our positions: We "knew" each other.

163

And of course there is comfort in that knowledge, dangerous though that comfort is. The unknown can be terrifying yet we fight against feelings of certainty. The danger of knowing others. It seems a strange thing to say! We want to know our students, but not in a way that makes us feel we can predict their thoughts and so limit them and our quest to know differently.

For some time now there has been resistance to the concept of feminist pedagogy. Several students are uncomfortable with its exclusionary "feel." All the students self-identify as women, are interested in social justice and comfortable with feminist ideas, but they are suspicious of feminist pedagogy. It is too narrow in its identifications. Sheila suggests "anti-oppressive" pedagogy instead.

"Sometimes we live no particular way but our own...."

I look around the classroom as students ask Sameeda questions and the conversation develops. I think about how the space, the very physical space of the classroom had conditioned and contained us. Students over the course of the semester have taken up their positions: theoretical and physical. Each student is in her accustomed and, one can only assume, comfortable place.

We want our students to be comfortable yet we have struggled with the idea of comfort. It seems a bedrock of our teaching that our students should feel safe. We all have to feel comfortable enough to take risks. We have to feel comfortable enough to be able to be uncomfortable in a productive way.

Sameeda talks about her home university, how men threaten her in the hallway, how her desire for education has ruined her as a woman for her aunts. The daily violence. The support and love of her father. As she speaks we are recast: Our discussions of feminism, feminist pedagogy, and intersectionality slip from their moorings. The impact of her language, her choice of words, her experience, and her voice are different for all of us, but we are all changed by it. We end the session knowing differently. I see a new path emerging out of the rut we had dug for ourselves.

"And sometimes we visit your country and live in your home..." And we never know when these moments will come.

I don't know what this change in atmosphere will mean.

There is freedom in becoming unstuck if only for a moment. Perhaps it is in these unpredictable moments that learning occurs. The moment passes but is not gone. The learning self is always unfinished.

"IT GOES TO SHOW YOU DON'T EVER KNOW..."
(HUNTER & GARCIA, 1972)

The stories we have told are everyday events. There is nothing extraordinary about a student sharing a personal experience or a presentation in class by a visitor. These are ordinary small moments in a teaching life, part of our on-going story of learning to teach. They talk of the ways in which the pedagogy and content of our teaching are in continuous negotiation with our lived experience and ideas about teaching. We have tried to show one way this negotiation works by starting the chapter with the question that very often comes at the end of a self-study: What have we learned? The chapter can be seen as a response to this question by showing that learning takes place in an imaginative space. We are not searching for propositional knowledge, but are more interested in the stance we take to our on-going teaching experience. We might say that our focus has moved from the epistemological to the ontological (Pinnegar & Hamilton, 2009).

Should we have predicted unpredictability as the central theme of this self-study? Is it surprising that our co/autoethnography has led us to value and appreciate the planned unpredictability of our teaching? Isn't this the very essence of our orientation? We self-identify as poststructural feminists and have spent the past few years reading and interpreting this work and its implications for teacher education. We have immersed ourselves in the scholarship of Ellsworth, Britzman, Lather, and St. Pierre. From poststructuralism, we have adopted the perspective that as Britzman (1993) writes, "all categories are unstable, all experiences are constructed, all reality is imagined, all identities are produced, and all knowledge provokes uncertainties, misrecognitions, ignorances, and silences" (p. 22). We have written about how poststructural feminism has helped us to embrace the uncertainty and unknowability of our teaching (Coia & Taylor, 2013). We are liberated as we have increasingly "given up on finding out 'exactly' what is going on" (St. Pierre, 2000, p. 477). We do not want our feminist work to become "routinized, static and predictable" rather we hope to "interrogate the enabling limits of its own practices, not to junk them but to shake them up" (Lather, 2006, p. 1). It is vital for us, as feminist teachers, to try and always be open, to never be fixed in belief or judgement. What better way to enact this than to allow for, to be open to, or to invite the unpredictable into our teaching. For it is in these moments that we have the opportunity to destabilize categories, to invent new identities, to try on diverse perspectives, to shake things up. As the Grateful Dead sing, "Nothin' shakin' on Shakedown Street. . . Don't tell me this town ain't got no heart. You just gotta poke around" (Hunter & Garcia, 1978).

The nomadic jamming we use in this chapter parallels the co/autoethnographic process enhancing our understanding of how we can live our feminism in the act of planning for unpredictability in the classroom. As nomadic jammers and co/autoethnographers, we rely on a type of improvisation that can occur when there is a trusting working relationship and a shared commitment to a reflective process that is not seeking the answer but rather possible interpretations. Utilizing the form of co/autoethnography we also crisscross between our teaching practices and our lived lives, between our individual selves and those in relation, between spoken and unspoken communication, and between teacher education and the arts.

This is a poststructural feminist understanding of the world. As Weedon (1987) succinctly puts it: "meaning can never be finally fixed. Every act of reading is a new production of meaning" (p. 134). We would add, that every act of writing is also a new production of meaning. We began this self-study a year ago, writing and talking, reading and listening to each other, to the students' voices, to our pasts and to what is happening around us. We have written over what we have written. You have in your hands a palimpsest. The traces of those first days thinking and writing are still discernible. For us this long-term writing and thinking together is the value of self-study. It is not so much making sense of what happened, but making meaning that has driven us. This is what it means for us to be learning selves, the selves of self-study.

There is no doubt that it is a confusing time to be a feminist. Feminisms abound. There are many ways to identify as a feminist but we, along our students, tend to find shelter in categorical absolutes and labels - we want to know who and where we are. We are so conditioned by the modern, humanist world in which we operate we find it difficult to disrupt fixed categories. We want definitions; we want to situate ourselves in our identifications. There is comfort in the definitive. But the unpredictable moments we have tried to capture in this chapter remind us to embrace a more complex understanding of feminism: to embrace feminisms. Flexibility helps budge us from our "stuck place" (Ellsworth, 1997, p. xi). Just as our chapter contains aspects of previous versions, so feminism has had what Kristeva (1986) calls "three generations": liberal feminism in which women want access to the patriarchy; radical feminism that celebrates what makes women unique and highlights difference or separation from men, and finally a feminism that embraces "woman as whole" where the orientation is not positioned in terms of the male/female duality. Like Kristeva, we wish to "occupy the signifying space of all three of the feminisms despite their contradictions" (Davies, 1999, pp. 38-39) and to navigate in between these feminisms in different contexts. What does this mean for our teaching and our commitments to social justice?

As bell hooks (2000) reminds us, "[s]imply put, feminism is a movement to end sexism, sexist exploitation, and oppression" (p. 1). Deceptively simple, this reminds us that teaching about feminist pedagogy as feminists must reveal a commitment to social justice. We have, in this chapter, essentially argued for a more difficult reading of feminism, a poststructural account with its shifting meanings and notoriously obtuse language. We seem forever to be drawn simultaneously to the simple and complex. Here, we must be ever mindful of St. Pierre's (2000) warning that "easy understanding and easy dismissal are both careless, even unethical practices since they betray" (p. 478) our commitments to social action.

The language of social justice is increasingly common in teacher education. Indeed, for many programs teaching for social justice forms part of the conceptual framework or mission. Often this is seen as understanding the importance of identity positions for learning. This commonly includes discussion of such issues as teaching children in poverty, or understanding linguistic differences between ethnic groups. In terms of gender this concern is addressed through questions such as "how can we help girls take up STEM subjects?", "What literature will encourage boys to read?" or "Are preferences for learning environments based on gender?" Questions that are not as frequently addressed are those that occur in our everyday lives and those of our students and their students: the subtleties of trusting someone for the first time, including someone new at your table in the lunchroom, or standing up for another or oneself. We suspect this is because teacher education has become exclusively about knowing how and knowing that, and not the type of ethical questions that occur when one focuses on relationships and wider societal issues.

We return once again to our initial question. What did we learn? We have realized that when we study ourselves teaching, the understanding of self must be central. Here we have taken a view of self as always discursively produced in language. The very act of producing this self-study has shaped our learning selves. As women teaching and thinking about gender and education, engaging in our nomadic jam, we found that in the ordinary there is the unpredictable and in the unpredictable we see much of our feminist practice and ideas. These cannot be reduced to techniques or strategies. Lather (1991) asks the right question, "How can . . . self-reflexivity both render our basic assumptions problematic and provisional and yet still propel us to take a stand?" (p. 44).

REFERENCES

Banks, I. A. (2004). *The algebraist*. London, UK: Orbit An imprint of Time Warner Book Group UK.

Britzman, D. P. (1993, October). *Is there a queer pedagogy?: Or, stop being [acting?] straight!* Paper presented at the Journal of Curriculum Theorizing Conference, Dayton, OH.

Coia, L., & Taylor, M. (2009). Co/autoethnography: Exploring our teaching selves collaboratively. In D. Tidwell, M. L. Heston & L. M. Fitzgerald (Eds.), *Research methods for self study practice* (pp. 3–16). Dordrecht, The Netherlands: Springer Press.

Coia, L, & Taylor, M. (2013). Uncovering our feminist pedagogy: A co/autoethnography. *Studying Teacher Education, 9*(1) 3–17.

Davies, B. (1999). *A body of writing: 1990-1999*. Walnut Creek, CA: Altamira Press.

Deaux, K. (2001). Social identity. In Worell, J. (Ed.) *Encyclopedia of women and gender, Two-Volume Set: Sex similarities and differences and the impact of society on gender,* (pp. 1059–1068). San Diego, CA: Academic Press. Retrieved from http://www.utexas.edu/courses/stross/ant393b_files/ARTICLES/identity.pdf

Deleuze, G., & Guattari, F. (1987). *A thousand plateaus: Capitalism and schizophrenia*. Minneapolis, MN: University of Minnesota Press.

Dylan, B. (1974). Simple twist of fate. In *Blood on the Tracks* (LP). Ram's Horn Music.

Ellsworth, E. (1989). Why doesn't this feel empowering? Working through repressive myths of critical pedagogy. *Harvard Educational Review, 59*(3), 297–324.

Ellsworth, E. (1997). *Teaching positions: Difference, pedagogy, and the power of address*. New York, NY: Teachers College Press.

Frankfurt, H. (1987). *The importance of what we care about*. Cambridge, MA: Cambridge University Press.

Gans, D., & Simon, P. (1985). *The Grateful Dead: Playing in the band*. New York, NY: St. Martin Press.

Hamilton, M. L., & Pinnegar, S. (1998). Conclusion: The value and promise of self study. In M. L. Hamilton (Ed.), *Reconceptualizing teaching practice: Self-study in teacher education* (pp. 235–246). London, UK: Falmer Press.

Holland, E. (2005). Nomadicism and citizenship. In A. Parr (Ed.), *The Deleuze dictionary* (pp. 188–189). Edinburgh: Edinburgh University Press.

hooks, B. (2000). *Feminism is for everybody: Passionate politics*. Cambridge, MA: South End Press.

Hunter, R., & Garcia, J. (1970). High time (Grateful Dead). On *Workingman's Dead* (LP). Warner Brothers Records.

Hunter, R., & Garcia, J. (1970). Ripple (Grateful Dead). On *American Beauty* (LP). Warner Brothers Records.

Hunter, R., & Garcia, J. (1972). Deal. On *Garcia* (LP). Warner Brothers Records.

Hunter, R., & Garcia, J. (1973). Eyes of the world (Grateful Dead). On *Wake of the Flood* (LP). Grateful Dead Records.

Hunter, R., & Garcia, J. (1978). Shakedown Street (Grateful Dead). On *Shakedown Street* (LP). Grateful Dead Records.

Korthagen, F., & Russell, T. (Eds.) (1995). *Teachers who teach teachers*. London, UK: Falmer Press.

Kristeva, J. (1986). Women's time. In T. Moi (Ed.), *The Kristeva reader* (pp. 187–213). Oxford: Blackwell Publishing.

LaBoskey, V. K. (2004). The methodology of self-study and its theoretical underpinnings. In J. J. Loughran, M. L. Hamilton, V. K. LaBoskey, & T. Russell (Eds.), *International handbook of self-study of teacher education practices* (pp. 817–869). Dordrecht, The Netherlands: Kluwer Academic Publishers.

Lather, P. (1991). *Getting smart: Feminist research and pedagogy with/in the postmodern*. New York, NY: Routledge.

Lather, P. (2001). Ten years later, yet again: Critical pedagogy and its complicities. In K. Weiler (Ed.), *Feminist engagements: Reading, resisting, and revisioning male theorists, in education and cultural studies*, (pp. 183–195). New York, NY: Routledge.

Lather, P. (2006, October). *(Post)Feminist methodology: Getting lost OR a scientificity we can bear to learn from*. Paper presented at the Research Methods Festival, Oxford, England.

Loughran, J. J. (2004). Learning through self-study: The influence of purpose, participants and contexts. In J. J. Loughran, M. L. Hamilton, V. K. LaBoskey, & T. Russell (Eds.) *International handbook of self-study of teacher education practices* (pp. 151–192). Dordrecht, The Netherlands: Kluwer Academic Publishers.

Moore, S. L. (2010). *Writing the past to create the future: Reconstructing the world of the classroom teacher*. Unpublished dissertation: University of Wyoming, Laramie, Wyoming.

Petersen, R. M., & Lesh, P. (1974). Unbroken Chain. (Grateful Dead). On *Grateful Dead from the Mars Hotel* (LP). Grateful Dead Records.

Pinnegar, S., & Hamilton, M. L. (2009). *Self-study of practice as a genre of qualitative research: Theory, methodology, and practice*. Dordrecht, The Netherlands: Springer Press.

Randall, V. (2010). 'Feminism.' In D. Marsh & G. Stoker (Eds.) *Theory and methods in political science*. Basingstoke, England: Palgrave Macmillian.

Semetsky, I. & Lovat, T. (2008). Knowledge in action: Towards a Deleuze Hamermasian critique in/for education. In I. Semetsky (Ed.), *Nomadic education: Variations on a theme by Deleuze and Guattari* (pp. 171–182). Rotterdam, The Netherlands: SensePublisher.

St. Pierre, E. A. (2000). Poststructural feminism in education: An overview. *Qualitative studies in education, 13*(5), 477–515.

St. Pierre, E. A. (2004). Deleuzian concepts for education: The subject undone. *Educational Philosophy and Theory, 36*(3), 283–296.

Taylor, M., & Coia, L. (2006). Revisiting feminist authority through a co/autoethnographic lens. In D. Tidwell & L. Fitzgerald (Eds.), *Self-study research and issues of diversity* (pp. 51–70). Rotterdam, The Netherlands: SensePublishers.

Taylor, M., & Coia, L. (2009). Co/autoethnography: Investigating teachers in relation. In C. Lassonde, S. Gallman & C. Kosnik (Eds.), *Self-Study research methodologies for teacher educators* (pp. 169–186). Rotterdam, The Netherlands: SensePublishers.

Weedon, C. (1987). *Feminist practice et poststructuralist theory*. Oxford: Blackwell Publishers.

"What is a jam band?" (2007). Archived from the original on 2007-01-24. Retrieved February 2, 2007 from Jambands.com

Wizard of Oz (1939). Retrieved from http://www.reelclassics.com/Musicals/Wizoz/wizoz2.htm

AFFILIATIONS

Lesley Coia
Department of Education,
Agnes Scott College,
Decatur, Georgia

Monica Taylor
Department of Secondary and Special Education,
Montclair State University,
Montclair, New Jersey

BIOGRAPHIES

Rabab Abi-Hanna is the Coordinator for Mathematics for Elementary Teachers at SUNY New Paltz, New York. Previously, she served as a mathematics consultant with elementary school teachers and administrators. Rabab has a B.A. and a M.A. with a concentration in Mathematics, and has reached the dissertation stage of her doctoral studies in Mathematics Education at Montclair State University. Her research interests include the influence of technology on elementary students' learning and teachers' classroom practices.

Linda Abrams is a doctoral candidate in the Teacher Education and Teacher Development program at Montclair State University in New Jersey. After receiving a B.A. in American and Women's Studies and a M.Ed in Social Studies Education, Linda served as a high school teacher and administrator in New Jersey for 24 years. Currently in the fourth year of her doctoral studies, Linda will begin her dissertation study, which marries her interests in action research, mentor identity and practice, with teacher education reform, in the spring of 2014.

Nathan D. Brubaker is a Lecturer in Curriculum and Pedagogy in the Faculty of Education at Monash University in Melbourne, Australia. He previously taught in the USA at the primary and tertiary levels. He teaches undergraduate and graduate courses in multicultural education and primary level curriculum, while supervising Masters and PhD students in teacher education. His research interests include preparing teachers to teach democratically, equitably, and inclusively through examining teacher educators' practices concerning classroom communities of inquiry, individualized grading contracts, and micropolitical dimensions of beginning teachers' experiences. His work on classroom authority, assessment, and inquiry has been published in various journals and books.

Allie Clemans is a Senior Lecturer in the Faculty of Education at Monash University in Melbourne, Australia. Allie's research spans diverse learning contexts such as workplaces, vocational education and training (VET), adult community education and tertiary education. Her focus is the professional learning of educational workers to develop teaching practices that transform adult learners. Her research interests also include lifelong learning and notions of employability.

Lesley Coia is a Professor of Education at Agnes Scott College where she teaches courses in comparative education, diversity, and gender issues. She has been involved in the self-study of teacher education practices SIG since 2002. With her co-author, Monica Taylor, she has published a number of self-studies that address feminist issues, including Uncovering feminist pedagogy: A co/autoethnography in *Studying teacher education: A journal of self-study of teacher education practices*. Her teaching and research focus on equity issues in education.

Charity Dacey is the Director of Teacher Education Admissions and Retention at Montclair State University in New Jersey. She earned a B.A. in American Studies and an M.S. in Organizational Leadership. After starting her career in education as a public high school special educator, Charity worked to recruit and develop new teachers in New York City and Prince George's County, MD. She is currently pursuing her doctoral studies in the Teacher Education and Teacher Development Program at Montclair State University. Her research interests focus on measures of teacher quality as indicated by initial admission criteria and differential theoretical approaches to assessment of learning.

Jacqueline Dauplaise is a Mathematics Teacher at Wayne Hills High School in New Jersey. Her degrees include a B.A. in Applied Mathematics, a M.A. with a Concentration in Mathematics, and a M.A.T. She has recently completed her doctoral coursework in Mathematics Education at Montclair State University. Her research interests encompass the influence of self-study on teachers' classroom practices, the affect of assessment on teaching practice, and Foucauldian analyses of power in the classroom.

Janet Dunn has a BA in Journalism and in Home Economics. Since obtaining her degrees she has worked in the technology industry in Silicone Valley in the San Francisco Bay Area. She currently is working with a technology consultant in the Northeast United States.

Rachel Forgasz is a Lecturer in the Faculty of Education at Monash University in Melbourne, Australia. In her research, Rachel explores the possibilities of theatrical performance as an embodied approach to self-reflexivity, especially as a way of engaging preservice teachers in reflecting on their emotional experiences of learning to teach. She publishes in the fields of embodied reflection, teacher emotion, and self-study. Rachel teaches in the areas of reflective practice and drama education and oversees the professional experience within several secondary teacher education programs.

Mary Lynn Hamilton is a Professor in Curriculum & Teaching at the University of Kansas. She is a co-editor of *The International Handbook of Self-Study of Teaching and Teacher Education Practices* (2004) and co-authored *Self-Study of practice as a genre of qualitative research: Theory, methodology, and practice* (2009) with Stefinee Pinnegar. Her research interests combine teachers' professional knowledge, issues of social justice, and the self-study of teaching practices.

Julian Kitchen is an Associate Professor in the Faculty of Education at Brock University, in Hamilton, Ontario, Canada. He is the author with Christopher Dean of *Professionalism, Law and the Ontario Educator.* Dr. Kitchen has published extensively on teacher education, Aboriginal education, and queer issues in education. He is the editor of the *Brock Education* journal and the co-editor of several books on teacher education practices, including *Narrative Inquiries into Curriculum Making in Teacher Education* and *Canadian Perspectives on the Self-Study of Teacher Education Practices.*

Jeffrey Kuzmic is an Associate Professor of Curriculum Studies in the College of Education at DePaul University in Chicago, where he teaches masters and doctoral level curriculum courses on the epistemology of assessment, the study of teachers and teaching, the history of curriculum practices, curriculum theorizing, and assessment of school curriculum. Dr. Kuzmic's research and scholarly interests focus on: democratic education, power, and inequality; gender, teaching, and curriculum; teacher identity, development, and professionalism; and the epistemologies of qualitative research methodologies, particularly in relation to self-study research. He is currently working on a book that seeks to revisit and reexamine his self-study research projects over the past decade in terms of their methodological and epistemological implications for post-qualitative research.

Stefinee Pinnegar is a teacher educator in the McKay School of Education at Brigham Young University, Provo, Utah. Her research interests focus on teacher thinking along with S-STTEP and narrative methodologies. In examining the development of teacher thinking, she has a particular interest in the development of practical memory in teaching. She co-authored *Self-Study of practice as a genre of qualitative research: Theory, methodology, and practice* with Mary Lynn Hamilton, is series editor for the *Advances in Research on Teaching* and is Acting Dean of *Invisible College for Research on Teaching.*

Kathryn Strom is a doctoral candidate in the Teacher Education and Teacher Development Program at Montclair State University in New Jersey and a research associate with the Teacher Professional Development Program at WestEd, a non profit agency. With a B.A. in Political Science and a M.Ed in Multicultural Education, Katie taught history and served in multiple school leadership capacities in urban schools in San Diego before pursuing her doctoral studies. Katie's current research interests include pedagogies grounded in social justice, rhizomatic and other non-linear research methodologies, and poststructuralism/feminist materialism in teacher education and self-study.

Pamela Schwartz has a BA in History and in English. Her original studies included secondary education, but she changed her focus to English, and during her graduate studies taught undergraduate courses in English. She worked for over 20 years in the Silicone Valley business world in the San Francisco Bay Area doing corporate training and some technical editing. She is currently working independently and pursuing her love of writing.

Monica Taylor is an Associate Professor in the Department of Secondary and Special Education at Montclair State University. Involved with the SIG since 2002, she has co-written several articles and chapters on co/autoethnography, a self-study methodology with Lesley Coia. Her research interests also include urban education, teaching for social justice, feminist teaching, and inquiry. Most of her teacher education work demonstrates her deep commitment to partnerships with K-12 schools. For the past three years, she has served as the lead faculty of the secondary strand of the Newark Montclair Urban Teacher Residency Program, which focuses on preparing math and science teachers for Newark public schools.

Deborah Tidwell is a Professor and Coordinator for the Literacy Education program at the University of Northern Iowa. Her research interests include reflective practice, issues of equity and access, and the use of visual representations in self-study methodology. She co-edited *Research Methods for the Self-Study of Practice* with Melissa Heston and Linda Fitzgerald and *Self-Study and Diversity* with Linda Fitzgerald. She serves on the editorial board for *Studying Teacher Education,* and recently guest-edited an issue on "Exploring the Transformative Nature of Self-Study of Teacher Education Practices" with Susan Elliott-Johns. Her recent work focuses on the processes used by young writers in expressing meaning, on the use of video conferencing in self-study research, and on self-study of teacher practice in literacy instruction for children with low incidence disabilities.

Lightning Source UK Ltd.
Milton Keynes UK
UKOW06f0839040416

271487UK00006B/95/P